WHAT PEOPLE ARE SAYING ABOUT

TORAH JOURNEYS

"Deep study and contemplation went into the writing of this work. Reb Shefa takes you into the House of Study of the heart and the soul and in this way engages the sacred creativity of the spirit."

Reb Zalman Schachter-Shalomi
co-author of *Jewish With Feeling* and *Credo Of A Modern Kabbalist*

In the days to come a new covenant will be written for us, one that is carved not in stone but in our hearts. (Jeremiah 31:33)

"These are those days. *Torah Journeys* is that covenant. If you dare be addressed by God — read it. If you dare be transformed by God — practice it."

Rabbi Rami Shapiro
Author of *The Divine Feminine*

"Torah Journeys is a remarkable book of profound depth. It has taught me much, drawing as the author does from the wells of different faith traditions in her life. Rabbi Shefa Gold is adept at teaching us how to grow spiritually using the Torah as the inexhaustible source. Please read this book if you too want to grow."

Archbishop Emeritus Desmond Tutu

"Even old places and familiar texts we thought we knew come alive again in this book of substance and deep spiritual refreshment. Here experience takes precedence over tired and literal dogmatic pronouncements and life comes alive again."

Theologian **Matthew Fox**, author of *A New Reformation: Creation Spirituality and the Transformation of Christianity*

WHAT PEOPLE ARE SAYING ABOUT

TORAH JOURNEYS

"The very word '*torah*' is from the ancient Hebrew vocabulary of archery. It means not the bull's eye, not the archer, not the arrow, but the process of aiming. This is what Rabbi Shefa Gold has given us — the truthful, artful aiming at the soul within. Within the Torah, and within each reader."

Rabbi Arthur Waskow, director, The Shalom Center; author, *Godwrestling–Round 2;* co-author, *The Tent of Abraham*

"No other contemporary teacher I know presents Scripture as so hands-on-accessible a tool for transforming personal suffering into happiness."

Sylvia Boorstein, author of *It's Easier Than You Think: The Buddhist Way to Happiness*

"Rabbi Gold opens each Torah portion in profound, new ways, pointing the way for us to find the Torah's most usable blessings, spiritual challenges, and sustainable practices for our own journeys. In Torah Journeys, Torah becomes a mirror for our lives and a tool for personal transformation."

Rabbi Tirzah Firestone, Jungian Therapist; author of *The Receiving: Reclaiming Jewish Women's Wisdom* and *With Roots in Heaven: One Woman's Passionate Journey Into The Heart of Her Faith*

"Torah Journeys is a wonderful opportunity to discover the depths of Jewish wisdom teachings through the guidance of a teacher who brings a perfect combination of heartfulness and skillfulness along with a passion for profound spiritual inquiry."

Rabbi David A Cooper, author of *God is a Verb*

Lynne Baker 2011

TORAH JOURNEYS:
AN INNER PATH TO THE PROMISED LAND

BY RABBI

SHEFA GOLD

Ben Yehuda Press
Teaneck, New Jersey

Published by Ben Yehuda Press
430 Kensington Road
Teaneck, NJ 07666

http://www.BenYehudaPress.com

For permission to reprint, including distribution of the material in this book as part of a synagogue or school newsletter, please contact:
Permissions, Ben Yehuda Press,
430 Kensington Road, Teaneck, NJ 07666.
permissions@BenYehudaPress.com.

Ben Yehuda Press books may be purchased for educational, business or sales promotional use. For information, please contact:
Special Markets, Ben Yehuda Press,
430 Kensington Road, Teaneck, NJ 07666.
markets@BenYehudaPress.com.

cover illustration ©Kit Hevron Mahoney www.brushstrokesstudio.com

ISBN Number: 09769862-6-4
ISBN-13: 978-0-9769862-6-3

Library of Congress Control Number: 2006935072

06 07 08 09 / 10 9 8 7 6 5 4 3 2

For Rachmiel

Like an apple tree among the trees of the wood.
In that shade I delight to sit
Tasting his sweet fruit.

TABLE OF CONTENTS

TABLE OF TORAH PORTIONS

ACKNOWLEDGEMENTS

I AM GRATEFUL...

...to *Rachmiel* for coming to Torah with Beginner's Mind and opening my eyes to the treasures hidden so obviously. Your keen eye, open heart and dedication to practice inspire me daily. Thank you for your amazing and skillful editing. Those long hours of careful reading and comment have been an extraordinary gift. I thank the Great Mystery that has brought you to me. We have birthed this miracle in sacred partnership.

...to *Eve and Larry Yudelson* for believing in my vision and challenging me to make it accessible to the world. Your sweet patience, understanding and determination have guided me through the process of manifesting my dream.

...to *Kit Mahoney* for her beautiful image which had been planted in my heart for many years. You have expressed in form and color, a hint of that which I give and receive – an invitation to walk the sacred path of Torah.

...to the "4-8-8ers" – *Arthur Waskow, Phyllis Berman, David and Shoshana Cooper, Shaya Isenberg, Bahira Sugarman.* Your steadfast companionship on this journey has given me a place to rest along the way.

...to my colleagues at the Institute for Jewish Spirituality. Thank you for giving me a place to be nurtured and challenged, where my practice and teaching might be strengthened and refined.

...to *Mickey Singer, Barbara Zacky, Rich Lenson* and *Judith Dack.* Your ongoing support and encouragement has sustained me through thick and thin.

...to *my students at Kol Zimra.* The opportunity to serve you has been a powerful force in my life. You call forth the Mystery from my depths.

...to *Paul Ray,* who saw who I was becoming and acknowledged the books that were waiting inside me to be written.

...to *my teachers at the Reconstructionist Rabbinical College* who provided me with the tools for digging in the treasure-house of my heritage. I especially want to acknowledge my teacher of Bible, Tikvah Frymer-Kensky (ז'ל) who encouraged my wildly creative musings while grounding me in serious scholarship.

…to *Melila Hellner* for illuminating the world of Midrash. Your delight in the text has inspired me to be an adventurer.

…to *Sylvia Boorstein* for your friendship that sustains me with its humor and depth.

…to *Reb Zalman Schachter-Shalomi* for your courage and example. You have opened the doors wide for me just by being true to yourself.

…to *Jeanette Gross* for your love and dedication as webmaster. Your hard work and loyal attention have helped bring these Journeys to birth.

…to *Lenny Grob* for teaching me that questions are holy.

Introduction

Torah is a spiraling mirrored pathway that is opened to us week by week. It is the *Sha'ar Tzedek*, the Gate of Righteousness, through which we may enter fully into our own lives.

For millenia, the reading of the Torah — the Five Books of Moses — has stood as a central Jewish practice.

At its core the reading of the Torah is meant to re-enact the Divine Revelation. In the Jewish tradition, the entire Torah is revealed to us in the course of a year.[1]

When I read Torah each week I search for the blessing in it; I receive the spiritual challenge and rise to meet that challenge; and I am guided in my practice.

Torah as Blessing

I have discovered a way of receiving Torah that transforms each line, each word, each letter into a blessing that infuses every moment of my life. This blessing is so alive within me that it calls out to be shared.

A young boy reluctantly studying for his Bar Mitzvah once complained to me. "Why do we have to read the same stories every year?" he whined. "What's the point?"

I undressed the ancient scroll and rolled it open to that week's reading.

"This is just the mirror," I said. "The real Torah is the Torah of our lives. Every week I get to see another aspect of my experience mirrored here. And every year when I read the same story, something new is reflected back to me."

Torah, defined in its narrowest sense consists of the five books of Moses – Genesis, Exodus, Leviticus, Numbers, and Deuteronomy. This definition can be expanded to include all the holy books – the writings of the Prophets, Joshua, Judges, Samuel, Kings, Psalms, Proverbs, Job, Ruth, Chronicles, Esther, Ecclesiastes, Daniel, Ezra, Nehemiah, Lamentations, the Song of Songs.

Torah is also understood to include not only the ancient writings, but also all the commentaries and responses to those texts, the commentaries on the commentaries, the laws that are derived from the text, the poetry and songs that have been inspired by those texts, and the stories that

[1] See appendix for Torah reading schedules, p.234

have emerged in the white spaces between the words that our ancestors have left us.

Every year I read the story again and something new is reflected back to me.

I am continually amazed by this "something new." The flow of blessing from Torah is nothing I could have imagined receiving. I grew up sensing that there was something tragic about being Jewish. I knew that my inheritance sensitized me to the suffering in the world and that there was something noble about this sensitivity. I knew that Judaism was so deep in my blood that it was useless to deny it or avoid it. So I accepted being Jewish as the work I was being given in this lifetime. Often I felt its weight as a burden that would either break me or teach me about some kind of strength that I could not yet imagine.

Judaism existed as the background to my spiritual search as I delved into the philosophies and practices of Sufism, Buddhism, Mystical Christianity, Native American Religion, Astrology, Tarot, the I Ching, Taoism, Yoga and various schools of Shamanism. I wasn't merely a dabbler. I surrendered to the transformative force that moved through each practice. I sought out teachers, studied the ancient texts, engaged in the process of retreat, and listened to the voice of Truth as it was filtered through different languages and cultures.

When my explorations of these practices and teachings gave me wondrous glimpses of the whole and holy, when they allowed me an experience of Unity that satisfied my deepest yearning, I was oddly disturbed.

"What does this mean about being Jewish?" I wondered.

If doing Sufi Zhikr led me to an experience of God, did that mean I must become a Muslim?

If Vipassana Meditation opened up a great spaciousness inside me, must I become a Buddhist?

This crisis of identity made me take long look at Judaism, my inheritance. I wasn't ignorant of Torah, but its doors hadn't opened for me.

From my experience with other traditions, I made an assumption that the same riches that I found elsewhere were hidden behind the locked doors of Torah. Every Tradition, I reasoned, must contain the tools to expand consciousness, to become fully human, to know God. This assumption guided me, kept me looking. Because, thank God, I had tasted that expanded consciousness in the context of other traditions, I knew what to look for.

Those doors have opened slowly over many years, by equal measures of effort and grace. Still, the transformation of Torah from burden to blessing seems nothing but miraculous. I am drawn towards simplicity and emptiness in my practice, and I struggled against what seemed like endless Jewish ramblings, thousands of years of accumulated clutter. I am an ardent feminist, and I struggled against the patriarchal and sexist attitudes behind the text. Having experienced the treasures of other spiritual paths I have become quite universalistic in my approach, and I struggled against the triumphalism and intolerance that I found in Torah.

Yet, here I am feeling completely blessed by my ancestors, feeling their permission to make the Torah my own. They accept my criticism with humility and ask for my compassion. And they invite me to dig deeper.

"Whatever you find here in Torah is also inside you. This is the map. You are the landscape."

My ancestors call me back to Torah again and again, saying, "Do you want to know what it means to be human? Then look here."

It has become our tradition to read the Torah publicly amid great ceremony. The scroll is brought out from its ark as if a grand queen is descending from her throne. When she is paraded around the Temple, everyone clamors to kiss the hem of her gowns. Then she is brought up to the reader's table and delicately undressed.

As the Torah lays there open, her robes are placed across her nakedness, and we are called for an "*aliyah*" – an opportunity to raise up our consciousness to the level of Torah and receive her blessing. In the traditions of Jewish Renewal, whatever text is read during your *aliyah* determines the nature of your blessing.

I was nearly 30 before I experienced my first *aliyah*. When I was growing up in New Jersey at a Conservative congregation, women were not allowed to come up to the Torah, so I felt somewhat of a distance from the whole ceremony of Torah reading.

When it happened, my first experience of *aliyah* was one of the pivotal moments that allowed the door of blessing to open.

My friend Abigail asked me to come with her to a little *shul* in Petaluma, California. She described the people there as "old socialist chicken farmers," which piqued my interest. When I entered, the first thing I noticed was that at the end of each pew, a beautiful woman's face was carved. I imagined that the Goddess Herself was standing guard amid the worshipers.

My friend and I were the only ones in the room younger than 70. A *minyan* of old chicken farmers looked at us with appreciation and curiosity. They soon determined that I would receive the first *aliyah*. I was the only one there who was a Kohen, which means that my father was of a priestly lineage.

I QUICKLY SCANNED the text that was to be read for my special honor, and my heart sank. Everything that I hated about Torah seemed to be crammed into those few lines. I can't recall what the words were exactly; I only remember my response.

I was cursing my bad luck when my name was ceremoniously called and the eyes of a dozen leftist chicken farmers were upon me.

I stood up beside the Torah and recited the opening blessing, numb with self-pity. The text that was chanted was filled with hatred and violence. Between the sound of those words I heard a loving voice whisper to me from someplace deep inside, "This is yours, too." I was startled awake then, and my heart opened.

For a moment, there was no one "out there" to criticize. There was no evil in the world, in history or in Torah that was not also inside me. I was being given the opportunity to wake up to the fullness of my humanity. The fierce blessing of Torah was being given to me as a gift to be unwrapped. Inside every blessing is a spiritual challenge.

MY *ALIYAH*, the raising of my consciousness to the level of Torah, freed me from the compulsion to reject what I didn't like in Torah. I could accept all of it as flawed, just like me. Ahhh, but in the awareness of our flaws we can become fully realized, which means we can choose to live from the truth of our interconnectedness, rather than from the places of fear and separation within us.

This was the spiritual challenge given to me inside the blessing of Torah.

In receiving the blessing of Torah, we can, like our father Abraham, "become a blessing." To be a blessing is to know and radiate the truth that our existence itself is holy.

TORAH AS SPIRITUAL CHALLENGE

JUDAISM IS A GREAT STOREHOUSE of treasures and blessing. And it is a vital, dynamic, living conversation that spans the globe and the centuries. Every generation inherits the accumulation of text, music, commentary, law, custom, recipes, and secret wisdom. And it is the responsibility of each generation to fully receive, re-interpret, add to the treasure and pass it on in a form that is more relevant and more alive to our present-day challenges.

This is the challenge we are given as we receive the Torah: to step right into the conversation in midstream. The miracle of Revelation happens in the conversation. And it is our sacred responsibility to hold up our end.

That word – responsibility – makes a lot of sense if you understand it as the ability-to-respond.

"There is a river; its streams water the cities of God, *Nahar p'lagav y'samchu ir Elohim.*"[1]

"What river is this?" asks Rashi, the great medieval commentator, who concludes that it is the river that flows forth from the Garden of Eden, the place where we all come from, the Garden of Delight.

The river that flows out from this garden of perfection is still flowing, but it has become an underground river that branches out in many streams beneath our feet. Right now as we read these words, it is flowing deep through the holy ground of our lives. It is the river that connects us with our Source and quenches the thirst that underlies all thirst.[2] This river of solemn joy, ever present beneath the surface, invites us to dig deep within this here and now to find the truth of our liberation. Judaism provides the shovel.

Our inheritance is a treasure chest filled with tools, created and refined for thousands of years, that can help us to dig beneath the surface of our lives; to find meaning here and now; to act in ways that reveal the essential mystery of Creation and our interconnection with all life.

When we are connected to that river of joy, then we have the strength and inspiration to participate consciously in our own evolution.

These treasured tools are language, story, culture, the rhythm of the festivals, music, meditative techniques and the ancient dreams that were born of the wilderness.

These tools are sometimes locked away, hidden behind a great misunderstanding. Although the river of solemn joy continues to flow on beneath us, we become dry and crusty, bitterly imprisoned on the surface of things. It is as if the great misunderstanding forms a concrete pavement which separates us from the ground of our being.

As a rabbi I often encounter this misunderstanding. People see Judaism as a set of rules and they come to me with questions about how they should live their lives. Their understanding is that if only these rules are closely followed, everything will be fine. "Tell me what is kosher and

[1] Psalms 46:5

[2] The image of the underground river was introduced to me by Matthew Fox in his teachings about Meister Eckhart

what is *treif*." "Tell me the words that should be said on this occasion." "How do I fulfill this obligation?" "What is the *Halacha*?"

The word "*Halacha*" means, "The Way," the Tao. It is the manifest spirit of guidance that helps us take the next step in our journey. Originally *Halacha* was something fluid. Torah was interpreted anew for each generation according to principles of goodness and kindness and justice. "Every day the Torah should seem to you as if it had been given on that day," says the Midrash.

The word *Mitzvot*, usually translated as "commandments," has in its Aramaic root the meaning, "connection." Through the *Mitzvot* we can connect with our Source. With every spiritual practice I do and with every prayer I say, I ask: Is this working?

Is it connecting me to that river of solemn joy, to the truth hidden inside this moment? Does this practice make me more compassionate? Does this prayer open my heart, expand the boundaries of soul, and connect me to others?

Or does it separate me, blind me to beauty, make me more judgmental, and dull my senses? If so, then it cannot be Torah, for Torah can only be "*Darchei Noam*,"[1] the ways of pleasantness. If it doesn't grow my love, then it isn't Torah, for Torah is a manifestation of the Great Love, the "*Ahava Raba*" with which God loves us.

Our generation, like each generation of Jews before us, must enter into the holy conversation of our tradition. It is a conversation that takes place across time and distance, and it dies if we refuse to hold up our end.

We must reach in to Torah, into the treasure of our inheritance, in search of answers to the questions of our time.

We bring to this conversation our dilemmas – the crises of body, heart, mind and soul that so urgently call.

As you seek to join this conversation, you must be careful of this common and insidious misunderstanding: You might think that receiving is a passive thing, that the truth is already formed, that someone else's Torah will speak to you, and that the Torah of the past will suffice. You might think that our tradition is inexorably fixed, and if it doesn't fit your sensibilities, then you are free to look elsewhere.

But that is to misunderstand that our tradition is a conversation, and that a conversation includes all who participate.

When we reach in to Torah, we receive its essence through word, music, or story, and then mingle that essence with our own desire. That mingling happens in the innermost reaches of the heart. To participate in this process we must cultivate and nurture an inner life. And we must

[1] Proverbs 3:17

create a life that is spacious enough that we can pay attention to the subtle shiftings of the heart, to the still small voice that is forever whispering to us the truth of who we are becoming. "*HaYom*," you will experience the infinite treasure of this present moment," promises the psalmist, "*Im b'kolo tishma-u,*"[2] if only you would listen to that voice.

Reaching in to the Torah means participating in a process, and becoming part of the conversation. It requires digging down beneath the soil of your everyday life and finding its holiness.

> **A student, expecting to hear a profound and esoteric answer, asked his Rebbe, "How can I best serve God?" The Rebbe replied, "You can best serve God with whatever you are doing at the moment."**

And here is the challenge: How can I make my life holy, moment by moment? How can I tap into that underground river that flows beneath my feet?

My way of reading Torah, of "doing Torah," is influenced by three streams.

The first stream is Martin Buber's philosophy of Dialogue which places the locus of holiness in "the Between," in the conversation, in the connection, in relationship. My relationship with the text demands that I bring all of my self — heart, mind, body, spirit, memory, aspiration — to the experience of Torah. It demands my full presence, which means sometimes setting aside old interpretations, and allowing the truth of this moment to emerge in the space between the text and myself. It means becoming vulnerable, acknowledging feelings that are triggered in me, following the trajectory of my associations as I ask myself, "What does this remind me of...?"

The spiritual challenge of Torah is to let it touch me, even when it makes me uncomfortable.

The second stream of influence is dream work. When I started paying close attention to my dreams, I began to learn their language and develop tools for translating that language into my waking wisdom.

I worked for a number of years leading dream groups. It was an amazing and enlightening experience. Each week one person would bring their dream to the group. On first reading, the dream often seemed so simple and we wondered what there would be to talk about for three hours. Every time, by the end of the evening it felt as if we had just begun

---

[2] Psalm 95:7

to mine its riches. So many pathways had opened, and we were always surprised.

One aspect of the technique we used was to pretend that someone else's dream was our own, to ask, "What would this dream mean if I had dreamt it?" Through my work with dreams, I learned to look beneath the surface, to pay attention to language, image and feeling tone.

There was a moment in my first year of rabbinical school when I realized that the Torah was so much like a dream. It is the dream of our people, the dream that illuminates our inner landscape, the dream that holds the key to our waking wisdom. That moment of realization felt like I was waking up and receiving a great gift. I held the Torah before me and asked, "What would this dream mean if I had dreamt it?" And the truth is I had… we have all dreamt this Torah into being.

To receive the spiritual challenge of Torah means to wake up and rise to the task of interpreting this awesome dream in ways that are useful to our lives, in ways that speak to this moment.

One way of understanding dreams is to see each element, each character in the drama as parts of ourselves. To dream is to manifest all the various and conflicting elements that make up our psyche, so that we can begin to truly know ourselves. Self-knowledge becomes then the key to self-realization.

I call this process of receiving the Torah as our collective dream, "Dream Exegesis."

When I come to a text, the first rule of dream exegesis is:

> **This is not about some other people who lived way back when. It is about what is happening inside me, at this very moment.**

And then I use the dream of Torah to send me to that truth within. I find that the further within I go, the more that oh-so-personal truth is actually a truth that is universal. I enter through the personal, and if I persevere, if I don't stop at the sentimental, nostalgic or historical, then I will be rewarded with a Wisdom that transcends the personal and connects me with the treasure of my humanity.

The third stream of influence comes from my experience with *aliyot* as they have been practiced in Jewish Renewal. This tradition is to "call up" to the Torah anyone who resonates with the themes of the text that is to be recited. Those who come up for an *aliyah* have the opportunity to receive a blessing that is connected with the theme of the text.

As this tradition evolved, I began to understand that every blessing holds within it a spiritual challenge. I must rise to the spiritual challenge in order to receive the blessing. I saw that coming up for an *aliyah* was not a trivial thing. It held the opportunity to rise to the challenge of Torah, to do the work that I was born to do, to step up to my potential. I can only do this through practice. In this way my spiritual practice is given to me through Torah. In receiving the blessing, I must discern the inherent challenge, and then rise to that challenge through my spiritual practice.

When I receive Torah as spiritual challenge, I must rise to the occasion. I call on the strength and the inspiration of my ancestors and I receive a vision of what is possible.

For me this is a truly joyful process. A challenge energizes me and pushes me to reach and expand beyond my current beliefs and opinions. I am called into the unknown.

Through the challenge of Torah I receive my life anew.

Torah as Guidance for Practice

My awareness, deliberate intention and loving attitude towards any particular moment of my life give that moment the power to grow into a spiritual practice. In that moment, I gather up my attention, focus the fullness of my energy, and surrender to the Presence that emerges from this particular here and now.

I am always breathing, but it is not until I bring awareness to the breath that it becomes a practice.

There are times I must deal with difficult or challenging relationships. It is only when I bring a particular intention to my part in the drama, and begin learning from the encounter, that nurturing those relationships becomes a practice.

Each morning, I make myself a cup of tea. When my attitude towards the making of tea is one of care-full reverence, then tea becomes a practice.

As soon as I go on "automatic" — lost in thought patterns, living from habit or becoming unconscious of my body or feelings — my spiritual practice is suspended.

Judaism is a spiritual path that seeks to transform each step of the way into a holy moment of blessing. To know each moment of my life as a spiritual practice is both energizing and humbling. It is energizing because practice gives relevance and meaning to even the smallest actions, and it is humbling because through the focus of practice, I am made aware of how much of my life I miss when I am distracted or scattered.

The first time I was seriously faced with the issue of practice was when I was eight years old and began taking piano lessons. I would sit at the piano each day and inside my head I could hear exactly what the piece should sound like. I would place my fingers on the keys wanting to play perfectly the first time.

The sound that I produced could scarcely compare to my expectations; it was so frustrating! I would cry at every single lesson. My piano teacher, Mrs. Held, who lived up the block, didn't know what to do with me. There was something fundamental about the idea of practice that eluded me.

Over the years I have come to realize that practice exists for itself, not for some imagined perfection. I can find joy in accepting myself exactly where I am. I can delight in the process itself as the music takes shape under my hands, in my ears and in my heart. I can give myself to the "Spirit of the Work."

It was only after many years of spiritual practice that the "Spirit of the Work" introduced himself formally to me. I was teaching a weeklong workshop at Elat Chayyim, a Jewish Retreat Center in the Catskills. Each morning I'd begin class by singing a *niggun*, a wordless melody, while people entered the room. This was my way of preparing the space, getting grounded and opening up to guidance.

On the second morning, nearly everyone was late. I closed my eyes and sang as people straggled in. Inwardly I was wrestling with my annoyance at the situation when I was startled by the feeling of a strong and expansive presence entering the space. I recognized his presence immediately. He introduced himself to me with the declaration, "I am the Spirit of the Work…and **I'm not staying**!"

Even though I was annoyed at my students for being late, I knew that I must argue with all my heart on their behalf and somehow convince the Spirit of the Work to stay. (Through this episode I was given a small glimpse of what Moses might have experienced as he defended the rebellious children of Israel before God.) I understood the value of the presence of this Spirit. Through my own practice, I have found that I feel both guided and empowered when I acknowledge the awesome power of the Work and approach it with respect and reverence.

The Spirit of the Work is an aspect of God that calls us to our potential. This Spirit requires effort from me, but it is a requirement that different than carrying a burden of obligation. When I am engaged in The Work, I am more fully my Self. The Work reminds me that I am completely ordinary and at the same time powerfully noble. The Work asks me to accept myself exactly as I am, while remaining open to the full force of the longing and desire within me that will give me the strength to move beyond my self-imposed limitations.

As a spiritual seeker I have learned that being given an important insight is like receiving a seed. That seed must be planted in the soil of my life and then watered and fertilized by my attention and practice.

In the study of Torah we can receive some amazing seeds, but if those seeds aren't planted and cultivated, they will remain fascinating, beautiful, disembodied abstractions. We will not be transformed by Torah until we commit to the practice that will grow the seed... which means that we are ultimately called to grow our own souls.

Once we intuit the blessing that is hidden in Torah and then discern the spiritual challenge that Torah lays before us, we are obliged to ask: "What is the practice that will help me to rise to this spiritual challenge and receive the blessing of Torah?"

Spiritual practice requires **intention, awareness** and **repetition.**

The word for intention in Hebrew is "*kavanah*." It refers to the direction of the heart. Energy pours through us all the time; when we consciously direct our hearts towards a purpose or value, the energy then becomes focused and clear. We can concentrate the power of our bodily passions, emotional moods, thoughtful insights, and visionary imaginings towards a single-pointed purpose. That purpose comes to guide us as our practice deepens and evolves over time.

Awareness is the aspect of consciousness that witnesses and investigates the immediate and ongoing effects of practice. In our spiritual practice we move through different states of consciousness. The rule of practice is this:

The awareness of a state magnifies its benefit.

Awareness transforms our practice from a series of spiritual experiences to the possibility of embodying, integrating, and living the spiritual truths of Torah in ways that heal and unify both our souls and our world. Through awareness we wake up to the blessings that are everywhere hidden. Through awareness we learn to acknowledge our resistance and then we'll know just where to apply our most loving attention.

Another important and sometimes misunderstood aspect of practice is repetition. Each time a practice is repeated there is an opportunity to take it deeper, to explore its subtleties, to receive new insights. Realizing my tendency for impatience, one of my teachers warned me that I needed to do a practice for three months before I discerned its effects, before I could evaluate whether it "worked." Sometimes I will teach a particular meditation and a student will respond in frustration, crying, "I can't do this!" or they might do it once and say, "Oh I know this ..." and stop right there. In both cases they have missed the meaning of the phrase, "It takes practice!"

Practices that appear quite simple can be deepened and refined over a lifetime. Imagine the old Tai Chi Master who repeats the very same movements that he learned as a child. As his practice matures, those simple movements unlock treasure upon treasure of wisdom and power and gradually reveal the secrets of embodied love.

Our practice gathers up the power and flash of temporary states of consciousness – spiritual experiences that pierce through the dullness of our "normal" trance – and harnesses that power to move us to a new stage of development.

Torah becomes a transformational force in our lives and the world when we move from just reading, thinking and talking about it to actually *doing* it. The "doing" of Torah is not a literal following of its commandments, but rather an actualizing of its Light. We "do Torah" by cultivating a dynamic and challenging practice that explores the "edge" of our learning.

Knowing and working your edge is an important aspect of practice. My edge can be found in the dissonance between what I know to be true and how I actually live.

In the language of Judaism our practice is guided by the *mitzvot,* which literally means "commandments." But what if the commandments don't come from "out there?" What if the Divine Commander is not separate from the inner core of my Being? What if God's will unfolds through even the smallest details of my life? What if these eyes, these hands, this heart, these ears are the vehicle for Divine vision, touch, love, and receptivity?

My obedience to the *mitzvot,* to my Creator, becomes obedience to the evolution of consciousness, to the manifestation of Love. The practice I establish depends on my willingness to wholeheartedly play my small but integral part in this cosmic drama.

Journeying Through Torah

My spirituality is very practical, so when I approach a text, I ask, "How can I read this in a way that will be useful?"

How will the study/experience affect my awareness, state of consciousness, sensitivity to others, or capacity to give and receive Love?

How can I dedicate the power of this text to the force of evolution that moves me towards loving awareness of the Whole of Life and its Holiness?

After my first year of studying Talmud intensively in Rabbinical School, I remember coming home to my husband who said, "You know, Shefa, you are much more argumentative since you started studying Talmud." He was right.

I was practicing the art of argument which cultivated a mind that was very keen, quick, and competitive. My fellow rabbinical students and I engaged in Torah study trying to "figure out" the text — master it — and become smarter somehow. We were all encountering an ancient Jewish neurotic pattern that whispered, "You'll never be smart enough…" which only made us study harder.

At some point I made a decision that I didn't need to get any smarter.

I needed instead to open my heart wider to the blessings of Torah that I knew were there. The powers of critical thinking were not going to unlock those blessings.

I needed to fully receive the spiritual challenge that Torah was offering me. I needed to to start learning to focus my courage, honesty and determination in order to rise to that challenge.

(I certainly haven't stopped learning, but my learning is fueled by a joyous curiosity rather than the neurotic quest for MORE knowledge.)

Instead of attempting to master Torah, I determined to surrender to its power and allow myself to be transformed by it. I decided to climb aboard and let Torah take me on a journey. The journey of Torah is the journey of the soul. Every soul travels the path of self-realization which is a process of enlightenment and expanding awareness. This is the path of the finite discovering its hidden infinitude, the Human waking up to its Divinity.

I lift myself up to the level of Torah and ask, "How can I read this in a way that will be useful for my life right now?"

Well, first I want to know, "What is this about?" Instead of just collecting lots of particulars and haphazardly piling them up inside me… I want to know where to put all these ideas, stories, laws, myth, history, and poetry. Entertaining the question, "What is this about?" enables me to contextualize and understand the purpose of each of those myriad details. I am able then to put the words of Torah to good use.

It is the same in conversation. When people talk to me, I first like to know what they are talking about. Then I can listen attentively and better process the information that is expressed by their words and presence. When I don't know what the topic is, I have a harder time listening and taking in the details.

I WEAR TWO very different kinds of lenses as I read Torah. One lens is like a magnifying glass that focuses in on specific words or phrases in which I sense hidden treasures of power and mystery.

As I read, my ears and heart are listening, watching for energy surges that happen when I am in the presence of veiled power or beauty.

I watch for difficulties in the text which appear like cracks on the smooth surface of the narrative. The cracks become doorways through which I enter to step inside the text. I know that what looks like a problem from the outside will become a portal to expanded consciousness if only I can find my way "inside." What begins as a contradiction proceeds into the realm of paradox. Paradox stretches the mind beyond its normal confines and is a sign that I am encountering the realm of ultimate truth.

The other lens I wear when I encounter holy text is panoramic — I see the whole weekly Torah portion at a glance.

I ask, "What is this really about?" I create a frame or context for understanding the purpose and meaning brought to my life by the text in this very moment. Sometimes meaning is revealed through the juxtaposition of seemingly disparate (though adjacent) texts, rather than looking at a passage by itself.

I HAVE ALSO USED the wide-angle lens, seeing as a whole each of the Torah's five books. This gives me insight into the entire flow of the Journey of Soul.

This framework has been useful to me in my journey: I offer it to you so that you can try it on and ask the question yourself, "What is this really about?" Asking this question is a sacred act. When I keep in mind (and heart) this reminder that the Torah is the story of my soul's journey and that it can help me navigate my way, then there is less chance that I will get lost or trapped in the myriad details of the text. I can dedicate my understanding of those details to the overall context and underlying purpose of this journey of Torah.

For me, the Book of Genesis is about INCARNATION.
The Book of Exodus is about LIBERATION.
The Book of Leviticus is about HOLINESS.
The Book of Numbers is about JOURNEY.
And the Book of Deuteronomy is about PRACTICE.

These over-arching themes help me to receive the words of Torah and put them to good use in my own process of self-realization, growth, healing and the unfolding awareness of my soul-journey.

THE BOOK OF GENESIS is about INCARNATION.

By Incarnation, I mean the flow of the Infinite into the finite reality of our physical world. Genesis first addresses the mystery of Creation, tracing the flow of pure potential as it becomes manifest. This is not merely a history of Creation; it is a description of a process that is happening now, at this very moment. "*V'nahar yotzei me-eden l'hashkot et hagan,*"[1] the river issues forth from Eden to water the Garden of our own Lives. The Divine blessing is flowing forth at this very moment and our job is to learn to receive it. In order to receive this blessing we must become fully embodied, fully Human.

Being Human means accepting yourself as part of a family (however complicated that is) and entering into the drama of identity, inheritance and belonging.

All of the family stories in Genesis lead us ever-deeper into the tangle and density of material existence. By the end of the Book of Genesis, our souls have journeyed "down into Egypt" where they lose themselves and become enslaved to the material plane. The Hebrew word for Egypt, "*Mitzrayim,*" means "the narrow places." *Mitzrayim* represents the narrow consciousness that sees the material world as "all there is."

THE BOOK OF EXODUS is about LIBERATION.

As Exodus begins, the pressure and narrowness of our slavery and conditioning call forth the diamond of prophesy in the image of Moses. He represents the spark of enlightened wakefulness at the very center of the dull hard husks of this material world.

As prophesy awakens, a groaning cry emerges from the heart of our suffering and is answered by God's loving perspective. "*Min hametzar karati Yah; Anani bamerkhav Yah.*"[2] From the narrow places I called out to God who answered me with the Divine Expanse.

---

[1] Genesis 2:10

[2] Psalm 118:5

The process of liberation begins with the awareness of our enslavement. This process then moves in stages, through plague and miracle as we explore the true meaning of freedom. At each point in the process – the crossing of the Sea, the journey through the wilderness, the gift of Revelation – we realize that we are not yet free. We discover that the bitterness of slavery has corrupted and poisoned us. The imprint of slavery exiles us into habit and the illusion of separateness.

Through the story of Exodus we remember the true meaning and purpose of freedom. Again and again God reminds us, "I brought you out of Egypt to BE YOUR GOD" in other words, "to be in relationship with you."

That relationship, that awareness of our connection to the Source and all Creation, is what sets us free. The last third of the Book of Exodus is about the building of the *Mishkan* (the portable Sanctuary), which is the place where the intimate connection with God can manifest. God says, "Build me a holy place so that I can dwell inside you and between you."[1] Through this inter-connectedness, you will know freedom.

In the *Mishkan*, we get a glimpse of freedom and we taste the holiness of connection.

THE BOOK OF LEVITICUS is about HOLINESS.

That taste of holiness comes and goes, leaving us with a fragrant memory and a yearning for sustained connection. Then the Priest or Priestess within us rises up to face the challenge: What is the meaning of holiness and how is it sustained? Is there a sacred technology that can keep us close to God? Are there principles of justice and love that can inform each step of the journey of soul and open our hearts to the Mystery that surrounds and fills our lives?

Our spiritual lives revolve around building a *Mishkan* within us and between us – a place for the Divine Presence to dwell. Yet even the *Mishkan* – our spiritual practice – is in danger of corruption, rigidity, deception and pettiness. How do we keep our *Mishkan* safe? How do we purify our intentions as we continue to build those holy places within and between us?

Often the Book of Leviticus speaks in the language of *Korbanot*, which is translated as "sacrifices," but literally means "the way of coming close" to God. *Korbanot* prescribe a system of addressing the many broken connections between human and Divine. Each *korban* describes a pathway of Return. Leviticus explores the nature of holiness – how to notice (and what to do) when we have distanced ourselves from the blessing of connection.

[1] Exodus 25:8

THE BOOK OF NUMBERS is about JOURNEY.

At some point on our soul's journey, we realize that it is indeed a journey. We realize that the destination is not as important as the path itself. The journey becomes holy as we open ourselves to its power to heal and transform us. The very act of becoming aware of the purpose of our journey changes the nature of each step. When we understand that the journey is meant to heal us and set us free from that which enslaves us on the inside, then each bend in the road becomes an opportunity for awakening.

The Book of Numbers, (called in Hebrew, *BaMidbar*, "In the Wilderness") begins with a census, representing the process of thorough self-awareness. The purpose of our journey cannot be fulfilled until we know who it is that is making this journey, and who it is we are becoming through our encounter with God in the wilderness. Only in the wilderness, the place outside of our civilized constructs of reality, can this transformation take place.

THE BOOK OF DEUTERONOMY is about PRACTICE.

In Hebrew the book is called *Devarim*, after its opening phrase, "These words." The oldest name of the book, however, is "*Mishneh Torah*, The Repetition of the Torah." In the book of Deuteronomy, the wisdom that the Soul has accrued along the path is repeated, refined, and given to us again so that we can make it our own. "These Words" are given to us through Moses, the aspect of prophesy. Moses stands at the borders of the Holy Land and looks back at the whole of the path we have traveled. From his broad perspective he can help us make meaning of "the long strange trip it's been."[2] Through meaning we are encouraged and strengthened in our practice.

This journey teaches us to live each moment of Life as Practice. Through Practice, we learn to love God with the fullness of heart, soul and might, whether we are sitting, standing, walking or lying down.[3] To love fully takes a lot of practice; and it is impossible to love God without loving and identifying with all of God's creatures.

Towards the end of Deuteronomy, God instructs Moses to give the people a song, "to put it in their mouths,"[4] as a way of truly remembering. The song is a practice of remembrance which is necessary because it is so easy to become forgetful, complacent, distracted, and, at times of unconsciousness, to turn to "other gods" such as comfort, fame, entertainment, wealth or security.

---

[2] Robert Hunter, "Truckin'," on the Grateful Dead album, *American Beauty*, 1970

[3] Deuteronomy 6:7

[4] Deuteronomy 31:19

When the Moses/Prophet part of us creates the song, the practice of remembrance, she must use all her intelligence, artistry and passion to craft a practice that is beautiful, compelling and alive with subtlety.

When I remember that Deuteronomy is about Practice, then I am compelled to put "These Words" into action.

Journeying through Torah is a way of sanctifying my own Life's path. Though each of our paths is unique, we travel together through the same shared text. Let the ancient stories shine their light, illuminate, magnify and bestow upon each of us our own particular blessing and spiritual challenge.

The Destinations of Torah Journeys

Through my own process and journey of writing this book, my enthusiasm has been kindled into a fire that warms and illuminates so much more than my Torah practice. It illuminates my entire life.

One afternoon, I was passionately explaining to my friend Miryam what I was writing. I wanted her to understand the method I was using in my approach to text.

"It's a rigorous practice," I said. "You can't sit back and criticize or blame what you don't like in the Torah. Instead, you must search for those same difficulties in yourself and then engage in a process of healing and purification. Instead of blaming, you have to take responsibility."

As I sat with my friend in the afternoon light ardently expounding my approach to sacred text, I heard a voice speaking ever so gently yet firmly in my right ear.

"And you could live your whole life that way."

The tone of this voice was so matter-of-fact, so patient, and so loving. I continued my conversation with Miryam, but in some deep place I had been awakened to a challenge.

What would it mean to "live my whole life that way?"

What would happen if I stopped blaming, and instead channeled the energy of blame into self-examination and wise response?

What would it mean to look for the blessing in each moment?

What would it mean to consciously receive the spiritual challenge of each moment, each interaction, every feeling, each relationship, each paradox... and accept that challenge wholeheartedly?

What would it mean to look for and commit to a practice that would help me to rise to that challenge and receive the blessing of each moment?

I thought I was writing a book about accessing the treasures of Torah and I wanted to share this amazing journey. Now I see the true purpose of Torah Journeys. It is an exploration of this method of encountering the text so that we can apply the very same method to our encounter with the texts of our own lives – the day to day struggles and surprises that Life sends us.

RETURNING HOME to New Mexico, I find out my flight has been cancelled, that the next flight is overbooked, and that I will be stuck in Dallas Airport with hundreds of frustrated travelers for who knows how long. Can I stop and look for the blessing of this moment? After all, it provides time to read, and an opportunity to serve others with a friendly countenance. Can I rise to the spiritual challenge? What a good test this is of my patience, and an equally fine opportunity to practice surrender. Can I find the practice that will help me? I can work on keeping my heart open through it all, maintaining self-awareness, practicing conscious breath, and doing walking meditation.

I read a newspaper and am filled with rage against the injustices perpetrated by people who wield power in this world.

Can I transform that rage into wise and righteous response, taking action that will be both effective and appropriate?

Can I admit to the places of apathy, despair, numbness or fearful divisiveness inside my own heart?

Can I accept responsibility for my complicity in this unjust system?

Or will my anger become self-righteousness, rigidifying into an "us-versus-them" perspective that will leave me powerless and ineffective?

THE PRACTICE of receiving Torah – all of it – and using the whole text as a mirror of the inner landscape, prepares me to know my whole world in the same way. Each of us is a microcosm of Reality. To know the vast realms of Self is to know the Universe. And when I glimpse the Great Mystery of All, I am sent within to know that wholeness from the inside.

This is a rigorous practice. You cannot sit back and criticize or blame what you don't like in the world. Instead you must search for those same difficulties in yourself and then engage in a process of healing and purification. Instead of blaming, you must take responsibility.

To take responsibility means to fully live the life you are given and take your place in the cosmic dance – to intimately engage with the reality before you "with all your heart and with all your soul and with all your might." It means to finally grow up into your full stature as Lover – accepting the lavish blessing and daunting challenge of this world while resting fully in God's supporting embrace.

To spend our whole lives gladly "growing up" — becoming a vehicle for blessing, rising to the challenge of our humanity, committing ourselves to practices of compassion and justice — this is the most wondrous, exciting, adventure-filled journey there is!

Genesis

Bereshit

Incarnation

Bereshit

(In the Beginning)

GENESIS 1:1-6:8

God creates the world.

THE BLESSING

EVERY SHABBAT CELEBRATES CREATION and thus the continuing re-creation of our world.

Creation begins with Light, *(Or)*, which is another word for consciousness. God wraps us within garments of skin, *(Or)*, which is Light *(Or)* made dense. Our physical bodies and the whole world that we see enfolds the Light of Creation. In this way, our world both reveals and conceals the Light of Creation.

Describing Creation the Zohar says:

> **"The silkworm wraps itself within and makes itself a palace. This palace is its praise and a benefit to all."[1]**

Our journey of consciousness/Light leads us through embodiment, the palace of existence, to Enlightenment, where God waits for us, ever present.

From the purity and innocence of Eden we journey forth through Duality (represented by the Tree of Good and Evil), through self-knowledge, suffering, and mistakes, towards the Tree of Life, a tree that is rooted in the Divine Reality, with branches that find their flower in our humanity.

THE BLESSING COMES as we receive a vision of "the palace" (physical reality) and let its praise sing through us. God is here, inside all Creation, radiant and waiting.

The teachings of *Kabbala* address the mystery of how the Divine becomes manifest, how the infinite enters the finite, how we might possibly bridge the chasm between God and Creation. *Kabbala* gives us the image of the Tree of Life with its roots in Heaven and its branches reaching into human awareness. The Tree has ten *s'firot* which form the pathways from the infinite to the finite. Each *s'firah* is perceived as a set of associated

[1] Zohar 1:15a; translated by Daniel Matt, *Zohar: The Book of Enlightenment*, Paulist Press, 1983

images that elucidate a certain quality such as Loving-flow, Boundaried-strength, Balanced Beauty, Endurance, or Sparkling-Glory.

The Tree of Life is a vehicle for Blessing. It is the connection between Heaven and Earth, between the infinite and the finite.

The seven days correspond to the seven lower *s'firot* of the Tree of Life. Each of these seven days and *s'firot* blesses us with its own gift. Moving along the pathway of the Palace of Creation, we discover God Herself wrapped within. As we get closer, we ourselves unwrap the Mystery of existence: the presence of God within everything.

With the creation of Light (consciousness, the dividing of light from darkness) we receive the blessing of *Chesed* – of Love and Flow.

With the creation of the firmament (the separation of the waters above from the waters below) we receive the blessing of *Gevurah* – Boundaries, Strength and Discernment.

With the creation of land, sea, and vegetation, we receive the blessings of *Tiferet* – Beauty, Harmony and Balance.

With the Creation of the sun, moon, and stars, we receive the blessing of *Netzach* – Endurance.

With the creation of fishes and birds, we receive the blessing of *Hod* – Sparkle and Variety.

With the creation of land animals and humans in God's image, we receive the blessing of *Yesod* – Foundation, Regenerativity, Creativity.

And with the creation of Shabbat, we receive *Malkhut* – the Indwelling Presence.

In receiving all these blessings we enter "the palace" where we may hear the praise of all Creation. Then, the power of our shining awareness, overflowing gratitude, and resplendent praise can send all of those sparks back to their Source.

The Spiritual Challenge

Our soul's journey begins with the question, *"Ayeka*? Where are you?" Hearing God's first question, Adam hides, saying, "I was afraid because I was naked." The spiritual challenge of this beginning time is to know that we are utterly naked and vulnerable. Yet rather than hide, we are challenged to stand in our nakedness. We are spurred to uncover our essence, to let go of everything that we've acquired to keep us safe. We are required to stand in our vulnerability, to open to the power that moves through us. This vulnerability allows us to experience the energy and flow of an ever-shifting and dynamic Reality. Suzuki Roshi calls this condition Beginner's Mind:

> **"...mind free from possessing anything, a mind that knows everything is in flowing change. Nothing exists but momentarily in its present form and color. One thing flows into another and cannot be grasped."[2]**

Even one moment of Beginner's Mind wakes us up to the knowledge that we always perceive the world through our own specific lens. Our first challenge is to examine that lens in order to learn its peculiar distortions and colorings.

The second challenge is to receive Creation as a gift, experiencing the complete, swirling re-creation of the world in this present moment. Instead of trying to figure it all out by acquiring more and more data about the world, our challenge is to simply open to the gift of each breath and enter the process of freeing our attention so that we can receive, in radical amazement, the newness of each moment. This receptivity is dependent upon being present and finding a heart of gratefulness for this very moment.

The third challenge lies in becoming co-creators with God. Knowing that the world is being re-created at every moment, and knowing that I am created in God's image, I am challenged to open myself to the flow of Goodness and to let that flow be expressed through the workings and play of my life. Then I can begin to know myself as a partner with God in the work of Creation. I can surrender the power of my imagination and the skills of my hands to the co-creative work of shaping a holy life. I am called into partnership.

---

[2] Shunru Suzuki, *Zen Mind, Beginner's Mind,* John Weatherhill, 1970, p.138

Guidance for Practice

I will suggest three practices for this week of Bereshit, *of beginning time, that might help us to rise to the spiritual challenges delineated above.*

Seeing the World without Its Clothes On

Sit outside in a place of natural beauty and power. Close your eyes and gently let go of every thought. Return to the knowledge that the world you perceive consists of the garments of God. Immerse yourself in the knowledge that there is a special God-light hidden inside everything. Resolve to penetrate the surface of Creation in order to know God who is "wrapped" within this palace of Creation. With each out-breath, allow the world to undress, with each in-breath, breathe in the light that shines out from within Creation.

An Exploration of Gratefulness and Receptivity

Close your eyes and focus on your breath. Let the breath slow and deepen slightly. With each in-breath receive the gift of your life, and then let each out-breath be an expression of gratefulness for the gift you have just received.

A Very Simple yet Powerful Prayer

Just speak two words directly to God. "Use me."[3] If you are ready to say these words, (on some days I know that I am not ready or available) then open your eyes and be attentive to the opportunities for service that present themselves during the day. Another way to say this prayer is:

"Hineni, osah et atzmi merkava l'shekhina" [4]
Here I am, transforming myself
into a chariot for Divine Presence.

[3] This practice was shared with me by someone who learned it from Rashad Field.

[4] I learned this phrase from Yitzhak Buxbaum's book, *Jewish Spiritual Practices.*

Noah

GENESIS 6:9 - 11:32

The world is destroyed by a great flood. Noah builds an ark and is saved along with his family and a sampling of each species. He is given the rainbow as a sign of covenant. His descendants try to reach Heaven by building the tower of Babel. The tower is destroyed and the people are dispersed.

THE BLESSING

OUR CONSCIOUSNESS HOLDS A MEMORY of utter catastrophe, of the death and rebirth of this planet. The story of the Flood represents this awareness which awakens us to the preciousness of Life. And the story ends with a the blessing of a great promise.

It is upon this blessing that our spiritual life rests. God touches our memory of devastation and says, "This will never happen again." She makes a covenant with all of life and places a rainbow in the sky as a sign of that covenant. "I will look upon the rainbow and remember."[1] The blessing of the rainbow is the remembrance, the assurance, that we are ultimately safe. This deep unquestioned sense of security and trust in the essential goodness and rightness of Reality becomes the foundation for the process of awakening. This sense is so basic that changing circumstances and events cannot disrupt it. A. H. Almaas calls this quality, "Basic Trust." Its presence allows you to relax and JUST BE with whatever is.

BASIC TRUST GIVES US THE CAPACITY TO SURRENDER, to let go of doubt and step into the unknown. As limiting ego-structures dissolve and we open to an expanded perspective, it can feel as though everything we know is falling apart. The rainbow reminds us that whatever happens, we are safe. Even when terrible things happen, when the outer structures are destroyed and we are seemingly paralyzed by fear, the rainbow appears and reminds us of a deeper safety. YES, EVEN DEATH IS SAFE! And that sense of safety becomes the springboard for our next step. This innate and implicit trust ultimately manifests as a willingness to take that necessary leap into the unknown. And so Basic Trust manifests in the courage to be with what is, and then instead of being a reactive victim

[1] Genesis 9:16

of circumstance, you learn to live your life from a deep wisdom, a wide perspective.

The Portion of Noah blesses us with yet another rainbow: the story of the tower of Babel. The tower of our arrogant singular purpose topples and we are given a rainbow of diversity in its place. As we seek to touch the Unity (prompted by hunger for mastery or control), we are answered with multiplicity. We are sent on the rainbow journey to acknowledge every shade of experience, to recognize the whole spectrum of what it means to be human. We are blessed with complex beauty, confounding paradox, and the opportunity to know and enjoy all the separate colors that together form the magnificent white Light of the One.

The Spiritual Challenge

The Slonimer Rebbe describes the three levels of faith (*emunah*):

> **There are three rungs of Faith (*emunah*): Trusting Mind (*emunat ha-mo'ach*), Trusting Heart (*emunat ha-lev*), but there is a rung still higher, Trusting with your limbs/ embodiment (*emunat ha-evarim*): where Faith (*emunah*) penetrates every fibre of your being, where horror can't seize you, for your whole body feels the protective divine Presence.**
>
> **Complete *emunah* occurs when it unfolds in all three dimensions. As King David said, 'My heart and my flesh [my body] sing to the Living God.'[2] Not just the heart, but also the flesh, our skin and our muscles, our bones and limbs also sing to the Living God, for *Emunah* suffuses our entire being.[3]**

The spiritual challenge is to suffuse our entire being with a sense of ultimate safety, to integrate into our very bodies, the promise of the rainbow.

---

[2] Psalms 84:3

[3] *Netivot Shalom*, *Parashat Beshalach*, pp.113-115; also, *Mo'adim*, seventh day of Passover, pp. 281-283. I learned this text with Rabbi Elliot Ginsburg and am indebted to his elucidations.

This sense of security is our inheritance. And yet at some point we become disconnected from our Source and lose our Basic Trust. We feel betrayed and lose our footing. The spiritual challenge is to re-connect with the truth of our safety, no matter what happens, so that we can again feel "held" by the goodness of Life, the Ground of Being. Then we can rest in the Divine embrace. Almaas describes the challenge like this:

> **"It means experiencing the factors which brought about the profound disconnection from reality, and experiencing repeatedly the fundamental truth of non-separateness, to the point where the soul can again rest in the knowledge of that truth. Each new experience of essential truth deepens the soul's contact with her own basic trust."[4]**

As we receive the blessing of the rainbow, we are challenged to remember God's promise and dedicate ourselves to living our lives in its light. Whatever blocks that light must be examined with compassion, and dissolved through dedicated practice.

When the tower of our singular will-for-power topples and we are left with a multiplicity of languages, systems, conflicting stories, and values, our path becomes confused and scattered.

Yet our spiritual challenge is clear. Diversity must not be ignored as we seek a vision of Unity. The shining vision of our Unity should not fade as we celebrate our differences. We must not betray the Many for the One, or the One for the Many.

---

[4] *Facets of Unity,* A. H. Almaas, Shambhala, 2000 p.27

Guidance for Practice

Sometimes experiencing God's faith in us allows us to find our own faith.

Faithfulness Chant and Meditation

There is a sacred phrase in the morning liturgy:

"Raba emunatekha"
How great is your faithfulness!

With this prayer, I acknowledge God's profound faith in me. God's faith in me soothes the trembling in my soul and awakens my own faith.

Chant this phrase for a while, directing your heart towards a loving Presence.

After some time, sit quietly and bring your attention to the soles of your feet. Feel God's loving attention seeing and knowing and loving every inch of your body, moving your attention up to the ankles, calves, knees, thighs… letting yourself be completely seen, known and loved… releasing any shame or hiddenness… allowing every part of you to be accepted by God's loving attention… moving your attention up to the genitals, belly, hips, waist, chest, arms, hands… letting God's gaze touch every wrinkle and crevice with complete acceptance… completely seen, completely known, completely loved… moving up your neck, face, between every hair on your head.

When you reach the top of your head, bring your attention to the breath, and imagine breathing in and out from every pore at once, your whole body alive with God's attention in you.

Complete the meditation by chanting *"Raba Emunatekha."*

(Thank you to Reb Zalman for his inspiration in composing this meditation)

Lekh Lekha

(Go to Yourself)

GENESIS 12:1 - 17:27

Abram is called to leave his home and go on a journey. When he reaches the Land that God shows him, Abram has to leave it because there is a famine. He goes down to Egypt and back again, encounters many challenges, receives the blessing of Malchitzedek and is given a Divine promise. He has visions and makes a covenant with God.

THE BLESSING

WE ARE BLESSED THIS WEEK WITH A MAP for the spiritual journey: the soul's path to awakening. I call it the "Covenantal Journey," because it describes the process of the maturation of the soul as it rises to stand in covenant with God. We begin this journey from wherever we are now. The invitation to embark is heard at the soul's crossroad, calling to all that would hear.

It is Rumi's invitation:

> **"Come, come whoever you are! Wanderer, worshiper, lover of leaving, come. This is not a caravan of despair. It doesn't matter if you've broken your vows a thousand times, still, come, and yet again Come!"** [1]

Rabbi Yehudah Leib Alter of Ger sees this as a journey of self-realization.

> **"Go to the Land that I will show you – where I will make you VISIBLE – where your potential being will be realized in multiform and unpredictable ways."**[2]

THE JOURNEY IS MAPPED IN SEVEN STAGES, mirroring events in the life of Abram/Abraham:

LEAVING – Abram leaves his home, family and everything familiar to set off for the unknown in order to "become a blessing."

We sever the fixed identification with body, small self, social identity, and begin to re-integrate our lost essence, reclaiming parts or ourselves that got lost during the socialization process.

---

[1] *The Illuminated Rumi* by Coleman Barks (Broadway Books, 1997). Rumi was a 13th Century Sufi Mystic.

[2] Rabbi Yehudah Leib Alter of Ger, *Sefer Sefat Emet al ha-Torah u-Mo'adim, Lekh Lekha.* I learned this text from Rabbi Art Green.

Disappointment – As soon as Abram arrives in The Land, there is a famine, which necessitates the journey down into Egypt and back again.

We discover that defeat can be a teacher as we learn to unmask even disaster as a blessing in disguise. The difficulties in our lives send us to our own depths where we find the core of our passion, vision, mission, and love.

Development – Abram becomes a warrior in order to redeem his captive nephew, Lot.

Becoming a spiritual warrior requires cultivating and honing the skills and courage that are required on the path. We nurture those qualities that will help us to redeem and maintain our own family ties.

Initiation – Abram receives the blessing of Malchitzedek who invokes "El Elyon" (the God Most High).

There are moments of epiphany on the spiritual journey when we receive an initiation, enter upon a wider perspective and enjoy access to a greater flow of blessing. Our identification with that which is "The Highest" — El Elyon — lifts us up to a new level.

Expansion – Abram looks to the stars (where before he looked to the dust) and receives a vision and promise of descendants and a place in the world.

We expand our sense of reality and know that we are connected even to the farthest star. This vision sustains us through times of contraction (when we lose our conviction of that deep and wide connection.)

Prophecy – Abram performs a powerful ritual and receives a startling vision, which reaches far into the future, through slavery and redemption.

All of the hard work of spiritual practice brings us to a place of Prophecy, where the structures of Time and Space dissolve, and we can see the whole of our journey in this expanded moment.

Covenant – Abram is called into covenant and receives a piece of God's name (the letter *hey*) incorporated into his own. As Abraham, he is given the *mitzvah* of circumcision as a physical sign of that covenant.

We receive the blessing of God's essence (Name) at the very core of our identity. Our calling is to reflect that core essence and allow it to shine through the prisms of our unique inclinations, experience, and personality.

The Spiritual Challenge:

Having a map and knowing that we are on a journey awakens us to the realization of the wondrous path we've traveled thus far, and to the road beneath our feet, which is fraught with dangers and strewn with treasures. We can use maps to orient ourselves, recognize landmarks on our way, discern when we've hit a dead end, and inspire us to chart new adventures.

Each blessing on the journey of Abraham holds a challenge for the soul. Leaving the known world without knowing the destination, our challenge is to trust the journey itself and to risk being "no one."

When we encounter disappointment or tragedy, we are challenged to surrender expectations and plant the seeds of compassion. Our lives become a journey of purification and as we are called into service, we are challenged to cultivate the qualities that are required for the work.

We are guided on the path just one step at a time as we seek out teachers, open to their wisdom, receive moments of initiation, and then spend years dedicated to integrating those moments.

Every initiation opens the way for an expansion of perspective and we are challenged to stay focused as we widen the view.

When those expansive states offer us moments of prophetic vision, the challenge is to allow those visions to transform our lives, moment-to-moment.

In accepting upon ourselves the covenant, the agreement to walk with God in simplicity and open-heartedness, we also take on the *mitzvah* of the circumcision of our hearts. Here the challenge is to continually cut through and release layers of distortion and defense that lay upon the heart, so that we can receive reality in its sparkling essence.

Guidance for Practice:

Reflection

Either write in your journal or share with a Spirit-Buddy[3] remembrances of your own life path that correspond to the seven stages of covenantal journey.

Leaving:

Disappointment:

Development:

Initiation:

Expansion:

Prophesy:

Covenant:

---

[3] see Appendix page 232 for an explanation of this aspect of practice.

Vayera

(And He Appeared)

GENESIS 18:1 - 22:24

Abraham is visited by three strangers who announce that he and Sarah will birth a son in their old age. Sodom and Gomorrah are destroyed.

THE BLESSING

THE FIRST WORD OF THE PORTION tells us that God has appeared. As a seeker of direct connection with the Divine, my heart leaps at the idea of this amazing event and I look for that revelation in my own life. We are blessed this week with a vision of God who comes to us in the form of three strangers.

Our attentiveness to these strangers will determine the extent of our blessing. If we are ready with open hearts, our eyes watching for opportunities to serve, if our humility is intact, and we have the energies and resources to express the natural flow of our generosity – then we will be given hope, and the fulfillment of our deepest desires. This openness to seeing God in the "the stranger" is rewarded abundantly.

IN STARK CONTRAST, we are presented with the story of Sodom and Gomorrah, places that represent hatred of the stranger. When God shares with our ancestor the imminent, terrible consequences of this hatred, we are meant to share in the wisdom, to learn from the tragedy.

When inhospitality and meanness rule, and the stranger is not honored, then Divine Presence is unrecognized and inaccessible. When that radiant presence which holds the world together is obscured, everything collapses.

EVEN THOUGH WE WITNESS THIS TRAGEDY, and learn the redemptive truth of how love for the stranger is a requirement for theophany, this same drama must unfold within our very own family. The lesson comes home.

The name Hagar means "the stranger." She represents the stranger in our midst. When we cast Hagar out into the wilderness,[1] her offspring becomes our enemy. When the stranger is banished, our opportunity for seeing God is squandered. The ability to see God passes instead to

[1] Genesis 21:10

the stranger, to Hagar. At the moment of deepest despair, "God opened her eyes."[2] She is blessed with a vision of God who appears as the living waters of life.

In receiving the blessing of *Vayera*, we are both the one who banishes the stranger, and the stranger herself. In finding the compassion to welcome the guest, to open our heart to the one who is different, the best tool we have is our memory of *being* the stranger ourselves. This memory moves us eventually to a re-integration of those two parts within us, the banisher and the banished.

Much later in the story, Abraham takes another wife named Keturah, which means "spice." The midrash says that this new wife is Hagar, returning, the-stranger-welcomed-home. She is transformed from a bitter, desperate stranger into a source of sweet fragrance.

Welcoming Hagar back into our hearts bestows on us the blessing of seeing God once more.

The Spiritual Challenge

Standing at the door of our tent, our first challenge is to remain alert, attentive, and open to opportunities for service. We can't just stand by and watch passively as life goes by; we must run to meet each moment with eagerness and joy.

To take this stance towards life means that I must do whatever it takes to be a clear channel for Divine Love. For me that means giving a lot of attention to self-nurturance – the right food, exercise, rest, meditation, play. The challenge is to love and take care of myself enough to be as effective an instrument I can be in serving others.

The stranger is not always easy to serve. She may be cruel, ungrateful, even unresponsive to your kindness. His manners may offend you. The challenge is to stay true to the spirit of service and to look for the Divine Mystery in every encounter, even if we are not being perceived or received in the way we'd like.

And when we, in our turn, are cast out and treated like a stranger, our challenge is to remain steadfast in our search for allies, and to avoid becoming bitter. Eventually, our eyes will be opened to the well of living waters that is ever before us, however obscured.

[2] Genesis 21:19

Guidance for Practice

Embracing the Stranger

Invite someone to your home. It may be a stranger, a friend who you don't know well, or an acquaintance. You can ask a friend to bring a friend of theirs along. Remember that welcoming "The Guest" is a spiritual practice that takes skill, style, creativity, concentration, and sustained open-heartedness.

In your encounter, be aware of the Mysterious Presence that enters your home when you act with graciousness and generosity. Bow inwardly to that Presence as you serve "The Guest."

Be open to any special message that your guest may bring to you.

Chayei Sarah
(Sarah's Life)

GENESIS 23:1 - 25:18

Sarah dies. Abraham buries her in the Cave of Machpela. Abraham's servant is sent to bring back a wife for Isaac. Abraham also dies.

THE BLESSING

IN THIS PORTION, OUR BELOVED ANCESTORS, Sarah, and then Abraham, die. It would seem that this is a story about loss and grieving. But the first word tells us that this story is about Life itself, perhaps the *secret* to the ripe, sweet harvest of Life's bounty.

According to midrash, Abraham found the cave of Machpela (which would become the place of burial) much earlier in his life. He came upon it while chasing an ox in order to feed the three strangers who brought the good news that Sarah was to become pregnant. He followed the ox deep into a cave where he found Adam and Eve stretched out on couches, candles burning near their heads. A sweet scent pervaded the cave. The blessing Abraham received was a glimpse of the very entranceway to paradise. It held the well-preserved legacy of his ancestors. The fragrance of that cave is what Abraham remembered when Sarah died.

SARAH TEACHES US the blessing of the fullness of life, the ripening of beauty. We learn that the time of greatest loss is also the time of most abundant harvest. Even as our hearts break in mourning, we receive (through that very-same broken heart) the legacy of our loved one, and we seek a way to secure that legacy, to plant it within us like a seed.

The blessing that comes of loss is hidden for us to find along the journey of our mourning. We are sent to our depths, to the cave of our ancestors. With courage we can walk into that cave, through the opening of our own broken hearts, to where *Adam Kadmon* – the primordial man and woman – lies waiting surrounded by the fragrance of Eden. When we breathe in that fragrance, we come back to ourselves in an ancient memory of who we truly are.

No matter how rich the blessing is that comes to us through loss, we are still in considerable need of comfort and healing. This portion tells us how to receive the blessing of comfort that will heal us.

Isaac, Sarah's son, goes out from Be'er-lahai-roi, the place that is associated with Hagar, the stranger. Our grief makes us a stranger to life and we dwell in isolation and alienation until we are ready to love again.

This preparation for love is described in Isaac's meeting with Rebecca. As a prelude to that meeting, Isaac goes out into the field to meditate. The word here for meditation is *la-su'ach*, which refers to the practice of "conversation" with God. The field, a place of spacious natural beauty, is the setting. Here we engage in holy conversation, pouring out our grief, anger and despair, listening deeply for God's voice. "*Min hametzar karati Yah, anani vamerchavyah.*"[1] (From the narrow places I called out to God, who answers me with Divine expanded perspective, the expansiveness of the open field.) The spaciousness that Isaac achieves in meditation allows him to lift his eyes and behold beauty and the possibility of love. In loving again we are comforted.

The Spiritual Challenge

There are many perils to the peace and integrity of the soul on the path of mourning. The bitterness, fear, and cynicism that sometimes accompany or follow experiences of tragedy and loss can become obstacles on the path of our soul's journey. When we react to the feelings of vulnerability that loss brings by building up defenses around the heart and fortifying the small self, we lose access to our own essence. That access is key to direct experience of God and to our ability to truly be of service.

The spiritual challenge at a time of loss is to surrender to the force of dissolution that grief brings, while harvesting the seeds of new life. After the seeds of legacy are planted, they are nourished by our practice and by what brings us comfort. As a gardener of the soul I want to grow compassion that will flower into acts of kindness and justice. This includes cultivating a compassion for myself that will allow me to receive comfort and be healed.

If we follow Isaac's example we will seek the open field and develop a practice of meditation that will allow us to lift our eyes and open our hearts to love.

[1] Psalm 118:5

Guidance for Practice

Find the Cave of Machpela within.

As you build the intention for an inner journey, chant these words:

***"ve-ikvotekha lo noda-u"*[2]**

And Your footsteps were not known.

At the end of the chant, dive into the darkness before you with the intention of finding the Cave of Machpela, the cave of our ancestors.

As you journey, pay attention to images and feelings. Go as far into the cave as you are called. Notice if anyone is there with you and allow that spirit to instruct you.

Ask for a gift and then open to receive it. When you have secured a gift, begin your journey of ascent.

When you reach the surface, describe or draw the gift you received and use it as an object of contemplation.

---

[2] Psalms 77:20

Toldot

(Lineage)

GENESIS 25:19 - 28:9

Jacob and Esau are born after wrestling with each other in Rebecca's womb. Isaac re-digs the wells of his ancestors.

THE BLESSING

WE CARRY within us the Great Duality, the fruit of the Tree of Good and Evil. Like Rebecca, we are pregnant with dilemma, with paradox. Carrying this contradiction can feel so painful that we forget that it is a pregnancy. We forget that we are in the process of birthing. In agony we cry out, "*Im Keyn, Lama Zeh Anochi?*"[1] (If life is like this... with so much suffering...Why *am* I?)

The blessing comes in the awareness that we are indeed birthing Life. We are always birthing ourselves.[2] The whole drama of Life moves through the narrow passage of our personal experience and we are stretched wide and torn open in the process. At some point, the contradiction within us will be made apparent. We will then have the opportunity of expanding to embrace the complex dilemma of our human situation.

TO BE FULLY HUMAN is to be connected to our lineage, to experience the presence of our ancestors within us. We receive the blessing of lineage by embracing the ancestors who live inside of us; we offer them our compassion and courage, we receive the merit of their efforts, and we learn from their mistakes. Through our love their power is freed, their wounds are healed.

Through the story of *Toldot* we learn to access our lineage. In his time, Abraham accomplished the great work of digging deep wells of spiritual sustenance, but by Isaac's time, the wells had become obstructed. Isaac lost access to the wealth of his lineage. In re-digging the stopped-up wells of his father Abraham, Isaac finds that the process is neither simple nor easy. In fact, he digs three wells before acheiving success – connection with the source.

---

[1] Genesis 25:22

[2] Later in our story (Exodus 3:14), God gives us his name – "*Ehyeh asher ehyeh,* I am becoming who I am becoming." We who are created in God's image share in this name and this status. We only exist in the process of "who we are becoming."

EACH WELL HAS A NAME that describes a marker on the journey towards deep connection:[3]

ESEK – "CONTENTION"
SITNAH – "ENMITY"
RECHOVOT – "SPACIOUSNESS"

FIRST WE DIG the well of *ESEK*/CONTENTION. We scrabble in a rocky argument with our inheritance, rubbing up against its hard edges, fighting its constrictions, and opening to its contradictions.

THEN WE DIG the well of *SITNA*/ENMITY. There we taste the contradictions of the tradition within us. When we come to know the suffering and struggles of our ancestors and the whole human family who have stood against one another, we cry out, "*Im keyn, lama zeh anokhi?*"[4] (If life is like this…(with so much suffering)…Why am I?)

AT THIS POINT, the very moment of birthing, we dig the well of *RECHOVOT*/ SPACIOUSNESS. The well of our ancestors becomes a fountain connecting the dark depths of our human story with the wide skies of awareness.

IN THE STORY of *Toldot* we learn of the tragedy of deception between brothers that results from the narrow belief in the scarcity of blessing. Our family is torn apart because of the tragic conviction that only one of Isaac's sons may receive his blessing.

This system of limiting blessing and creating hierarchy is born of the belief that love and blessing are finite, that there are winners and losers. This idea is drawn from the well of CONTENTION.

When I deceive my brother or attempt to steal the blessing from my sister, I am drawing on the well of ENMITY (whose waters are poison) which will only drive me to greater thirst.

From the well of SPACIOUSNESS comes the wisdom that our fates are bound up with one another. Your loss, your suffering, is also mine, and true blessing is shared. At the well of spaciousness I slake my thirst with the knowledge that the source of blessing knows no bounds, and that we are each capable of accessing that blessing directly.

---

[3] Isaac's efforts to access the wells of his father so clearly mirror my own struggles to receive my Jewish inheritance – the treasures of Torah.

[4] Genesis 25:22

THE SPIRITUAL CHALLENGE

IN THE MIDST OF PAIN AND STRUGGLE, the spiritual challenge is to remember to ask the question, "What am I birthing?"

Pain narrows our awareness, disguises itself as the whole of reality, saps our strength and makes us forgetful of the holy process of birth. Our only path to divinity is through our humanity. When pain presents itself we must remember that it is a doorway. The only way is *through*.

Each contraction brings us closer to new life. The challenge is to remember the promise of life even as we cry out, even if our cries are filled with despair. The cry will open the ancestral well. Bearing the pain of our humanity, digging through *ESEK*, through *SITNAH* to the well of *RECHOVOT*, we can receive the legacy of our mothers and fathers who struggled and birthed new life.

THE SPIRITUAL CHALLENGE of drawing from the well of our ancestors is to receive their essence and make it our own. There is always the danger of getting caught in the forms that we have inherited without tasting and knowing their essence. We must let our own unique creative flow be invited and opened by the legacy that we inherit.

GUIDANCE FOR PRACTICE

RE-DIGGING THE WELLS OF OUR ANCESTORS

WRITE A LIST OF YOUR BELIEFS about yourself and your world.

QUESTION THEM. Who are you and what is the nature of your existence? Notice all the contradicting beliefs that you carry within. Where did these beliefs come from? Which of them remain useful?

INVOKE THE PRESENCE OF YOUR ANCESTORS before your prayer. Ask for their encouragement, support and inspiration.

GO OUT IN A PLACE OF SPACIOUS NATURAL BEAUTY AND SING directly to God, the Source of life. Raise up your voice with or without words, without care for its pleasantness or correctness, just releasing the cry that is in you. Let your voice express the truth of where you are right now in the process of birthing yourself.

Vayetze

(And he went forth)

GENESIS 28:10 - 32:3

Jacob goes on a journey, guided by dreams and visions, and develops a relationship with God.

THE BLESSING

JACOB'S JOURNEY IS BLESSED at its outset with a dream and with a moment of awakening. In the dream God shows Jacob the stairway that connects the realms of Heaven and Earth and then gives him a promise. Through this blessing we ourselves become that stairway, that connection, with our feet planted in the foundation of Earth and our crowns open to the expanse of Heaven. Through us the Divine flow pours down into the earthly realms. Through us the pleasures and miseries of earthly experience are offered up to The Divine Expanse.

When I become available to this flow, I am awakened to the most awesome and transformative truth. God was here all along and I didn't know it. THIS is none other than the House of God. THIS is the Gate of Heaven. This very moment and this place here where I stand is at once God's home and the doorway to all realms.

Our journey brings us the blessing of *zeh* – "This." In becoming fully present to this moment – Here and Now – the Presence of God is revealed.

IN THE STORY OF *VAYETZE*, Jacob tries to negotiate with God. Perhaps he misunderstands the promise that was given to him in the dream. Perhaps he has forgotten the moment of awakening and become frightened. He wants assurance that the right food, clothing and peace will be available to him on his journey.

We all would like to have our blessings offered to us in ways that seem comfortable and familiar. Caught in our fears and desires we miss the true promise.

THE PROMISE: I will give you *HAMAKOM*, "the place," the land of your life—to possess, to know, to inhabit, cultivate, refine. The awesome place that I give you is none other than the House of God—I live there at the heart of every molecule and I will shine out through the windows of your own eyes when they are open to this truth. And this awesome place is the

Gate of Heaven – connecting all realms and dimensions, Heavens and Hells – connecting you with your wildest dreams.

I will give you descendants. You will be a delicate flower held up to the wind. You will be blown open, that your seeds may scatter and take root, blossoming in places you could not imagine. The winds of history and circumstance and coincidence will spread your essence, your song, your sigh, mixed with the pollens of desire, to the far corners of the world. Your fragrance will waft through the farthest garden.

Through you and your descendants, all the families of the earth will be blessed.

I am with you. I do not promise that it will be comfortable or that you will not suffer. I do not promise that you'll never be hungry or feel despair. I do not promise that your heart will never be broken. My promise is simply that I am with you – in your suffering, your hunger, your despair, through your wandering, your stumbling, your confusion – (I am with you), "*Anokhi Imach*"[1] – even when you feel abandoned.

The Spiritual Challenge

The spiritual challenge of *Vayetze* calls me to fully engage in the journey, to be taken up by the adventure of living, to open my heart to guidance with each step, and surrender to the momentum and flow of my story. At the same time I must realize that I have already arrived. Each step, each moment is an arrival. God is in THIS place, THIS moment, and all that I have to do is to become present. Each side of this paradox holds a spiritual challenge, as does the paradox itself.

I recently met an old man on the streets of Berkeley who said that the spirit of his grandmother sat on his shoulder and gave him guidance. She counseled him that the three most important qualities to cultivate on the journey of life were **courage**, **curiosity** and **compassion**. Though the man seemed a bit odd, this grandmotherly advice has been valuable for me.

The challenge of journeying requires that I become a student of life, receiving each new circumstance, landscape, or dilemma as an opportunity for learning. My courage will allow me to overcome the paralysis that sometimes accompanies fear, so that I can take the next step. My curiosity will lead me onward and infuse the journey with joy. And compassion will open my heart, connect me with others, and heal the wounds that life inflicts.

[1] Genesis 28:15

This adventure of life is a journey towards God-realization. My commitment to exploration and travel on the roads that unfold before me is absolutely crucial to this realization... and yet... God was here all along and I didn't know it. God, the ultimate reality is in THIS. This place, This moment. The challenge is to stand still with enough calm and spaciousness to be fully present to Presence itself.

I live in the paradox of journey and arrival – finding stillness in my journey, yet continuing to follow the path of awakening as it unfolds in the stillness.

Guidance for Practice

Vayetze *guides me towards two practices that illuminate both sides of the paradox. One works with the quality of presence and the other helps us onward with the journey.*

Heaven and Earth Breathing

The purpose of this practice is to become the connection between Heaven and Earth, and to expand the heart wide enough to contain both.

Prepare for the practice by breathing gently in and out of the heart. Once you are centered in the heart, begin by inhaling into the heart and exhaling down through your body into the Earth. Then inhale up from the Earth, bringing the energy of Earth into the heart. After a slight pause in the heart, exhale upward through the crown of your head into the Heavens. Then inhale the energy of the Heavens down through your crown into your heart.

Continue this pattern. Each time you exhale down into the Earth, send the breath a bit deeper. Each time you exhale to the Heavens, send the breath a bit higher. And each time you inhale the energies of Heaven or Earth into the heart, expand the heart to receive those energies. Do the practice for at least five minutes and end with breathing gently in and out of the heart.

Walking Meditation

Find an easy and quiet place to walk. Begin by finding your balance and stillness, feeling the earth support you.

As you begin to walk bring your attention to the point of contact with the earth. Stay completely present in each step, noticing the shifting of weight, and the air against your skin.

Enjoy each step. Walk as if you were kissing the earth with your feet.

After at least ten minutes, come to stillness and focus your attention on the breath.

Vayishlach
(And He Sent)

Genesis 32:4 - 36:43

Jacob wrestles with a mysterious being on the banks of the Jabbok. He is injured and is given a new name and finally reconciles with his brother.

The Blessing

Jacob's journey follows the course of the ego's development. Due to the nature of physical embodiment, the soul develops an ego to deal with our helplessness as infants. The ego emerges in response to the challenge of having to squeeze a vast soul into a particular and limited form.

The small self (Jacob) is sent on a journey to rediscover its essential nature – Soul. Jacob, as ego, is the wheeler/dealer employing every manipulation to get what he needs to survive. On the journey home to the land of the soul, there comes a point where all the manipulations of the ego become useless and irrelevant; and one must stand naked and vulnerable before the truth. In that moment it is possible to receive the blessing of a closer identity with soul, allowing greater access to the inner realms and opening the doors to a deeper level of self.

As Jacob journeys home, his past deceptions haunt him and he must confront his own twin brother, the one he had so cruelly deceived and desperately fears. Jacob's fear is multiplied by guilt and shame about being such a con-man. All his manipulations have only strengthened the false self, and that false self must shore itself up with defenses, for it projects the only reality that the ego knows.

Before meeting Esau (who embodies Jacob's past catching up with him), Jacob (as ego shoring up the false self) does everything possible to ensure his own survival. Jacob gathers intelligence, prepares a stratagem of escape in the event of battle, sends a generous gift of appeasement, and prays to God. Finally, after all his manipulations, Jacob is left alone.

All night long Jacob wrestles with a mystery. All his cunning and defenses are wrested from him that night. He is held in the grip of truth as layers of false self fall away, revealing, at the break of dawn, the soul's hidden radiance.

All through the dark night we wrestle until our wrestling becomes a dance, and the dance an embrace. At dawn the embrace calls forth a blessing. We are given a new name, and that name represents our true essence. Our new name is the call of the soul. Who am I beneath this personality? Who was there before birth and will survive physical deterioration and death? By identifying with that aspect of existence, which is eternal, we can let our personality be shaped and refined by the power, wisdom and perspective of soul.

The blessing of that dark night on the banks of the river Jabbok is in the name we receive. A true name signifies and holds our essence. It calls forth our true power and sends us on a path towards remembrance.

The Spiritual Challenge

Even after Jacob receives the blessing of his new name, "Israel," a reminder of soul-identity, he is still Jacob. For the rest of his story he is called by both names. Even after moments of profound awakening we oftentimes slip back into the habitual manipulations of ego. Even as we awaken the power of soul, we find ourselves tangled in the web that our ego has woven.

Jacob's sons continue his pattern of deception. Even as Israel he must deal with the karmic legacy of his past. The spiritual challenge is to anchor ourselves in the glimpses of soul we receive. From such points of remembrance, we can face the challenge of acting righteously and responding from our soul wisdom in this moment, despite our shortcomings and flaws.

During Jacobs's night of wrestling with a mystery, he is injured. Through that injury, God reveals to Jacob the true nature of his flaws. The touch of that moment of Truth leaves him with a limp, a constant reminder. Thus the inflated ego is humbled. We all need to be vigilant of the tendency of the ego towards inflation and self-deception. As we learn to accept the limitations of our physical, emotional and intellectual powers, the infinite spiritual reality is opened to us. As those doors open, the spiritual challenge is to let go of past identities as we step out of the confines of small self and expand into the unknown.

Guidance for Practice

Our tradition speaks of five levels of soul:

Nefesh – **the separate self that is completely identified with the body**

Ruach – the self that begins to open to divine inspiration

Neshama – the self that opens to the awareness of the interpenetration of human and Divine, each breathing its essence into the other

Chaya – pure undifferentiated Life Force

Yechida – the self that is completely identified with God

THE PRACTICE FOR VAYISHLACH IS TO RECOGNIZE EACH OF THESE ASPECTS OF SELF IN OUR OWN EXPERIENCE.

I understand *Nefesh* as the place where most of us learn to live–in separateness–confined to a narrow paradigm of Reality. In moments of alienation I can feel the pain of being stuck in *Nefesh.*

And then there are moments of inspiration where the *Ruach HaKodesh*, the Holy Spirit blows into my life, expanding my awareness to the level of Ruach. Here I am moved and my heart opens to the possibility of a wider reality.

The place of *Neshama* is the doorway into higher consciousness, and that door is opened through the practice of God-breathing. Through this practice we can receive glimpses of *Chaya* and *Yechida.* Those glimpses can be planted as the seeds of soul growth.

GOD-BREATHING:

Close your eyes, sit comfortably and focus all your attention on the breath, following the complete inhale and exhale.

Feel yourself surrounded by God and when the inhalation is happening receive the breath as God breathing in to you.

Let your exhalation be an emptying of self, breathing out from the center, creating a space within you to again receive the Divine essence.

Continue for at least ten minutes.

Vayeshev
(And He Dwelt)

GENESIS 37:1 - 40:23

Joseph tells his amazing dreams and is thrown into a pit by his jealous brothers. Then we turn to the story of Tamar, Judah's daughter-in-law. After Tamar is widowed by two of Judah's sons, he withholds his third son from her, leaving her in limbo. She tricks Judah by disguising herself as a prostitute. Tamar is rewarded for her efforts with the birth of twins.

THE BLESSING

"HERE COMES THE DREAMER," say Joseph's brothers as they plot his murder. "We shall see what will become of his dreams!" In this week of *Vayeshev*, we will look to our dreams to see what has become of them. For in following those dreams, and risking everything, the blessing of our lives may be received.

Joseph, the dreamer, knows that the troubles he encounters are sent to him by God. He knows that blessing comes disguised and it is his mission to see through that disguise, to unmask the blessing even if it takes a lifetime. Somehow Joseph is blessed with the knowledge of his own radiance. He has always known that he is loved, that he is special and that he has a rich destiny to fulfill.

What prevents us from receiving the blessing of our *own* shining essence? What has dimmed our radiance, belittled the greatness of our souls and obscured for us the truth of just how we fit in to the great puzzle of life?

THE TORAH TEACHES US THAT GREATNESS is born through unlikely circumstances; destiny unfolds in unexpected ways. Interrupting the story of Joseph is the drama of Tamar from whose blood will come King David and the messianic consciousness to heal the world.

Tamar, caught in the injustice of a cruel system, breaks all the rules, and acts from the knowledge of her own beauty, truth, and radiance. Tamar refuses to give up her dream. She risks her life to allow our dream to be birthed through her. The two children born to Tamar as a result of her dream-following and risking-taking are named "Breakthrough" (*Peretz*), and "Radiance" (*Zerach*).

Joseph too is blessed with the powers of Breakthrough and Radiance that come from following dreams. *Vayeshev* returns us to his story and it is our story as well. Fate seems to play a strange game, lifting us out of slavery, letting our beauty shine, and then sending us back to the dungeon. Yet even in prison, the dreams keep us alive and will eventually open the doors to freedom and power.

The Spiritual Challenge

Sometimes the gift of our uniqueness becomes a burden. When we receive the glory of our unique destiny, there is a danger of estrangement. We may feel lonely or alienated from societal norms. It is hard to know how to manifest our dreams when we feel so isolated. We guard ourselves from the envy of others by hiding the gift, even from ourselves.

The disjunction between ordinary life and the life of our dreams can send us spinning off too far in either of those directions. We may not have the words or the confidence to express our dreams, and so dishonor or discount them. Or we might become so in love with our dreams that we want to live only there. We can become so involved with the drama of our unique destiny that we forget our humility and interconnectedness. There is a danger in knowing that you are special, but forgetting that everyone else is just as special, just as beloved of God.

The spiritual challenge of *Vayeshev* invites a well-known Hasidic paradox into our pockets. In one pocket the message says, "For me the world was created." In the other pocket the message reads, "I am but dust." When I become too intoxicated with my own dream, I reach into the pocket of Dust. When I forget the dream I reach into the pocket of World. Sometimes I just keep both hands in my pockets, touching both truths, bathed in glory, and laughing at myself.

Guidance for Practice

As we honor Joseph, the master of dreams, it might be a good time to honor our own dreams – both the sleeping and waking ones.

Recollecting

Before you go to sleep, ask for a dream and then place a notebook and pen near your bed.

In the morning, write down whatever you remember from the dream, even it is just a fragment. Let the images received in your dream inform your waking life. Share them, draw them, write about them, and learn from them.

Joseph teaches us that all interpretations belong to God. When we honor the dream, and clear a space for it to grow in our lives, its Divine Truth will blossom and bear fruit.

Chant: Waking Dream

The practice of chanting is a good way to prepare the mind for a waking dream. Begin by preparing an imaginary altar before you. Place on that altar the memory of your earliest idea of what you wanted to do or be in your life. (I wanted to be an explorer – a mountain climber.)

Chant these words:

***"ma yihiyu chalomotav"*[1]**
What will become of his dreams?

Send the energy of the chant onto the altar of memory. Let the chant be a question that reaches your soul wisdom. (Make up your own simple melody.)

Chant for at least 10 minutes, then sit in the silence afterwards and just listen. Pay attention to any images or feelings that arise.

[1] Genesis 37:21

Miketz
(At the End)

GENESIS 41:1 - 44:17

Joseph gets out of prison by successfully interpreting Pharaoh's dream. He rises to power in Egypt. He has a dramatic encounter and reunion with his brothers who had wronged him.

THE BLESSING

THE FOUNDATIONAL STORY of our people is the story of leaving Egypt, going from slavery to freedom. This journey home is the story of consciousness evolving from narrowness and separation to expansion and awareness of its identity in the One. If the book of Exodus follows this journey of liberation, then Genesis is the story of how we got into that state of enslavement in the first place. And this portion of *Miketz* holds the key to that enslavement.

In the language of the soul, enslavement is the process of incarnation and the complete identification of ego with the material world. When the soul loses its conscious connection with the infinite, then it is "in Egypt," (in constriction). *Miketz* reminds us how we got there, how we got stuck, how we got lost in the illusion of a limited reality. The blessing hidden in *Miketz* is that whenever we descend into the tangle of incarnation, we take with us the seeds of liberation.

It all happens so innocently. Joseph is raised up into power through his wisdom and psychic gifts. On behalf of Pharaoh, (the status quo), he gathers the wealth of the land during the time of plenty, and then sells it back to the people during the time of famine. Because of the system that Joseph sets in place, the wealth of the land is redistributed and the people become completely dependent on Pharaoh. As this system of dependency evolves, whoever is at the lowest socio-economic level becomes vulnerable. Joseph's own people are the ones who will suffer and be enslaved by the system of power and wealth that he himself set in place.

AS WE DESCEND with our people into the bonds of physicality, we take with us the seeds of our liberation. We see in Joseph, the dreamer, a heart that still suffers and loves, despite the hardships that he has endured. Through Joseph, we struggle with power, and slowly make peace with our past. Through Joseph, we struggle with our past and slowly make peace with power. In Joseph's heart, the two sides of his father's legacy are revealed. The side of Jacob, the schemer, plays the game of getting even, while the side of Israel, the God-wrestler, weeps with the glimmer of a love that transcends bitterness.

The bones of Joseph (his deepest essence) will be buried in Egypt, as seeds of liberation and awakening. Joseph is recognized by Pharaoh as "the one in whom the spirit of God lives."[1] The bones of Joseph represent his deepest intention, buried under the illusion of Egypt.

The Spiritual Challenge

When Pharaoh perceives the spirit of God in Joseph, he puts a ring on his finger, dresses him in fine linens, lays a gold chain on his neck, gives him a new name and an Egyptian wife. The challenge of power and wealth is that you become bound to serve the one who confers it upon you. You become invested in defending the system that keeps your wealth and power intact. If you can constantly remember that God is the true Source and know that it is really God that you serve, then your wielding of power will express the divine attributes of justice and compassion. This remembrance becomes more difficult when, like Joseph, we are carrying old hurts. Whatever is unhealed in us becomes an obstacle to the pursuit of justice, obscures the heart of compassion, and keeps us locked in patterns of manipulation.

Even though the "Spirit of God" is in us, we spend most of our time listening to the command of Pharaoh, who has put the ring on our fingers and the gold chain around our necks.

We are tangled up in a system that is inherently unjust. We can work towards establishing a more equitable distribution of wealth. And we can honor and protect the seeds of liberation that are in us – our compassion and open-hearted vision of the preciousness of every being. When we carry old hurts and the bitterness that surrounds those wounds, then our every attempt to do justice is distorted by a sensation of pain. And so the spiritual challenge is to heal those deep places of bitterness. In that healing, the Spirit of God in us is made manifest.

[1] Genesis 41:38

Guidance for Practice

Healing a painful memory

We call on the Source of Love within us to facilitate our healing.

Begin by calling on a memory, a painful scene where you felt yourself the victim of some injustice. When the scene becomes vivid, freeze the action, place a frame around it and lay the scene on an altar before you.

Bring your attention to the breath, and breathe from the place you imagine is the deepest point within your heart. That point exists beyond the separate self and connects an infinite reservoir of Divine energy to your own radiant heart.

Breathing in and out from that deepest point, begin creating a field of energy around you. Imagine an egg completely surrounding you. Send energy out from your core to fill up that egg, charging it with God-force. You might see it as a particular color – white, gold, pink – whatever color you see, let it grow fuller with each breath, and stay anchored in the source at the center of your heart.

After at least five minutes of deep heart breathing, when the egg is fully charged, bring your attention back to the framed memory on your altar.

Imagine that there is a plug at the bottom right-hand side of the picture, and pull out the plug. Let all the color drain out of the picture. Replace the plug. Imagine a plug at the top left-hand side of the picture and take out the plug.

Pour the light from the charged egg shaped field around you in to the picture. Let the scene of your memory be filled with this light of Power and Presence.

Examine the picture again and notice what has changed.

Complete the practice by returning to heart breathing, again establishing that egg of light as your field of God-power.[2]

---

[2] I thank my teacher, Ellen Dosick, for inspiring this practice.

Vayigash
(And He Came Near)

GENESIS 44:18 - 47:27

The story of Joseph and his brothers continues to its resolution. Jacob descends to Egypt and is reunited with Joseph.

THE BLESSING

WHEN JOSEPH'S BROTHERS LEARN that he is still alive, they must go and tell their father, but they are afraid that he will die of shock upon learning the truth. They are afraid that this news will be too great a blessing, and that Jacob's soul will fly out of him upon hearing it. They argue with each other about who will deliver the news.

There is a legend that recounts the solution to their problem. Jacob had a favorite grand-daughter, Serach, who was the daughter of his son Asher. Serach was a musician with a gentle voice and a powerful spirit. Her songs were a healing balm for Jacob during his dark nights of wrestling. Whenever he called for Serach, she sang for him and he was comforted.

It was agreed that only Serach would be able to reveal this great news, because when Jacob's soul, overcome by blessing, flew out, Serach would be able to sing a song that would call his soul back to this world.

THE SONG THAT SERACH SANG to Jacob was the most beautiful melody she had ever sung. Everyone that heard it wept with joy because in it Joseph's spirit was revealed. The melody carried Joseph's beauty, pain, longing, love and devotion. Her words told the story of his journey and it was woven with his dreams. Serach's song also told the truth about the whole family, a truth that would have been hard to hear if it were not delivered with such purity.

When Jacob heard Serach's song, his soul indeed flew out and left this world... but it was called back by the beauty of her song. For this gift, Serach was rewarded with a very long life. It is said that she sang through 400 years of slavery in Egypt.

When the people were about to leave Egypt, they were at first held back by their promise to bring Joseph's bones along with them. Fortunately, having lived long enough to both witness Joseph's burial *and* be present at the time of the Exodus, Serach located exactly where Joseph was buried, and the liberation could begin.

THE SPIRITUAL CHALLENGE

WE, LIKE JACOB, WILL REMAIN ignorant of the greatest blessing – the miracle of life itself – unless we can receive that blessing in beauty. The truth of our lives will remain mute and invisible unless it becomes a song. The vast miracle of our existence would be overwhelming if received unadorned, and all at once. It would tear us open, and our souls, set free, would fly. Yet, artful glimpses of that same vast miracle gradually expand our capacity to know the truth. The spiritual challenge that we share with our father Jacob is to prepare ourselves to listen for the song of truth and blessing, and to let its beauty call us to deeper living.

We, like Serach, will be rewarded for our song. Our reward will be the ability to preserve the precious memory (of the *etzem,* which means "bones," or "essence") that will eventually lead to freedom. And we are challenged to keep singing, to keep the memory and blessing alive in our song, even through our darkest days of slavery.

ALL THE SPIRITUAL CHALLENGE and blessings of *Vayigash* rest on a pivotal moment – the moment when Joseph reveals himself to his brothers. He steps out from behind the mask of power, the mask of the false self, and weeps aloud. These are the tears of profound relief and of love unbound. This moment of expansion is the result of Joseph's embrace of a paradox. Two seemingly contradictory truths live inside Joseph, and when he can hold them both, then the true self is set free from artifice.

LATER IN THE STORY Joseph describes this moment to his brothers. "You meant evil against me, but God meant it for good."[1] On some days we acknowledge the deep woundings that we have suffered; we mourn the loss of innocence; we confront the face of evil. And on some days we absolutely know that those very same wounds are the source of our compassion and our power; we celebrate the essential rightness of the path of Life in all its turnings, understanding that what feels like evil is an aspect of the goading force that unfolds the soul to its true breadth.

And there comes a day when both these perspectives exist at once. On that day joy and anguish meet within us and the resulting alchemical reaction explodes the boundaries of the false self. On that day we are set free. This freedom allows us to come out of hiding, to finally tell the truth and reveal ourselves.

---

[1] Genesis 50:20

Guidance for Practice

The Torah of Moses is there to point us to the Torah of our lives. Each of us is given an amazing story, set in a world of suffering and redemption, tragedy and miracle. The false self keeps itself in power through deceptively shoring up of one side of the paradox, favoring it over the other. Only when we can live within the seeming contradiction, expanding to embrace the paradox of our existence, can the true self be revealed.

Paradox Meditation

Use a concentration on the breath to center yourself in a meditative state.

When you reach a place of steadiness and calm, call up a scene in your life when you felt victimized. When you can really feel the feelings of that time, shrink the scene till it can fit into the palm of your left hand. Hold it and feel its weight and color and texture. This is the hand that knows "you meant evil against me." In it you hold your anger, vengeance, indignation, grief.

Set that hand aside for a moment and bring your attention to your right hand. This is the hand that knows that "God meant it for good." This hand holds the wide perspective, the wisdom and the compassion that has come from your suffering, the opportunities for touching the deeper ground when the rug was pulled out from under you. Feel in this hand the joy, curiosity, strength and courage that have emerged from your particular life-dilemmas.

Widen your focus until you can feel both hands at once. Notice the difference in weight and feeling-tone.

Slowly bring your two hands toward each other. Notice whatever resistance is present and keep moving them towards each other. When your two hands touch, pay particular attention to whatever images or words arise and to the feelings in your body. (I'm always completely surprised by what emerges in this practice.)

Share what you have found with a trusted Spirit-Buddy.[2]

---

[2] see Appendix page 232 for how to use this aspect of practice.

Vayechi
(And He Lived)

GENESIS 47:28 - 50:26

Jacob, on his deathbed, gives a blessing to each of his sons.

THE BLESSING

"JACOB LIVED," the portion begins, and the story reveals a deathbed scene where instead of saying that "Jacob died," it says he was "gathered into his people"[1]...into us. The blessing that I receive from *Vayechi* is the knowledge that Jacob still lives within me.

After wrestling with an angel on the banks of the Jabbok, Jacob received a new name. That moment represented a spiritual transformation. "Your name shall no longer be Jacob, but Israel, for you have striven with beings divine and human and you have prevailed," said the angel.[2]

Yet, until the very end of the narrative of Genesis, Jacob is called by both names. Even at the moment of death he is referred to as "Jacob." Jacob's story tells us something quite profound about the nature of spiritual transformation. And it helps us relate more realistically to our own process of transformation.

LOOKING AT YOUR OWN JACOB, you might find certain qualities that seem to be wired into your personality. You might be a worrier or you might be impatient, argumentative, controlling, or manipulative. When you begin to have experiences of expanded consciousness, you are given the name "Israel" and you take on a spiritual practice that proceeds from that new identity. But "Jacob" never really goes away. Through our practice we learn how to manage that worrier, that impatient one, that manipulator. We can learn to have compassion for the fearful source of that voice. After many years of committed practice I realize that the voices of Jacob-within-us may never be entirely silenced, but as the Israel-in-us grows, those Jacob voices lose their power to compel and we are no longer tricked or trapped by their arguments.

When I receive the blessing of the knowledge of where Jacob lives within me, then I can recognize his voice and gently refuse his advice, looking instead to Israel, for wisdom, passion and courage for my journey.

---

[1] Genesis 49:33

[2] Genesis 32:29

The Spiritual Challenge

Vayechi gives us an extraordinary scene of Jacob on his deathbed initiating each of his sons on their path, naming the particular medicine that they will carry. Depending on how that medicine is used, it can be either a blessing or a curse. To carry a particular medicine into the world always means navigating a delicate spiritual challenge, for the power of your medicine can either heal or destroy.

Each of Jacob's sons are gifted with a totem – an image, quality, or animal that can be their teacher in the spirit realms. We carry within us all the medicine of our ancestors:

the Unstable water of Reuben,

the Lion of Judah,

the Harbor of Zebulon,

the Strong-boned ass of Issachar,

the Snake of Dan,

the Warrior of Gad,

the Prosperity of Asher,

the Deer of Naftali,

the Wild Ass of Joseph

and the Hungry Wolf of Benjamin.

Each image is a pathway through which power can move through us into the world. The spiritual challenge is to call on that power as we become healers, to use that power with awareness, and dedicate it to holiness – for the good of all.

Guidance for Practice

This spiritual practice concerns the art of being in relationship both to the place of Jacob within you and to the place of Israel. Both must be named and acknowledged.

Chant for Honoring Jacob and Israel

Address these words in chant to each part:

"*Mah tovu ohalekha Yaacov*"
How good are your tents Jacob

"*Mishkinotekha Yisrael*"
your *Mishkan* (dwelling-place) Israel

Find those two places within you as you chant. The difference between a tent and a *Mishkan* is that a tent is always temporary and limited. A *Mishkan* is where the Presence of God dwells eternally. It contains infinite space. The voice of your true soul calls forth from the *Mishkan* of Israel, and to its presence you sing:

"*Mah Tovu!*"
How Good!

The tent of Jacob, though limited, though temporary, is also good. It has sustained you, sheltered you in the wilderness and kept you safe. To that place you sing:

"*Mah Tovu!*"
How Good!"

Shefa Gold

EXODUS

Shemot

LIBERATION

Shemot

(Names)

EXODUS 1:1 - 6:1

The Israelite tribe grows while enslaved to Pharaoh in Egypt. Moses is born, is raised in Pharaoh's court, and eventually rebels and goes to live as a shepherd in Midian. He receives the call to prophesy, is given God's name and returns to Egypt to free his people.

THE BLESSING

As WE ENTER THE BOOK of Exodus, we live ever more consciously the story of our liberation. This story happens in the timeless present. It stirs the soul to its awakening. Only when we can know and experience the journey from slavery to redemption each day can we truly taste freedom and enjoy the milk and honey that is our inheritance.

Our blessing, the possibility of liberation, is born at the time of greatest travail. Moses is born within us at a moment of despair when we have been beaten down, constricted, forced into the narrowest possible definition of self. That seed of truth and vitality is hidden away and then placed in a *teva,* an "ark."

What distinguishes an ark from a boat is the absence of sail or rudder. It is a vehicle that is completely surrendered to fate, to God's Will. As with Noah's ark, the hope of a new world, a new kind of consciousness, is set afloat. The Ba'al Shem Tov reminds us that the word for ark, "*teva*," also means "word." The word filled with potential is set adrift on the river of Life.

THIS IS HOW OUR JOURNEY towards consciousness begins. The inner seed of prophecy, filled with our true essence, is surrendered and entrusted into the hands of God, via the primal waters. From there it is embraced by the journey, blessed with experience, education, nourishment, and inspiration, sent to distant lands, initiated into foreign wisdom, and shown the secrets of the wilderness.

We are prepared for prophecy by the landscape of our lives until finally, one day, we stumble upon the same bush that we have passed a hundred times. This time, our eyes open to perceive its fire. In that extraordinary moment of blessing, God calls us by name twice,[1] breaking through the outer self to the inner essence that has been waiting. And that inner essence responds, "*Hineni*."[2] Here I am.

We are called into presence by the sudden knowledge that the ground upon which we stand is holy. We are commanded to take off our shoes, for nothing must come between us and this sacred ground. We are called into prophecy as we receive the great name, which is the Ground of Being – *Ehyeh Asher Ehyeh*.[3] Standing on that ground we are sent to do the work of liberation, freeing ourselves from societal expectations of what is deemed "normal."

The blessing of *Shemot* sends us to a work that to "normal mind" seems impossible.

The Spiritual Challenge

For 400 years the people of Israel suffered the oppression of Egypt. Only when the sigh and the cry and the groaning were sent forth could the process of liberation be set in motion. God waits for that cry, and that cry only happens when self-awareness is achieved and the spirit is set free to be heard, remembered, seen, and known.[4]

The spiritual challenge of *Shemot* is to cultivate the awareness of our own enslavement. Consciousness must precede the cry that awakens the God-force of liberation. To be heard by God is to let the inward sigh become an outward cry. That cry breaks the pattern of enslavement, shakes up the status quo until the memory of covenant is jarred awake. To be remembered by God is to remember the presence of God within. To be seen by God is to lift the veils of self-deception. To be known by God is to move beyond pride and shame, to surrender to the Unknowable.

When the God-force is set in motion by our cry, our lives become the scene of miracle. Moses the Prophet, Aaron the Priest, and Miriam the Artist are awakened to power, and then Pharaoh will be challenged. When that happens, when Pharaoh's power is threatened, he takes away

---

1 "God called to him out of the midst of the bush, and said: 'Moses, Moses.'" (Exodus 3:4)

2 Exodus 3:4

3 "And God said to Moses: 'I AM THAT I AM' (*Ehyeh Asher Ehyeh*) and He said: 'Thus shall you say to the children of Israel: I AM has sent me unto you.'" (Exodus 3:14)

4 These are the verbs used to describe God becoming aware of the oppression of the Israelites (Exodus 2:24-25).

the straw that we used to make the bricks of our enslavement, and the task before us becomes even harder.

The spiritual challenge of awakening becomes even more difficult, yet unavoidable. We see how slavery (living from our conditioned responses) has deadened the senses, drained us of vitality, kindled our doubt. Our usual strategies for survival are not working anymore. There is no turning back.

Guidance for Practice

Becoming aware of our enslavement: Identify an area or aspect of your life that is a source of stress, a pattern of thought that leads you into negativity or despair, a particular way of relating that you know isn't productive. You might identify a habitual response that is rooted in insecurity or fear, an addiction, or a place of resignation or bitterness within you. Just sit with the feeling of that enslavement. Don't fight it or deny it. Just let it sink in and feel its weight.

Finding the cry within us: Look underneath that weight and find a sound, a word or a phrase that is buried beneath your despair, resignation, bitterness or fear.

Being Heard: Open your mouth and let that sound, word or phrase out. Repeat it again and again, exploring and varying pitch, volume, and tone. Let your cry tell the Truth that has until now been silenced. This may take some time. Do not stop for at least ten minutes.

Remembered: In the silence that follows your cry, bring your attention to the breath and imagine the breath moving directly into the space inside your heart center. As the heart expands to receive the breath, invite your ancestors to sit inside your heart. Feel the power of their deepest longing within you. Receive their blessing.

Seen: Imagine yourself as a very young child. Surround your vision with your most tender compassion.

Known: Imagine yourself very old at the moment before a peaceful death. Breathe out your entire life. Breathe in the unknown.

Va-eyra
(And I Appeared)

EXODUS 6:2-9:35

The story of Moses in Egypt continues as he confronts Pharaoh and tries to free the Israelites from slavery. God brings the plagues against Egypt. Pharaoh's heart is hardened again and again.

THE BLESSING

THE BLESSING OF *VA-EYRA* comes to us as God's self-revelation.

"I am YHVH – I am Being itself. And yes I am the same one that your ancestors perceived as El Shaddai, the very same One. All the names you have called Me are aspects of the One, and now you are ready to receive a glimpse of the Whole, that Unnameable One.[1]

"You will see Me and know Me through the process of liberation that you are about to experience... Freedom is the key to knowing Me... Through this process I will bring you to fulfillment, to a state where you can receive the divine inheritance, which is the knowledge of the divine spark at your core. I am YHVH. I am Being itself."[2]

In receiving the blessing of *Va-eyra,* I place my journey in the context of cosmic process. I know that every tragedy I suffer and every delight I enjoy moves me towards the fulfillment of the divine promise. As each face of God appears to me, I can see it in the greater context of the One. Each day in my prayers I can remember (with the *Sh'ma*[3]) that all conceptions of God (*Eloheynu*) are aspects of YHVH, which is Being itself.

ONE WAY THAT I WILL OPEN myself to the view of the One is by witnessing the plagues – which represent the manifestation of divine power split off from its wholeness. In Kabbala, the Jewish mystical tradition, that wholeness is represented by The Tree of Life which is made up of ten *s'firot* – divine aspects that mediate between the infinite and finite realms.

When one of these *s'firot* is broken off from the whole of the Tree, evil comes into the world. The ten plagues correspond to the ten *s'firot.* Each

[1] "And God spoke to Moses, and said to him: 'I am the LORD; and I appeared to Abraham, to Isaac, and to Jacob, as God Almighty, but by My name YHWH I made Me not known to them.'" (Exodus 6:2-3)

[2] Exodus 6:6-8

[3] "Listen (*Sh'ma*) Israel, YHWH our God, YHWH is One!" (Deuteronomy 6:4)

plague is an aspect of the God-force that is broken off from the Tree. Its separation from the Tree of Life makes it a "blessing in reverse." The energy is twisted, distorted, and loses its intelligence; disconnected, this energy no longer serves the Whole.

In preparation for our freedom, which derives from the perception of the Whole and our inter-connectedness, we witness the destructive power of separation, as each aspect of the God-force breaks itself off and becomes distorted. Blood is a symbol of Life, but in excess becomes its opposite. Z'ev Halevi describes the plagues as "an overbalance of life that becomes deadly to itself." [4]

The blessing that comes from witnessing plagues (those tragic situations of obvious and deadly imbalance) is the awakening of the inner force of conscience that turns us towards wholeness and balance, and thus towards freedom.

The Spiritual Challenge

When Moses tells the people what God has said, they cannot hear it. The inability to hear and respond to the promise of freedom, to the truth of Oneness, and the self-revelation of God, is attributed in the text to "short spirit" and "hard slavery."[5]

At the center of our liturgy is the prayer that says, "Listen! *Sh'ma!*" Listening is the first step in the process of liberation. *Va-eyra* reveals to us two main obstacles to listening, and here our spiritual challenge is laid out.

The first challenge to listening is "shortness of spirit." This is sometimes translated as "impatience." The process of liberation requires great patience and discipline to take the small, necessary steps that will not necessarily relieve our immediate pain. Resolute patience is required to fully rest in the present moment as it is. This full acceptance of "what is" awakens the power of our presence and allows the process of transformation to unfold. Here is the paradox: One must patiently BE… in order to BECOME.

Hard slavery is the second challenge to the kind of listening that could lead us to freedom. We can become so tied to our work that our busy-ness is the driving force forming our identity. In this atmosphere, we can't stop long enough to listen. Listening is only possible when there

[4] *Kabbala and Exodus* by Z'ev Ben Shimon Halevi (Weiser Books, 1988) p.72

[5] Exodus 6:9

is a degree of stillness and spaciousness. When life is experienced as a constant struggle, the barrage of stress prevents us from receiving the flow of grace that might move us out of bondage.

When we witness the plagues – aspects of the God-force that have been separated off and distorted, we are initially moved to compassion. In the face of immediate suffering and need, our hearts are wrenched open. But when the immediate danger is past and we have recovered from the initial shock, our hearts tend to close again in complacency. We get used to the world in its imbalance and develop strategies that will ensure our short-term survival. This is called the "hardening of the heart." It is accomplished by narrowing the focus, deadening the senses, and denying any feelings that might threaten the status quo.

The spiritual challenge of *Va-eyra* is to keep the heart open in the face of prolonged suffering and to let the seeds of freedom grow in the darkness. Once you identify the ways in which your heart has hardened, the challenge is to bring beauty and tenderness and compassion to the heart, to soften and penetrate the layers of defense that have been built up around it.

Guidance for Practice

What is accomplished through the following practice is patience, spaciousness and presence. And in the process you will encounter and get to know your impatience and busy-ness.

Deep Listening[6]

Find a quiet place.

When you hear a sound, don't identify or interpret that sound. Instead, notice its pitch, volume, rhythm and tone. Don't make any judgement about it. When you find yourself identifying, interpreting or judging, just gently let go of those thoughts and listen even more deeply. Open yourself up to receive the sound fully. Don't reach out for the next sound. Wait for it to come in to you. Give equal attention to the outer sound and to the inner space that's receiving the sound.

Listen for at least ten minutes.

---

[6] Thanks to Pauline Oliveras for her teachings about Deep Listening.

Bo

(Come On In!)

EXODUS 10:1-13:16

The story of the Exodus from Egypt continues.

THE BLESSING

THE BLESSING OF *BO* IS OUR FREEDOM. We finally take that first step out of the narrow spaces of *Mitzrayim* and become conscious journeyers touched by the dream of awakening.

Freedom in our tradition is not merely "freedom from," freedom *from* oppression, suffering, or servitude. It is "freedom to," freedom *to* be in direct relationship with God our liberator. Being in that relationship means serving the One, the Whole, the Holy. Our freedom depends on this servitude.

At the beginning of the portion God speaks to Moses, the prophet within us, and says, "*Bo*! Come on in! I am waiting for you inside the heart of Pharaoh. The heart of Pharaoh is inside *you*. It is the place that has grown heavy with the weight of life's experience. It is the place that has hardened – its outer shell cynical, and its inner layers made of fear and unhealed grief. Through this heart of Pharaoh you must come if you are to know Me, if you are to find your freedom."

THERE IS A STORY about some jealous angels who are asked to hide the spark of the Divine in the world.

> **"Let's put it atop the highest mountain," offers one.**
>
> **"No," says another, "The Human is very ambitious; he will find it there."**
>
> **"Well then, let's bury it beneath the deepest sea."**
>
> **"That won't work either," another chimes in. "The Human is very resourceful. She will even find it there."**
>
> **After a moment's thought the wisest angel says, "I know. Put it inside the Human heart. They will never look there."**

And so the spark of God is hidden in the heart of Pharaoh where we are kept out by the heaviness that has accumulated, by the hardness that we meant for our protection. Sometimes that spark will speak to us from within, and say, "*Bo*! Come on in. I have been waiting for you for so very long."

WHEN WE COME THROUGH the heart of Pharaoh and enter in to those depths within, the blessing we receive is freedom and protection from the Angel of Death, whose only realm is the surface of things.

We are called into consciousness during a "night of watching," a night of vigilance.

We are blessed with a ritual of celebration and renewal so that we can re-experience the miracle of freedom with a feast of *Matzah*, unleavened bread. *Matzah* represents our essential self before it is "leavened" with ego.

THE SPIRITUAL CHALLENGE

THIS WORLD IS FOREVER CALLING US to the surface of things with its drama, seduction, humor, and entertaining dilemmas. Constantly bombarded with stimulation, we begin to rely on that stimulation to keep us from boredom, and dreaded emptiness. The spiritual challenge of *Bo* lies in the cultivation of a rich inner life. The obstacles to inner-ness, and depth, are represented by the heart of Pharaoh, the obstruction through which we must pass on our way to freedom.

How do we address the weight of our burdens? How do we acknowledge the hard shell of a self-image that has become too small? There are moments when the burden is lifted, when the hard surface softens, and the heart of freedom is revealed in its glory. Even as those moments fade I lift them up with my awareness and my gratefulness. I keep the memory of that inner vastness and hold it as witness against a world that pretends to reflect the whole truth.

ONE OF THE KEYS to freedom lies in Moses' insistence that the whole of the people must be freed together. When Pharaoh offers freedom if the feminine and child parts are left behind in bondage, Moses refuses, for he understands that to be free is to be whole and integrated. When Pharaoh offers freedom to the people if they will leave their animal selves behind, again Moses refuses, knowing that without the acknowledgment of all aspects of our selves, we cannot serve God.

The challenge before us is to accept and honor all parts of the self as the pre-requisite to freedom. In answering the call of *Bo,* we are led onto the path of healing and wholeness.

Guidance for Practice

There are two practices for this week of Bo.

Softening the Heart Music Meditation

Set aside some time alone to come through the Pharaoh-heart within you and dwell for a time in the space within.

Choose a piece of music of great beauty that you believe may have the power to lighten the heaviness of your heart and soften its hard surfaces. (Beethoven's Seventh Symphony works for me.) Make sure that you will be undistracted and very comfortable.

Before you begin, light a candle and dedicate this time to holiness and wholeness. Be aware of the places of cynicism in your heart or tension in the body and allow the music to gently penetrate those areas. Be aware of emotions that rise to the surface and allow them to be released.

Use the breath to direct the power of the music into the places of heaviness and hardness.

At the end of the piece, sit in the silence and allow the music to reverberate through your body. Enter through whatever doors that have been opened and rest inside.

Blessing Pharaoh

When Pharaoh finally lets the people go, he asks for a blessing. Perhaps we will not be entirely free until we can find the blessing for the part of us that is the tyrant, for the part of us that oppresses the spirit and has kept us in slavery, chained to a familiar constricting habit. That blessing can only come from self-compassion and self-forgiveness.

Compose a blessing with which to bless the Pharaoh-within as you move from slavery to freedom.

Beshallach
(When He Sent)

EXODUS 13:17-17:16

The Israelites cross the Red Sea and celebrate with song and dance. They are sent on their journey and given manna for sustenance which appears daily. If one takes more than he can consume that day, it rots and turns wormy. The Israelites receive Shabbat. They start complaining.

THE BLESSING

IN *BESHALLACH* WE ARE SENT on a journey of purification. The path seems impossibly circuitous, doubling back on itself, spiraling around and through every place of darkness within us – untangling the residual knots of our enslavement. We must take with us the bones of Joseph.[1] The Hebrew word for bones also means "essence." As we journey forth we carry the essence of our lineage, the bare bones of wisdom which we will flesh out with our own experience.

Our blessing is the wilderness, the landscape that will allow us to recreate ourselves in the image of freedom! The journey will call forth all of our strength and reveal every flaw. This is the kind of blessing that Ram Dass calls, "Fierce Grace." It begins in miracle as we walk on dry land in the midst of the sea.

Thus every spiritual journey begins. In the midst of the turbulence of this world, and in spite of our fear, we somehow find the courage to take one loving focused step and then another, with each step finding our footing on a path that only reveals itself step by step. But we DO it! We don't let the fear stop us. We cross into the wilderness leaving behind the safety of slavery – a life of conditioned response.

WE CELEBRATE THE MIRACLE of this crossing with a song and a dance that become the force of "sending" (*beshallach*). The power of the song and the magic of the dance propel us into the wilderness. The song lays out a formula for Salvation. My strength, "*Ozi,*" and the Song of God, "*ve-zimratYah,*" will be my salvation.[2] The blessing of Beshallach comes in the balance of these two aspects.

Ozi is the force of will that I bring to this crossing – the place inside me that desires freedom and truth, and will do anything for its attainment.

[1] Exodus 13:19

[2] Exodus 15:2

Ve-zimratYah is the part of me that knows how to surrender, that opens to the rhythm and melody of God's Song and gives itself unconditionally to "what is." The blessing comes in the balance of will and surrender.

With too much will, I isolate myself from the flow of Divine Grace that moves the world. With too much surrender, I become passive and abdicate my responsibility for full partnership with God in the work of Liberation. Too much will or surrender, and I might have drowned in the sea. In the marriage of my strength of will and a surrender to the God-song, the sea of confusion splits open and the dry land appears beneath my feet.

This internal balance of will and surrender comes to us slowly through practice and by learning from our mistakes. The blessing of Manna and the blessing of Shabbat are given to us as practices we can use to perfect this balancing.

Manna is the miraculous sustenance that is given to us each day. I may only gather what I can eat this day. If the force of my will grows too strong, it feeds my ambition and I will try to gather more than I can use. I will want to have enough manna for a week, a year, a lifetime, and from the will's point of view I can never have enough.

When I follow the impulse of ego-driven or fear-based will, all the surplus manna that I have gathered will rot. And so I must learn to gather only what this moment requires. Realizing that ultimately, I am not the one in charge, I surrender in faith to the taste of this day's bounty. (The Midrash tells us that manna tasted different to each person.)

The will is required in order to gather in sustenance and distribute it justly in our world. That force of will in us must be continually strengthened and refined. And on the sixth day we gather in a double portion in preparation for Shabbat, the day of surrender. The blessing of Shabbat is given to us as a practice of re-balancing and of integrating the gifts that we have been given.

The Spiritual Challenge

After the miracle of our crossing, we journey for three days into the wilderness and our thirst begins to plague us. The waters that we find here are bitter. Our resistance to stepping into the void disguises itself as complaining and rebellion. We are tasting the bitter waters that have accumulated inside us during the years of slavery. This is the place in us that is in the most need of healing and purification.

During the course of a week-long retreat, it takes about three days for "normal" consciousness to drop away, for the cluttered mind to begin to clear, for the body to release its rigid posturing. Then I am confronted with whatever bitterness that has accumulated inside me.

That bitterness might be projected on outer circumstance. "The food is terrible." "My bed is too soft." "My back hurts." "The teacher isn't very clear." "Perhaps this isn't my practice after all." "I'll never do it right." "I should just go back home, this isn't for me."

Beshallach sends us to our own bitterness that we might be healed. In order for this healing to occur, we must acknowledge the bitter murmurings and compassionately yet firmly set them aside, making room for Moses, our capacity for wisdom, to act. God shows him a tree, which Moses then throws into the bitter waters, rendering them sweet. The spiritual challenge of *Beshallach* is the sweetening of our own bitter waters. If those waters are not sweetened, they will poison us, and sell us back into slavery. ("I'm going back home, this isn't right for me.")

The tree that Moses uses to sweeten the waters is the Tree of Life. Whatever bitterness we carry (difficult memories, regrets, grudges, or disappointments), will be transformed when touched by this tree. So what does it mean to cast the Tree of Life into our pool of bitterness?

The Tree of Life has its roots in Heaven and its branches spread out into our lives. It is the bridge connecting the infinite mystery with this finite seemingly imperfect world. When I take hold of that tree, I am touching the truth of my connection to the Source of all Life. In touching that tree I connect myself with all of Creation.

When I can grasp that perspective, I can understand that my small pool of bitterness is only a drop in the ocean of the great being that we are together. My fixation on that small drop is what makes the water seem bitter to me. As the Tree of Life expands my perception, the spiritual challenge is to let go of the drop and become an ocean, vast and sweet. This is the healing that God-consciousness brings. "I am YHVH who heals you" – from the disease of feeling separate and abandoned.

Guidance for Practice

The Song of Celebration

We have all made miraculous crossings in our lives. Recall a time when you took a leap of faith, when you took a chance and crossed over into a new way of being in the world. Remember a time when you left the slavery that you knew and set out into the unknown. If you made a crossing and did not stop to celebrate, to sing your own Song of the Sea, and to call the women out to dance with their timbrels, then you have not been properly "sent."

This song of celebration isn't optional. It is necessary to the journey. This song will carry us into the wilderness. This dance will energize us for the journey.

Bring yourself back to a moment of miracle that was not fully acknowledged. It is not too late.

Honor your crossing with a song of praise, a dance, a poem, an offering. Share it with a Spirit Buddy.[3]

The Practice of Manna

Manna teaches us to appreciate what is before us without reaching for what is next.

Practice an eating meditation by creating a special meal for yourself and eating it slowly, in silence, one bite at a time, savoring its gift of flavor and texture and nourishment.

Acknowledge the Source of this food with blessing and trust each bite to bring you complete satisfaction before reaching for the next bite.

Gather in the manna, the miracle of this food through your concentration on the sensations of smelling, tasting, chewing, and swallowing. Slow the whole process down so you can notice everything about the food and your capacity to enjoy and be satisfied.

---

[3] see Appendix p. 232 for an explanation of this aspect of practice

Yitro

(Moses' Father-in-Law)

EXODUS 18:1 - 20:23

Yitro advises Moses. The Israelites come to Mount Sinai and experience the Revelation.

THE BLESSING

THE GREAT BLESSING THAT COMES TO US this week of the portion of *Yitro* is the blessing of Divine Revelation. When, in our wanderings, we come to Sinai, God speaks to each of us directly. The mountain of revelation appears to us on our journey when we are ready to receive the awesome truth of our connection to the Source, to each other, and to all of Creation.

In that moment of Revelation, it becomes clear:

Obviously, God is the true reality;
bowing down to my own illusions would be silly.

Of course, I cannot hurt any other living thing
without hurting myself; we are a part of each other.

Of course, there is no need to steal;
who is there to steal from, but another member
of the larger self of which I too am a part?

In that moment of revelation it will become clear that the desire that has created such turmoil within me is based on an illusion of lack; connected to all of Creation,
I am rich beyond measure.

And certainly, my father and mother must be honored; they are my own flesh and blood and they gave me this precious life.

And yes, in that moment of revelation the beauty and sanctity of Shabbat becomes clear; how else can I remember this moment of freedom that revelation brings if not by stopping and receiving the miracle of Creation anew each week?

There is no need for commandments at Sinai. The moment of revelation is a moment of clarity that informs how we live. In that moment of clarity all boundaries between self and other dissolve; all of our senses confirm the fact that consciousness can expand beyond culturally set boundaries and expectations. Living according to the commandments is a natural by-product of the Divine Revelation. Having experienced Revelation, it no longer makes sense to live any other way.

At Sinai it seems that we see the sound of thunder and hear the flash of lightning. Sound and light are revealed to us as energy. A whole new way of perceiving energy is awakened in us at that moment of revelation. With this new perception, even the thickest darkness cannot obscure the truth that we have been given.

God says, "I have carried you on eagle's wings and brought you back to Me." God, as mother eagle lifts us up out of our limited perceptions and shows us a perspective of the whole. When we take that view to heart, our lives are transformed.

The Spiritual Challenge

How do we prepare ourselves for the moment of revelation? How do we find our way to Sinai? The portion begins with a visit from Yitro, who is father-in-law to Moses and also his teacher of the mysteries of the wilderness.

Yitro comes to prepare Moses for Sinai. The old master of the wilderness watches how Moses lives, how he tries to do everything himself, and yet is never alone. Yitro says, "This is crazy. You're wearing yourself down with this life of yours. You sit alone and yet people are around you all the time. You need to change the way you do things."

Yitro instructs Moses in the laws of empowerment – how to see and call forth the qualities of leadership in others, and how to share in the joy and the burden of being human. If you sit alone with the burden of Truth, it will weigh you down. And if you are serving people from morning till night, you cannot become a proper vessel for Revelation.

I often say, "My first practice is sanity." Sanity for me is the condition that allows for the full functioning of my body, feelings, thought and awareness, which then allows me to be present for revelation. Sanity requires just the right balance of solitude and service, spaciousness and stimulation.

If Yitro came to you in his wisdom and observed the course of your day; if he had a chance to watch how you balanced the requirements for wholeness, what might he say to *you*?

Guidance for Practice

Requirements for Sanity assessment Practice

Make a commitment to sanity and wholeness by taking Yitro's advice to heart. Be honest about your personal requirements for sanity. What must you do each day in order to stay whole and alert? Sometimes we only learn about these requirements when we do not fulfill them and find ourselves out-of-balance, unable to be present for the miracle around us.

The practice for this week of Yitro is to do an honest accounting of:

our minimum daily requirements,
our minimum weekly requirements,
our minimum monthly requirements,
and our minimum yearly requirements,

for solitude, silence, wilderness, learning, music, dance, meditation, pleasure, beauty, nourishment, intimacy, rest, retreat time—whatever it is that is required in order to feel truly whole and fully alive.

After contemplating your requirements, write them down and share them with a Spirit Buddy. Then take out your appointment book.

Whenever I teach a workshop on spiritual practice I say that this is the holiest book there is. It's the one you consult every day and really live by. When you make a specific commitment to a practice, write it in that holy book. Then do it, just as you would take responsibility for fulfilling any other commitments written in that Holy Appointment Book.

By making a commitment to your own wholeness you send a clear message to God that you are available, that holiness is your priority.

Mishpatim

(Impeccabilities)

EXODUS 21:1 - 24:18

The Israelites are given and accept a series of laws to live by.

THE BLESSING

MISHPATIM BLESSES US with the power of discernment, as we attempt to live our lives in balance with Divine justice and love. We are blessed with the holy task of being present, vigilant, and kind, that our actions might be in agreement with the vision of wholeness and connection that we received at Sinai.

We embark upon this holy task in the context of the value system of our particular culture, time and place. The Torah gives us an example of a people struggling to express a loving and exacting justice in their world. In order to follow the example of our ancestors, we must discern the principles of justice and apply them in OUR lives and in OUR world.

For instance:

> **"If you take a neighbor's garment as a pledge, you must restore it to him before nightfall because that's his only covering and where is he going to sleep? When he cries to me I will hear, for I am gracious."[1]**

In other words, kindness supersedes the rules of property. Empathy for the neighbor who might shiver through a cold night is what is really important. We are given the assignment of being God's ears as we listen for and respond to the cries of the poor and oppressed. Whenever we resort to the logic of "what's mine is mine," God reminds us that "All the Earth is Mine."

Mishpat is usually translated as "rule," "judgment," or "ordinance." When I encounter this word, I understand it as "impeccability." When the Toltec Shaman, Don Juan, cautions Carlos Castaneda that he must be impeccable, he is trying to impress upon his student the utmost importance of staying alert and aware of the consequences of one's actions. Every word and deed ripples out to affect the whole — so the welfare of the whole must be considered.

This consideration extends through time as well as space. How will my actions benefit or harm generations to come?

[1] Exodus 22:25-26

We are blessed with the responsibility of being scrupulous with what we consume, what we waste, and how our lives impact the planet. This responsibility helps us to stay awake and aware of our potential to destroy as well as create. *Mishpatim* strips us of any excuses for cruelty or apathy. Even our enemy may count on our help when she is in need.

The Spiritual Challenge

When a *mitzvah* is repeated in the Torah, it's a sign to pay close attention. When it is repeated 36 times, we know that not only is that mitzvah important; but it stands as a central spiritual challenge on our journey. We are commanded not to wrong or oppress the stranger. This mitzvah appears twice in *Mishpatim*. The first time we see this commandment we are charged to keep it because we ourselves were once strangers in the land of Egypt.

This reasoning does not quite hold. Those who suffer oppression often themselves go on to oppress others. Whatever hurt I suffer becomes the source of my destructive powers. The wound that is layered over with scar tissue makes me insensitive to the suffering of others. To acknowledge the pain of others, I would once again have to feel my own.

Parents who abuse their children have most likely been abused themselves. The chain of suffering continues. Each subsequent generation seeks revenge for the misfortune it has endured. We inherit the myth of "good guys" and "bad guys" so that we know exactly who to blame. The stranger in our midst is always a likely target. We are caught in this cycle of oppression in which our suffering festers and grows inside us, becoming a weapon of continued blame and retribution. Yet the spiritual challenge remains: How can I transform my suffering into compassion for the stranger?

We receive this commandment again in the very next chapter; this time it comes with further clarification. "Do not oppress the stranger, for you know the soul of the stranger, for you too were strangers in the land of Egypt."

The clarifying phrase – "*ve-atem yedatem et nefesh ha-ger...*" (for you know the soul of the stranger) – gives me the key to the door of compassion. The verb "*yada*" (to know), signifies intimacy. When I encounter the stranger, I am commanded to know her soul, to step inside her skin, to see that his pain, his joy, is not different than my own. This moment of *knowing* breaks the chain of oppression.

When I encounter the suffering of the stranger it can be an opportunity for me to approach and begin to heal the place inside myself that remembers suffering. From that place of newfound wholeness I can then work for justice and become a healer of the world's pain. The secret ingredient is profound connection with the other. Gazing into the soul of the stranger, compassion is born. This compassion embraces your own suffering as well as the stranger's. Remembering what it was like to be the stranger, the spiritual challenge is to let your heart open first in compassion for yourself, and then expand to encompass the reality of the stranger who stands before you.

Guidance for Practice

Facing the Opression in our Midst

So often the ones who are the most vulnerable in our communities are the ones who become invisible. The spiritual practice for this week of Mishpatim is first to find out who those people are.

Begin by finding out about organizations in your community that help the homeless, the orphan, the widow, the stray animal, the poor, the stranger, the immigrant, the disabled.

Seek out the *tzaddikim*, the "righteous ones," who are doing the work of justice and love, who might help you open the eyes of your heart to the stranger in your midst. Find out where the need is the greatest and let your heart pull you.

Get involved, whether through giving, joining, hands-on work, or prayer for those who are lost at the lowest rungs of our society.

The spiritual practice for *Mishpatim* is to ask yourself: "Who is it that I may have stopped seeing because their poverty, disability, or despair makes me uncomfortable?"

Have compassion for yourself as you move through those uncomfortable feelings. You know what it is to be the stranger. Awaken the memory and let it help you grow into the fullness of who you are.

As a young child, I would lie in bed at night and listen. I was sure that I heard the sound of the whole world groaning. No one else seemed to hear it and after a while I stopped listening. Now I know that the sound I heard was real—and if I become deaf to it I will also miss the great joyful song of praise that all of Creation is singing to its Creator.

Terumah
(Offering)

EXODUS 25:1 - 27:19

The people are given instruction concerning the building of the Mishkan, the movable sanctuary that they are to carry throughout the wilderness journey.

THE BLESSING

OUR JOURNEY TAKES US AT LAST TO THE THRESHOLD of a great mystery. God has brought us out of Egypt, the place of narrow perception, for one reason: "to be Your God," to exist in holy relationship. For this is the key to freedom: a conscious connection to the reality that lies beneath the surface of things frees us from the bonds of the material world and allows us to expand beyond the arbitrary limits of our particular conditioned perspective.

Yet freedom is elusive. When we left Egypt in search of it, we were blocked by the great impossible sea. When we crossed the sea and fled to the wilderness, we encountered within us the enslaving attitudes and habits of rebellion and complaint. And even after we stood at Sinai and received that moment of clarity, we still fell back into the habits of busy mind and cluttered heart.

And so God says to us, "Make for Me a holy place so that I can dwell inside you. Yes, it is possible to stay connected with me at all times in all places, even as you engage in the life of the world." When we make a place for God to dwell in our lives, then we will never again be trapped in the illusion of separateness. God will be available and accessible to us in the innermost chamber of the heart and in the inner dimension of all Creation.

SPIRITUAL PRACTICE is about making our lives into a *Mishkan*, a dwelling place for Divine Presence. About one third of the Book of Exodus consists of the detailed instructions for building the *Mishkan*. As we build our spiritual practice, the details are important. The purpose of the *Mishkan* is to send us to the space within where we can receive the Mystery of Presence. Just as a great poem points us towards a truth that is beyond mere words, so the beauty that shines from the *Mishkan* of our lives illuminates the beyond that is within us.

The portion of *Terumah* begins with the invitation to explore and discern the true generosity of our hearts. For the *Mishkan* cannot be built solely out of a sense of duty, obligation or debt. Only the willing and generous heart can participate in this endeavor. The willing and generous heart is fueled by love and carries the motivation needed for spiritual practice.

What makes the artist choose one color over another? What inspires the composer to create a song that can open the heart? Where does the sculptor get her vision of the form that lies buried inside the block of marble? What moves the writer to express the inexpressible? Here is the blessing of *Terumah*: When the heart is willing and there is a commitment to the work, then the Divine Spirit will show us the pattern, the blueprint, the plan, the inspiration that births beauty into the world. And that beauty is designed to send us back to the Source of its inspiration.

The Spiritual Challenge

As artists of the holy we are given the spiritual challenge of opening to the creative flow and becoming a clear channel for Divine Will. To prepare for this purpose, we must heal our hearts that have contracted in stinginess born of fear. *Terumah* means "gift," and ultimately the only gift we can give is ourselves, our full and available presence in each and every moment of our lives.

I remember a moment, years ago, when I was so vehemently disappointed in the circumstances of my life that I ran outside into the desert at three in the morning and screamed at God through the thick darkness, "What do you want from me?!!!!"

I was absolutely shocked to hear an answer within me whispering, "Everything! How else can you become a servant of The One?"

Giving everything means accepting this moment, making myself completely available for the experience of being human – all of it, the torturous grief and jubilant triumph. It means not hiding or shrinking away from the experience of this "Now." It is, after all, a two-way invitation that is being offered. I am making a home for God to dwell within me, and I am listening for God's invitation to come home, which is to know this world as God's house and to enter into it completely. With this gift of my presence, my wholeheartedness, I build the *Mishkan*. How else can I become a servant of the One?

We are called upon to sanctify the vessel of our lives, to become empty. Yet at the same time the spiritual challenge is to make those vessels so incredibly beautiful and compelling that Spirit will be drawn in to them.

Guidance for Practice

Holy Ark Meditation

Sit quietly and bring your attention to the breath. Imagine the breath entering directly into your heart and expanding your awareness of the space within.

With each breath, let that space expand. Bring your breath in to the very center of that space and imagine that you are breathing in and out of that very center.

After about ten minutes of concentrated breathing into the heart space, introduce the image of the Holy Ark sitting at the center of your heart. On either end of the Ark two winged cherubs face each other.

Bring your attention to the point between them. From that holy space between, the voice of the Divine Presence speaks. Concentrate on that point and listen.

Tetzaveh
(You Shall Command)

EXODUS 27:20 - 30:10

Tetzaveh *describes the inside of the Mishkan, the implements and clothing of the Priests, and finally, the ceremony of Priestly consecration.*

THE BLESSING

WHEN I WAS A CHILD ATTENDING SYNAGOGUE I was fascinated by the *ner tamid*, the "Eternal Light," that hung above the ark. No matter if I was bored or sad or confused, the *ner tamid* filled me with hopefulness and curiosity. Everything changes; everyone dies; yet here was a light that would shine on regardless of circumstances. No matter what storms of doubt I suffered, this small light was constant. Through winds of change, through the tumultuous rains of my shifting experience, the *ner tamid* did not falter or flicker. I took refuge in this light and found it within me. *Tetzaveh* begins by blessing us with the light of eternity. We learn that this light, which is consciousness itself, requires our daily attention.

As *Tetzaveh* goes on to describe the vestments of the priests – the *ephod*, breastplate, robes and crown – we see that all the same colors and materials that went into building the *Mishkan* now adorn our bodies. Each of us is clothed in the garments of the Holy Indwelling, reminding us again that God has made Her home within us. We are blessed with wisdom of the heart, and from that wisdom flows forms of expression and creativity that radiate beauty and honor.

TETZAVEH DESCRIBES THE CEREMONY OF CONSECRATION, as we become priest and priestess in service to *Shekhina*, the Indwelling Presence of the Divine in our lives. In honor of our devotion to this sacred work we wear fine linens of luminous gold, shining blue, royal purple and passionate scarlet, and precious jewels engraved with the sacred names of our beloveds. Blue pomegranates and golden bells adorn the hem of our robes, and every detail is meant to remind us that this beauty has a purpose.

Across our foreheads each of us carries an inscription that hangs down from the crown of our priesthood. It says, "*Kadosh Le-YudHayVovHay*" (Holy for God) who is, was and will be the Ground of Being. When we get distracted or confused, it is possible to look at the forehead of a friend and see their lives inscribed for Holiness and remember what we too are working for, and why we are alive.

The Spiritual Challenge

Teztaveh offers us the spiritual challenge of consecration to the priesthood. We are called to be a "nation of priests," and a "light unto the nations," and are given the opportunity to take that priesthood upon ourselves consciously and dedicate our lives to serving the One, the Whole, the Holy.

Within that challenge, the first requirement is a daily practice of tending the *ner tamid,* the light of consciousness. This is the steady practice of awareness that underlies all other practice. Slowly, I begin to identify not with the self that is continually changing, but with the one who is paying attention to all these changes. When the flame of awareness is burning steadily within me, it illuminates the act of perception, rather than just the object being perceived. At this point, I can begin to discern the lenses through which my perception becomes distorted; I can realize when a passing mind-state has colored my reality.

The challenge lies in glimpsing the pure light of consciousness and seeing that light refracted into the ten thousand colors of our subjective experience. That experience of reality and its drama of mortality is so interesting, so compelling, so seductive that it blinds us to the light of the eternal shining through it all. It is only through the dailiness of practice – the repeated touch of the eternal, the persistent effort of the heart, the frequent affirmations of a wider expanse – that we can begin to free ourselves from the trance of our particular drama and enter into the holiness of conscious presence that crowns this world.

As priests and artists of the holy, we are commanded to honor that holiness by awakening the wisdom of the heart. The wisdom of the heart manifests in our love of beauty, because the function of the beautiful is so central to the life of holiness. Beauty has the power to send us to the Source. That same beauty can also trap us at the surface if we are not conscious of its power and purpose. We can consciously use the elements of this world (color, texture, fragrance, sound, light, movement) to open the doors to all the worlds.

The danger lies in falling in love with the forms themselves, worshiping the words, the ritual, the idea, the artistry, rather than what all those forms are pointing us towards. Our spiritual challenge is to adorn and surround ourselves with a beauty that will inspire us to see the whole world as a mirror for God's Holiness.

Guidance for Practice

The practice of preparing for Shabbat can be an opportunity to awaken the wisdom of the heart and become priests or priestesses in service to the Shekhina, the Indwelling Presence that makes itself known through the radiance of Shabbat.

Chant in Preparation for Shabbat

As you get ready for Shabbat, use the sacred phrase that lifts up your intention for holiness. As you clean the house, repeat the words:

Lich'vod Shabbat

For the honor of the Sabbath

As you're cooking a delicious meal...*"Lich'vod Shabbat."*

Even while washing the pots and pans... *"Lich'vod Shabbat."*

While setting the table... *Lich'vod Shabbat."* Then as you shower or bathe, washing off the worries of the week, you can chant, *"Lich'vod Shabbat."*

Remember the elaborate vestments of the priests and their intention for holiness. As you pick out your clothes and dress, let it be a ceremony of intention... *"Lich'vod Shabbat,"* "I adorn myself for the honor and radiance of this day."

Choose a fragrance that you only wear on Shabbat and anoint yourself with it saying... *"Lich'vod Shabbat."*

Finally when you are ready and come to the table, treat it as a holy altar, remembering that with the Shabbat candles you are consecrating this day with your delight.

Ki Tisa

(When You Lift/Count)

EXODUS 30:11 - 34:35

Ki Tisa *begins with the law of the half-shekel that all must contribute, and continues to describe the implements for the Mishkan. It goes on to tell the story of the Golden Calf.*

THE BLESSING

THE *MISHKAN* IS THE SANCTUARY INSIDE US, the holy place wherein the Divine Presence dwells. And the *Mishkan* is also built between us. God dwells in our midst whenever we make a profound connection with each other. In loving relationship and community, the Divine Mystery reveals itself. With the offering of the half-shekel, we are called to build this aspect of *Mishkan* together.

Ki Tisa tells us that everyone, no matter how rich or poor, is commanded to make an equal contribution. Those half-shekels that are collected are used for the casting of the sockets of the sanctuary, the pieces that hold it all together. What a blessing to know that my half-shekel is necessary and valued. And what a blessing it is to look around me and acknowledge that everyone has something to contribute that will hold the "Structures of the Sacred" in place. (I am not alone in my contributions, nor may I withhold my presence from this sacred task.)

THE HALF-SHEKEL is called "a ransom for your soul," for your soul is truly in danger if you do not consciously contribute to this *Mishkan* of community and acknowledge the equal value of each and every one of us. We can only build this holy place *together.* And we cannot sustain a spiritual practice that is blind to our interdependency with all of life.

The half-shekel we contribute is a reminder of the truth of our interdependency. Giving it consciously, we are saying, "Count me in!" Just by being alive and present I become an integral part of this glorious community. My half-shekel redeems me from the illusion of separation. The blessing of the half-shekel is that it saves me from inflation and self-importance… after all it's only a half-shekel, only a miniscule part of the whole. And the blessing of the half-shekel saves me from invisibility or demeaning of my self-worth… after all my contribution is of equal value to everyone else's, and the *Mishkan* could not be held together without it.

Ki Tisa goes on to bless us with the attention to the details of the instruments of the *Mishkan* – the laver, the anointing oil, and the holy incense. For the task of constructing and crafting our spiritual practice and the structures of our religious life, God turns from Moses, the prophet, and from Aaron, the priest, and instead appoints Betzalel who is the artist. The true artist within us and among us is filled with the spirit of God and is blessed with wisdom, understanding and intimate knowledge. She also has acquired the skills to express her inspiration. The name Betzalel can mean, "In the shadow of God" *(Be-tzel-El)* or it can mean "the Divine Egg." *(Betza-L-El)* Our artistic, creative life is sheltered under the wings of the *Shekhina* and incubates the Divine potential.

The Spiritual Challenge

The instructions and descriptions of the building of the *Mishkan* constitute the climax of our journey to freedom. When you have built a place in your life for the Divine Presence to dwell, then your ongoing and growing relationship to the Eternal frees you from the enslavement of the conditioned mind.

Ki Tisa inserts into the middle of the *Mishkan* texts the most serious spiritual challenge to our freedom. That challenge is represented by the story of the Golden Calf, which our tradition points to as exemplifying the quintessential sin.

I've wondered sometimes… what was so bad? After forty days of waiting, the people grew restless and afraid. Moses was, after all, the exclusive mediator between God and Israel. His absence left an unbearable void and so the people cried out to fill that emptiness with an image that would comfort them.

The only way to understand the Golden Calf is to compare it to the *Mishkan*, for the building of the *Mishkan* is the context for this story. The *Mishkan* exists for the space within it. It is a structure that is built to send us to that holy inner-ness. All of its beauty, color and design are dedicated as a nexus point between the Human and Divine, between Heaven and Earth. The important part is not the outer form, but what is inside, for that is where God speaks to us. The further within you get, the more holy is the space.

In contrast, the Golden Calf is solid, existing of and for itself. We supply the gold, but then the Calf seems to take on a life of its own. Aaron describes the process saying, "I cast the gold into the fire and out came this Calf!" The Calf has no interior space. It glorifies itself. It is "full of itself." It represents the most dangerous hindrance in the life of spiritual practice: that of worshiping and staying attached to the forms, rather than allowing those forms to send us inward to the essence, as is their purpose.

This is the spiritual challenge of *Ki Tisa*. How can I dedicate my life to spiritual practice without turning the forms of my practice into an idol? The difference between building a *Mishkan* or a Golden Calf is sometimes very subtle.

Sometimes when I think I'm building a *Mishkan,* I'm really making a Golden Calf. I remember once performing some music for a very appreciative audience. During the first verse of the song, I felt the holiness that the song was creating. I, along with everyone in the room, felt invited into that holy space. By the second verse, I was thinking, "Wow this is great. Everyone loves it. The sound system is terrific; my voice is really 'on' tonight. And this is really a great song." By the end of the second verse I realized that instead of building a *Mishkan*, I was making a Golden Calf; the song had become a monument to itself and to me. By the third verse, I made a resolve to build a *Mishkan* again, to get out of the way, and to dedicate my voice and the song to the Great Mystery. I'm certain that no one in the audience perceived the invisible struggle that went on within me.

As a rabbi, I sometimes fall into the role of advocate for Judaism or Jewish practice because I have tasted its treasures and they have opened the "doors of perception" which have brought me to the precipice of the Great Void that is God. The danger is that we can come to love Judaism more than we love God—who is beyond any religion or practice. The Torah, the tribe, the prayers, the language can become a Golden Calf, glorifying itself, binding us to its power and beauty.

There is a story that when Moses went up the mountain and stayed for forty days, God personally inscribed the Torah onto the tablets that Moses carried. They were made holy by the signature of the Divine. When Moses descended the mountain carrying these holy tablets, he saw below him the people worshipping and celebrating the Golden Calf. Moses cried out to God, "Look at what our people are doing! If I bring them this Torah inscribed with the Divine hand, they will make this into an idol too. They will worship *it* instead of You!"

God heard the cry of Moses and sent a strong wind, which blew the stone tablets out of his hand. They smashed at his feet into a million particles of dust, each particle inscribed with the signature of God. Then God sent all the winds – north, east, south and west. They lifted up those holy particles, each inscribed by the hand of God, and scattered them across the wide world until a fine dust covered our planet.

"If the people wish to know Me," said God, "they can ponder and appreciate My Creation. When their eyes are opened, they will see My handwriting everywhere."

GUIDANCE FOR PRACTICE

As we engage in the sometimes tedious work of building the Mishkan of our spiritual practice, there are moments when yearning overtakes us and like Moses, we cry out to God, "Let me know Your ways! Let me behold Your Presence!"

Sometimes God answers us by revealing Her qualities – Compassion, Graciousness, Patience, Forbearance, the Great Love, or Honesty. We can only perceive these Divine qualities when we begin to cultivate them in ourselves.

CULTIVATING DIVINE ATTRIBUTES

THE SPIRITUAL PRACTICE FOR THIS WEEK of *Ki Tisa* is to look for the seed of a Divine attribute in your own life.

ASK IN PRAYER, "What quality is needed right now in my life?" For that is how God wants to reveal Himself to you.

WHEN YOU DECIDE ON A QUALITY, try to discern its obstacle. For example, if you are cultivating patience, every time you feel impatient, explore the root of that impatience. Is it rooted in fear? If so, what are you afraid of? If you are cultivating honesty, look carefully and with the utmost compassion at the impulse to deceive yourself or others. When was this impulse born in you?

DURING THIS WEEK OF KI TISA pay careful attention to the seed of this Divine quality growing in your life.

LOOK FOR OPPORTUNITIES to demonstrate it, to water that seed with your attention.

WHEN OBSTACLES ARISE (and they will), observe and explore them carefully, holding yourself with tenderness and compassion.

Radiance Practice

Another practice for this week of Ki Tisa *is the practice of Radiance. When Moses came down from Mount Sinai his face shone with the light of his Divine encounter. It is an important practice to learn – to shine forth the Inner Light that has been kindled by our practice.*

Every period of retreat, prayer, or meditation can be understood in five stages. When those stages are recognized and honored, our practice can become a more powerful blessing for the world.

The first stage is an inward turning: we become self-aware and open the doors to our inner life. A certain stillness becomes necessary in order to discern the subtleties of the heart.

The second stage is ascending: we are lifted out of normal discursive mind, out of our narrow perspectives into an expansive and sometimes ecstatic panorama.

The third stage I call unity: the place beyond words or concept, the pure experience of Being.

The fourth stage is called descending: it is about embodying the Holy, bringing that holiness into form and idea.

And the final stage is radiance: when we learn to open the inner source of Light and allow it to shine through us into the world. The body becomes almost transparent and each breath becomes an instrument of light, inhaling into the center of our source point within the heart and exhaling with the intention of shining that light into the world.

Vayakhel

(And He Assembled)

EXODUS 35:1 - 38:20

Vayakhel describes the building of the Mishkan.

THE BLESSING

VAYAKHEL DESCRIBES THE ACTUAL CONSTRUCTION of the *Mishkan.* Our spiritual work is laid out before us; our enthusiasm is kindled.

When Moses calls the people together for their final instructions for building the *Mishkan,* we are first warned that there must be a holy rhythm to our lives. We are blessed with the knowledge that rest and reflection are absolutely necessary to the success of this project. Without the practice of Shabbat, we are warned, this work, even though it is holy work, will kill us. The blessing of Shabbat makes our work possible. Work becomes life-giving and wholesome only when it is balanced with Shabbat.

In the practice of Yoga, each series of poses is followed by a resting pose to integrate and fully receive the benefits of the preceding postures. The practice of Shabbat fulfills this same purpose, creating a space to receive, integrate, and deepen the benefits of our spiritual work. For six days we work at building the *Mishkan* and on the seventh day we can enter into that Holy dwelling and simply receive the Divine influx.

VAYAKHEL BLESSES US WITH THE AWARENESS of the true nature of the heart that is unconstrained by fear. Even though the disaster of the Golden Calf is still a fresh memory, Moses can look out at us and see that our true nature is ruled by a generous heart. When he calls on the gifts and talents and generosity of the people, he does not do so only for what they come to offer to the communal project. He is calling the people to know their own gifts and to experience the blessing of a generous heart.

When we can experience the flowing and giving heart, freed from the constraints of fear, we begin to know and trust ourselves as if for the first time. We can relax and let go of worries about not having or being enough, because the experience of flowing generosity feels effortless and infinite. *Vayakhel* tells us that Moses had to ask the people to stop giving because they had become so intoxicated with their experience of generous flow. We are reminded that together we have more than enough to complete the task of making a place for God to dwell among us, between us and within us.

The Spiritual Challenge

At the entrance to our sanctuary the laver is built. Here we wash and prepare ourselves for the holy encounter. The laver is made from the mirrors that the women bring.

When I was 22, I went on a three-week trip kayaking down the Green River in southern Utah. It was quite an adventure and those 3 weeks proved to be transformative. Besides getting my first real experience of wilderness and solitude, it changed the way I perceived myself. For those three weeks I didn't look at a mirror and so began to know myself from the inside–out. Without the daily reminder of outer appearance and the worry about how others might see me, I discovered my inner beauty and strength. I was surprised by a new image of myself that arose in the context of my relationship to water and rock and sun. I had become used to believing what others saw and reflected back to me. A new woman emerged that hardly resembled the image that others perceived or that I perceived through their eyes. The mirror had lied to me. It merely showed me the surface.

In our culture where it seems we (women especially) are judged by our appearance, we are given the spiritual challenge of knowing ourselves from the inside. We bring our mirrors as offerings to build a vessel of purification. Washing ourselves of others' projections and expectations, clearing away judgment and the need for approval, wiping away shame, we clean every pore of its need for artifice, till the skin can let our radiance shine through. Only then will we be ready to encounter God in the Tent of Meeting. We must offer up the judgments, criticism, and vanity that obscure our depths. The spiritual challenge of *Vaykhel* asks: How do we transform the mirror—our self-image—into an instrument that prepares us for the Divine encounter?

A distorted self-image can be an obstacle on the spiritual path yet this obstacle can be transformed. I once had a dream that I was dying. All of my friends and family were gathered around me. Some of them were grieving; others trying to heal me. Everyone was caught up in the escalating drama.

I excused myself to go to the bathroom and there I looked into the mirror. I was for the first time profoundly grateful for the face that had served me through my incarnation. I felt some remorse at how I had wasted so much time worrying over that face (Did it look alright?) or avoiding it (I didn't want to be vain).

Finally I could see myself—the self that was shining through from my eternal soul—and I felt great peace with who I had been and who I was becoming through the passage of my death.

When we are freed from the obsession with self-image, we can become playful with the gifts of incarnation. We can play with style and color and texture, bringing joy to the image we project and letting it express the truth and uniqueness of the inner dimensions of beauty that we encounter on our journeys. Without the worry about 'how I look,' or about 'how others might see me,' I am free to explore and expand my understanding of beauty. I can be grateful for the face I have been given and I can allow it to shine with God's radiance.

Guidance for Practice

Inner Reflection: A Mirror Meditation

After a period of prayer or meditation, gaze into a mirror.

Let yourself gently release any judgments that arise.

Try staring into one eye, then gradually expand your focus to include your whole face.

Then stare into the other eye, gradually expand your focus.

Look for the spark of your uniqueness. Continue to let go of judgements. Who is it that looks out from behind this face?

Watch the outer face transform as the inner face emerges.

Pekuday
(Accounts)

EXODUS 38:21 - 40:38

An accounting is given of all the work and materials used to build the Mishkan. The Mishkan is dedicated.

THE BLESSING

PEKUDAY BLESSES US WITH AN ACCOUNTING of all the work we have done to build a spiritual life. All the components are there. The effort and artistry and riches that have gone into this life-project are made visible to us. This is why I came here… to do this work.

I look back at my journey and remember the days when my resistance to the work took up most of my attention. I still have days like that. Yet today, as I bask in the blessing of *Pekuday*, I can remember, above the din of my whining and complaint, that this is the work that I was born for. In the big picture, there is nothing more compelling or that gives me more joy than to make a place for the Divine Presence to dwell among us, between us and within us.

To this project I have brought the gold of my love and the silver of my shining desire for Truth. I have made hooks and sockets to connect me with the whole of Creation. I have brought every color of my changing moods, offering them up to that which is eternal. I have mined carnelian, turquoise, topaz, sapphire, emerald, agate, onyx, jasper, crystal, lapis lazuli, and amethyst – in the Ground of My Inheritance. I have faceted these jewels with tools of mind and heart. I have chiseled, cleaned, and polished these collected treasures and arranged them for my descendants.

And this *Mishkan* that I have built, and that we have built together, will, with its beauty, send us to the holy dimensions where God dwells beyond conceptions, beyond form or religion.

THE SPIRITUAL CHALLENGE

LEGEND TELLS US that all of the components for the *Mishkan* were completed to Moses' satisfaction and he blessed all the Israelites who had created such beauty… yet the people had to wait for three months until it was erected and consecrated. Those three months of waiting might well have been more difficult than all the time spent in creative work.

THIS IS THE SPIRITUAL CHALLENGE that confronts us when we learn that we are not, and have never been, in charge of the timing of God's grace. Without that grace all of our efforts are worth little, because we are building this *Mishkan* for it to be filled with Divine Spirit. And Spirit moves in ways we cannot control. We can only create the space. We can only invite that Presence in. This waiting time is a period of gestation. It is the darkness and cold of winter. It is the long wait for spring.

Moses was told to wait for the first of Nisan, the month during which we are liberated from the narrowness of Egypt and the time of the re-creation of the world. In Nisan, color and life return to the Earth; flowers begin to show their buds; the grasses sprout their new green; the miracle of re-birth surrounds us. During those cold dark months of winter waiting, it seemed like nothing was happening, but now we realize that beneath the ground, beyond our awareness, miracles were stirring. The waiting time was necessary to this re-birth of possibility.

Still, this waiting time is a test of our faith and patience, in which we ask: "I have done all the 'correct things.' I have been faithful to my practice. I have followed the rules. I have crafted each piece of the *Mishkan* with beauty and precision. I have said the right words and acted righteously.... So why has Grace not descended? Why hasn't my life come together in the way it's supposed to? Why do I not feel loved and appreciated? Why is it still dark and cold? Why is the world still filled with misery?"

During this long winter waiting, all the voices of impatience emerge as the spiritual challenge of *Pekuday*, and Faith rises to that challenge as we learn to wait and intuit the miracle that is stirring beneath the frozen ground.

WE CAN STUDY THE NATURAL WORLD to understand the process of our own spiritual growth. I was studying at a yeshiva in Jerusalem in March of 1991. It had been the wettest winter remembered in a hundred years. I walked into my Midrash class and Melila, a very special teacher and wise soul waited for us; everyone could tell she was very excited. "Class is cancelled," she shouted. "Everyone, go to the desert above Qumran. All the flowers are blooming."

My classmates went home, happy to have the day off. I raced to the Central Bus Station and boarded a bus for Qumran. There I climbed up above the desert floor to the heights that offered views of the Dead Sea in the distance. I sat on a rock and looked around. The desert heights, once barren and brown, now were covered with flowers. I tried to think of a color that wasn't there… and I couldn't. Every color that I could imagine was accounted for. Seeds that had been buried in the hard dry desert ground for a century were blooming.

All afternoon I sat there and did the work of *Pekuday*, the accounting for this *Mishkan*. I wondered what seeds were buried in me. Every color nurtured my faith.

Guidance for Practice

Meditation Practice

I receive Pekuday *as guidance for the deepening of my meditation practice. When the work of the* Mishkan *was finished, the Glory and Presence of God filled the space that had been prepared by the work. Each day I sit in silence, open myself and become available to the Mystery.*

In meditation we become the Mishkan. *When the presence of God filled the* Mishkan, *even Moses was not able to enter. In meditation there is fullness that is empty of content. As I sit and gently let go of thoughts, even Moses, the part of me that is brilliant revelation, prophetic message, answer to all great questions cannot enter the Mishkan. All content is excluded from the holiest of places, along with passing thoughts of breakfast, aches and pains, things to do, meditation tips. Everything is surrendered with the intention of becoming empty so that I might be filled. And because God is no-thing… then every-thing of content, no matter how compelling, is not God, is not the Source.*

Sitting down on my meditation cushion, there is initially an accounting that must take place. This is the first part of the practice of *Pekuday*. I must become fully present. All of my gifts must be called up and dedicated to the practice of direct encounter with the Source.

I stretch out the sore places in my body so that energy can flow through me unobstructed.

I do a number of breathing practices so that the rivers of soul can flow freely and I can connect with the reservoir of Life-force at my core.

I open my heart, call forth the power of my intention and refine my ability to focus through prayer and chant.

And then I sit. "*Dom l'Yah, v'hitcholello.*" "Be still," Psalm 37 tells us, "and wait for God."

The final sentence of The Book of Exodus, the manual for our liberation, tells us that we must cultivate an awareness of God's mysterious presence, characterized by the Divine cloud in the day and an inner fire at night. This awareness will guide us throughout our journeys.

Shefa Gold

LEVITICUS

Vayikra

HOLINESS

Vayikra
(And He Called)

LEVITICUS 1:1 - 5:26

The book of Leviticus begins with the Laws of sacrifice for the individual, the congregation and the priests.

THE BLESSING

AS WE STEP INTO THE BOOK OF LEVITICUS, we move to another level of spiritual development and pause to take stock of our journey. Genesis can be read as the descent of the soul and its contraction into physical form. It is the story of incarnation and as the story ends we find ourselves enslaved in the narrow perspectives of physical reality.

Exodus then shows us the path of liberation, the awakening of the soul to its true essence, which interpenetrates the Divine Essence. God must find a way into our hearts and we must find a way into the heart of Reality... which is God-consciousness. The story of Exodus ends with the building of the *Mishkan*, which is the vehicle for this interpenetration. Through the *Mishkan* we learn that our Freedom depends on our connection to God and our willingness to make a holy space within us and between us for God to dwell.

How can we sustain this connection, this state of holy freedom?

This is the question addressed by the book of Leviticus. So often the complications of life seem to draw us away from the perspectives of holiness. We become alienated, distracted, complacent, blind to what is essential; deaf to the music at the core of silence; numb to the mystery that dwells at the heart of this life. Our daily struggles sometimes close us off from the flow of the Great Love.

The blessing of *Vayikra* is the call to come into harmony, balance, connection and intimacy with the God who has freed us for this love... and not only to return, but to establish for ourselves a system of continual returning.

THE MEDICINE that *Vayikra* gives us for the dis-ease of our alienation from God is described in the language of *Korbanot*, the "sacrifices." Literally, *Korbanot* means "bringing ourselves near" again to God. The *Korbanot* were a powerful and effective means of engaging all of the senses, witnessing the power of Life and Death, and then sharing a sacred meal in the Presence of God. The result was experienced as total purification

– removal of obstructions and a re-connection to the flow of God's love and presence. And for a time this was a spiritual technology that worked well.

The Spiritual Challenge

Our tradition tells us that prayer now takes the place of the sacrifices. The spiritual challenge of *Vayikra* is to make our prayer-life as powerful, as intense, and as effective as the sacrificial system was for our ancestors.

Can the word of a prayer engage the senses fully? Can we taste it? Smell it? Touch it? Feel its blood? Hear its music and the silence within it? Witness its passage into the void? See in it the shadow of death and the spark of life? Do we leave our prayer feeling purified, our burdens lifted?

Our ancestors celebrated their new state of connection by sharing a sacred meal with the priests and with God. After praying in community, can we also make our celebrations holy? Can we eat these sacred meals — our *Kiddush* and *Oneg Shabbat* gatherings[1] — knowing that each bite of our feast is also tasted and enjoyed by God?

Guidance for Practice

The Altar of Prayer

Vayikra describes a number of different kinds of sacrifices, each one directed towards correcting a specific imbalance or disease of soul. This week our practice of prayer will be guided by the images of Vayikra as we lay our words on the altar of sacrifice. Each spiritual disease from which we suffer removes us from God's Presence. Our practice of prayer is meant to bring us close again.

We will first discern the particular disease that keeps us distant from God. Then we will chant the sacred phrase that carries the power of Korban, the power to release the obstacles that keep us separate. Each sacred phrase holds a particular medicine that can restore our connection to the whole of Creation and return us to God's loving embrace.

---

[1] *Kiddush*, literally "sanctification," and *Oneg Shabbat*, literally "Sabbath joy," have come to refer to the celebrations following Sabbath services, which can range from simple cake and soda to elaborate sit-down meals.

OLAH עולה

THERE IS A PARTICULAR SPIRITUAL AILMENT THAT MANIFESTS AS AN INFLATION OF THE SELF. The mind is consumed with ME. Everything seems to depend on ME. I am obsessed by MY memories, MY plans, MY importance, MY spiritual path, MY sickness, how I might manipulate the world to MY benefit. The medicine for this condition must sometimes be drastic—namely, the complete nullification of self.

The *Olah* is the burnt offering that is completely consumed by fire. Through the *Olah* we experience the complete surrender of the self to God's will.

In prayer, the *Olah* is the total surrender of "ME" into the Divine fires. When the self is entirely given in prayer, we may experience a moment of terror as the self dissolves. In that moment of dissolution, God welcomes the gift of our return and breathes in the sweet savor of our fragrance (which is the self distilled into its pure essence). God then breathes our unique essence back into us that we might be re-created. In that moment of Divine pleasure, we experience a great and sublime relief.

"Re-ach nicho-ach L'Yah"

a sweet savor unto God

(These are the words that I savor and contemplate as a sense of self returns to healthy balance in relationship to the cosmos that is birthing me.)

SH'LAMIM שלמים

THERE IS A PARTICULAR SPIRITUAL DISEASE THAT AFFLICTS US WHEN WE ARE CORRUPTED OR INSULATED BY OUR WEALTH AND GOOD FORTUNE. It manifests as complacency and stinginess, as a lack of passion or sense of wonder.

The *Sh'lamim* is an offering of thanksgiving. It expresses our sense of wholeness and is given in response to the Grace we receive. Our giving allows that Grace to flow through us. This offering always culminates in a sacred meal shared with the givers, priests and God.

In prayer, the *sh'lamim* flows from our acknowledgement of the amazing richness of Life. Through this offering, generosity is kindled in the heart. Giving becomes the natural response to receiving. My fullness overflows into the world and goodness is multiplied as it is shared. I let my prayer express this wondrous overflow.

***"Kosi r'vaya"*[2]**

My cup satisfies...overflowing

(These are the words that remind me that I must become a vessel through which the abundance can flow.)

CHATAT חטאת

THERE IS A PARTICULAR SPIRITUAL DISEASE THAT IS CAUSED BY CARRYING THE BURDEN OF PAST MISTAKES. It causes us shame which cuts us off from God's love. We become defensive and seek to blame others.

> **The *Chatat* is an offering that lifts from us the sorrow of our errors. When awareness reveals that we have acted unconsciously, and thus have unintentionally done damage to others, our remorse can be transformed into resolve. The *Chatat* celebrates this moment of clarity, purifying us from the obscuring effects of guilt or shame, empowering us to turn towards God, towards reconciliation and wholeness.**

In prayer, the *Chatat* is the heart-song that sings us free from the shame of our errors, and turns our mistakes into clear instructions for repair and holiness.

***"Hashiveynu Elekha v'nashuva"*[3]**

Let us turn to You and we will be turned

(These are the words that I use to extricate myself from the web of guilt and open me to the healing power of forgiveness.)

Note: *We are all at all levels of development at once. No one level has precedence over another. Each comes into focus as we identify with that level.*

---

[2] Psalms 23:5

[3] Lamentations 4:21

Tzav
(Command)

LEVITICUS 6:1 - 8:36

Tzav consists of instructions concerning the sacrifices and how to install the priests in their service.

THE BLESSING

WE ARE COMMANDED TO BE A NATION OF PRIESTS, to take responsibility for the holiness of our world, to be healers, and when necessary to stand between Life and Death, bridging the finite and the infinite. *Tzav* addresses the priest in us and so its blessing is in calling that priest forward.

TZAV BEGINS with the instructions for keeping a perpetual fire burning on the altar. Without the constancy of this fire, all of our sacrifices, our prayer, our holy work would cease. This fire on the altar of our hearts is the pre-requisite for all spiritual practice. *Tzav* directs us in the tending of that innermost fire. If the fire should go out, our priesthood will be worthless.

TZAV ENDS with the ceremony that consecrates our priesthood and sends us to our holy work. During this ceremony we are blessed with the blood of the ram of consecration on the ear, the hand, and the foot:

> **ON THE EAR that we might hear and respond to the cry of the oppressed and to the still small voice within our own hearts.**
>
> **ON THE HAND that we might dedicate ourselves to doing justice and making beauty.**
>
> **ON THE FOOT that we might walk carefully and deliberately on the path of pilgrimage.**

The Spiritual Challenge

Tzav asks us to enter within and inspect the condition of the innermost fire upon the altar of the heart. We are challenged to look at our lives and ask the serious and probing questions about what supports that fire as well as what puts it out.

The fire itself speaks to me and says, "You must provide the spark. Be with the people who spark your creativity and enthusiasm. Keep reading and learning. Seek out places of beauty. Let yourself be challenged by difficult and interesting projects. Make music and colorful art. Travel to exotic places. Find reasons to celebrate."

Seeing that I am listening, the fire grows bolder saying, "And I need space to burn. Spacious air. The breath of life. Spirit. Wind. Open spaces. If you schedule every minute of your day; if you fill the silence with words; if you clutter up your life with so much stuff… how can you expect me to have enough space to burn?"

The fire begins to open to me and so I speak to her directly. "What will you use as fuel? What keeps you burning?"

The fire flickers brightly at my question and whispers, "The love that you give and the love that you receive… that is my fuel. For love is as fierce as death… no river can sweep it away."[1]

"And one more thing," says the fire, flashing righteously, "you must remove the dead ashes every day. I cannot burn clean and pure if the refuse of the past is allowed to accumulate within you. Each morning you must remove that which is old and done."

Guidance for Practice

Journey to the Fire on the Altar of your Heart

Begin your journey by sitting before a candle and staring into the flame. Let your breath deepen and slow.

Look into the heart of the flame (for at least ten minutes). When the flame has burned its image into your eyes, close your eyes and see the flame inside your heart. Whenever you lose the image within, open your eyes and let the outer flame send you to the inner fire.

---

[1] Songs of Songs 8:6-7

When you can see or feel the inner fire clearly, ask it some questions about what it needs to burn brightly and continuously. Ask the fire about what will spark her; ask about what kind of spaciousness she needs; ask her about what will be the fuel to keep her burning continuously.

Let the fire instruct you concerning the removal of ashes.

Write down the answers you receive.

Shemini
(Eighth)

LEVITICUS 9:1 - 11:47

Just before the priests are to be installed, Aaron's two sons, Nadav and Avihu offer "strange fire" before God and die in the process.

THE BLESSING

THE STORY OF THE STRANGE FATE of Aaron's sons Nadav and Avihu can be read as a warning... or as a promise.

On the face of it, it looks like they did something very wrong and were punished for it, thereby leaving us with a stern warning: You must play by the rules...or else! The text states that they, "offered strange fire which God had not commanded them. And fire came forth from God and consumed them and they died before God."[1]

But perhaps Nadav and Avihu did not do anything wrong, but instead did something extraordinarily right. Perhaps death was not a punishment, but instead a passionate Divine embrace of beloveds.

Moses conveys God's explanation of the event to Aaron with these words: "Through them that are near Me, I will be sanctified; and upon the face of all people I will be glorified."[2]

These are not the words of an angry God. Those who were close to Nadav and Avihu are forbidden to mourn them. Is this because God is celebrating their return?

WHEN I RECEIVE this story as a blessing, Nadav and Avihu's death becomes a demonstration of the power of transformation. I look for the place within me that is willing to offer up everything, directly from the impulse of the heart, without being asked, without conforming to what is deemed normal. The fire that I give seems strange because it is unmediated by religious convention. I give the strange raw essence of my passion, my fire, and then I am transformed through my giving. God takes me, rather than my gift. And isn't this just what I had intended? I ask to be taken, used, transformed by the force that is constantly re-creating the world. I surrender self, form, knowledge, even religion that I might be returned to my Divine essence.

---

[1] Leviticus 10:1-2

[2] Leviticus 10:3

Shemini blesses me with this possibility, this promise: There comes a moment when all rules, procedures, methods, even my spiritual attainments are stripped away from me, and all I have left to give is my self. In that moment my giving is entirely unselfconscious. It is a gesture of pure soul yearning to return to its essence. In that moment of selflessness, the glory of God appears upon the faces of all people. In fact it is everywhere.

The Spiritual Challenge

After recounting the story of Nadav and Avihu, which is about ecstasy, wild abandon, supreme intoxication, *Shemini* goes on to describe the path of discernment, responsibility and sobriety. Our spiritual challenge is to embrace the wisdom of both of these paths.

The path of sobriety requires that I do everything possible to keep myself clear so that I may be of service. I must clear myself of prejudice, distortion, pride, despair… anything that might cloud an accurate vision of the truth of this moment or weaken my power to respond.

I must be careful about what I consume and what words I say. I must monitor my state of consciousness because it is the lens through which I perceive the world.

The path of sobriety requires an impeccability that is inspired by knowing that this day might be my last.

The path of ecstasy requires that I be willing to surrender everything so that I might be held in the Divine embrace. On this path my sense of separateness dissolves. There is a happy confusion of subject and object.

It is necessary to learn to walk both these paths in the realization of holiness. Our sobriety gives us the strength and wisdom to hold and channel the ecstasy. Our ecstasy challenges rigidity and brings vitality to the heart of our sobriety.

In *Shemini* the reason that is given for our quest for holiness is that we must become like God, our Source. Becoming holy is, then realizing who we truly are. Towards the end of *Shemini* we are given this spiritual challenge:

I am YHVH (the Ground of Being) your God;
Sanctify yourselves and be holy
For I am holy.

Guidance for Practice

Chant

The practice of chant can combine the exacting discernment of the path of sobriety with the wild abandon of the path of ecstasy.

Set aside 10 minutes for this practice at the end of your regular meditation or prayer. It is best done when the mind is already somewhat settled.

Let yourself be drawn to a sacred phrase from liturgy or scripture that has some power for you right now. Begin to chant it with a simple melody.

For the first 5 minutes focus all of your attention on the sounds of the phrase, first the consonants, and then the vowels. Notice exactly how each sound feels in your mouth, what kind of breath each sound requires. Notice exactly where in your body each sound resonates.

With each repetition of the chant, focus more intently. Be a scientist of sound investigating each consonant and each vowel to discern its effect on your energy.

For the last 5 minutes, let go of all focus and let the chant chant you. Surrender to its transformative power.

Tazria / Metzora
(She Will Bear Seed)

LEVITICUS 12:1 - 13:59
LEVITICUS 14:1 - 15:33

This portion details the laws concerning purification after childbirth and the laws concerning Tzara'at. *It goes on to describe just how the one who has been healed must be welcomed back to the community.*

THE BLESSING

THESE CHAPTERS ARE CONCERNED with the delicate times when one's condition necessitates a period of separation from communal life. How does that separation happen and how is that person later re-integrated into the community?

Tazria begins by discussing the condition of a woman immediately after childbirth. She is blessed with a time of separation and then given a path for returning. I understand this condition not only in the context of childbirth, but in regards to the creative process. During a time of intense creative output, as with childbirth, a person steps outside the boundaries of time and space. She touches the realm between the worlds where *ayin* ("nothing") gives birth to *yesh* ("existence").

In that place between worlds she is completely taken up by the process of birth. The artist lives inside the poem, painting, or song, and the rest of the world, for a time falls away. The blessing of *Tazria* is in knowing that there will again be a way of returning to the community, to normal life. The time of alienation, which is necessary for the creative process to unfold, is also finite. The artist may return and bring with her the riches that she has mined and be re-integrated, welcomed back, and appreciated by her community.

DURING THE PROCESS of re-entry, the mother, or artist, brings two offerings, a *Chatat* and an *Olah*.

The *Chatat* is the offering that celebrates the purification from unintentional sin. If during my time of separation and focused creativity I have by necessity neglected other parts of life, I can be cleansed of guilt and blame, and with the offering of the *Chatat* be re-connected with the life of the community.

The *Olah,* the burnt offering, is completely consumed by fire, completely given. After creating something wonderful and being consumed by that process there is a danger of identifying your ego with your creation. When that creation is praised you may become inflated; when it is criticized you may become defensive. The offering of the *Olah* is a way of completely giving your creation to God, to the wholeness of the cosmos.

There are many times in life when it may be necessary to seclude oneself for a time. *Tzara'at,* which is usually translated as "leprosy," can be understood as a difficult inner psycho-spiritual passage that manifests as a disturbance on the surface. Someone with this condition needs to separate himself from the community for a time in order to pay close attention to those inner changes, which are the causes of the outer confusion. At a time of inner growth, it might feel like your life has become too small. There is a chafing or an irritability, and it is time to 'leave the camp.' It is time to go on a retreat.

The blessing of *Metzora* comes to us as the force of re-integration, symbolized by the priest, as it reaches out to you in your place of alienation, recognizes your transformation and brings you back to the community. In the ritual of re-entry, two birds are brought. One is killed, to symbolize the old self that has died; and one is set free in the open country to express the re-born self flying free into an expanded life.

The Spiritual Challenge

Often, a person's growth happens on the inside before it manifests in the outer world. The spiritual challenge lies in navigating this awkward time of dissonance between inner and outer. During this time the two realities must be reconciled. It is an uncomfortable time because there is a tendency to resist change and that resistance can manifest in the physical body. Retreat time is required in order to attend to and integrate the inner changes.

The spiritual challenge of *Tazria/Metzora* is to know when to separate yourself from the community and to know how to return.

The separation depends on having a community/relationship/family who honor and trust the process. This means that they understand the process of retreat as necessary and valuable to the life of the community.

When someone 'leaves the camp' to do the inner work that is calling them, they will be fully available upon their return and will have an integrated wholeness to give back to the community.

The process of retreat requires paying attention to the subtle messages of the soul in an atmosphere of spaciousness, without the everyday distractions and demands of the outer life. For some it may seem selfish to take this time for yourself, but it really is a **requirement** in the life of service.

Guidance for Practice

Retreat Practice

Plan a one-day retreat for yourself.

Prepare food in advance, shut off the phone, clear your space or go out into Nature.

Leave the 'camp' of your normal life. Spend the day in prayer and meditation, listening to the promptings of your heart.

Find two stones. Bring them back with you when you return to the 'camp' of your normal life.

Arrange for a friend to welcome you back at the end of the day and listen as you articulate and integrate your experience.

Hold one of the stones you brought back with you and describe the part of yourself that you have outgrown, that is dying, that has ceased to be useful.

With all your strength throw that stone away as far as you can.

Hold the remaining stone and describe the place in yourself that is new, that wants to grow in your life.

Keep that stone and place it on your altar as a reminder of this day.

Complete the ritual by sharing a sacred meal together.

Acharey Mot

(After the Death)

LEVITICUS 16:1 - 18:30

We are given a description of the Yom Kippur ritual and then laws concerning the holiness of our diet and sexual relationships.

THE BLESSING

OUR PORTION BEGINS with a description of a complicated ceremony of purification performed once a year by the High Priest on Yom Kippur. The purpose of all expiatory rites was to maintain the purity of the sanctuary, preparing it as a place where the Divine Presence could dwell.

Understanding that the *Mishkan* can be found inside us and that the High Priest also resides there, *Acharey Mot* can be received as a clear reminder of the responsibility to keep our hidden sanctuaries functioning. The inner *Mishkan* functions as our place of access to the infinite flow. This is the place where we can touch God inside us, and the presence of God can touch our lives moment to moment.

Some of our ancestors realized that a ritual of purification performed just once a year might not be enough to keep us open to the Divine flow. They instituted the celebration of *Yom Kippur Katan* ("Little Day of Atonement") each month on the day before the new moon. This transformed the dark time of the month into a time of purification so that the sanctuary within could be cleared and a space could be prepared for the Divine Presence as the moon returned to the night sky.

THE BLESSING of *Acharey Mot* is the opportunity to purify our inner sanctuaries at regular intervals, whenever necessary... once a year, once a month, every week... or perhaps each night. There will always be imperfection, mistakes in our human stories. And after seeing and speaking the truth, there will always be Divine forgiveness.

AFTER DESCRIBING THIS RITUAL of purification, *Acharey Mot* continues with instructions about holiness in eating and in sexual relations. Decisions about what we eat and with whom we engage in intimacy must be made as part of our pursuit of holiness, which means our motives must be pure, our intentions clear, and the implications considered regarding our actions and their effects on the whole.

Accepting the blessing of God's Presence within us means that we must be continually purifying the body as Divine dwelling place. We do this by honoring the holiness of the physical body and by guarding against its desecration in regards to habits of eating and sexual behavior.

The Spiritual Challenge

During the ritual of purification, two goats are brought. One is designated "for God" and is slaughtered as a *Chatat*, a "sin offering." The other is marked for Azazel. After laying upon its head all the sins and transgressions of the people, the second goat is sent into the wilderness to Azazel. Whoever or whatever Azazel is, he holds the key to our purification.

Someone would be designated for this job of escorting the goat to Azazel in the wilderness. He was the one charged to move between the civilized world and the wilderness. I've always imagined myself as that "*ish itti*" – the "man of the moment" – performing that job.

The designated escort knew this secret: All of our sins can be traced to the wild part in us being lost, misdirected or suppressed. If the wild, the ecstatic in us is not honored and allowed its vitality, it will find outlet in cruelty and violence. When the "*ish itti*" escorted the goat with all of Israel's sins on it in to the wilderness, he was returning that misdirected energy back to its source.

Our spiritual challenge is to find that wild place inside us and through ecstatic practice, give it voice and space and an honored place in our lives. If we do not, it will get twisted and become a destructive force. Returning the goat to Azazel is allowing the wild part of us its wilderness, its place to be free.

Guidance for Practice

There are two practices for this week of Acharey Mot.

Yom Kippur Katan

Each night during this week of *Acharey Mot,* grant yourself a mini-Yom Kippur.

Review your day noting each interaction.

If you have hurt another, make a resolution to apologize or compensate that person.

If someone has hurt you, resolve to forgive them.

You may want to recite this traditional prayer:

Eternal Friend,
Witness that I forgive anyone
Who hurt or upset me
Or who offended me
Damaging my body, my property
My reputation
Or people that I love;
Whether by accident or willfully,
Carelessly or on purpose;
With words, deeds
Thoughts, or attitudes;
In this lifetime
Or in another incarnation –
I forgive every person,
May no one be punished because of me.[1]

Maintaining Holiness

During this week of Acharey Mot pay special attention to how and what you eat and how you use your sexual energy.

Let each act of eating or sex be an expression of your holiness.

[1] Translation by Rabbi Zalman Schachter-Shalomi in *Yedabber Pi: A Weekday Siddur–As I Can I Say It* (2006), p.35.

Kedoshim
(Holy)

LEVITICUS 19:1 - 20:27

Kedoshim consists of instructions for holiness, including moral injunctions, ritual laws, and our attitude and behavior towards every aspect of Creation.

THE BLESSING

OUR JOURNEYS HAVE TAKEN US TO THE CENTER OF TORAH, where we enter into the mystery of the holy. Leviticus is the middle book and *Kedoshim* is the middle portion. Here we are blessed with a vision of holiness, a vision of what holiness might look like here in our world, in our everyday lives and at the center of our awareness. *Kedoshim* blesses us with an intimate knowledge of the source of that holiness. The reason we must be holy is that God is holy. After every injunction this reasoning is alluded to through the words, *"Ani YHVH,"* ("I AM THE UNPRONOUNCEABLE GROUND OF BEING/BREATH OF LIFE").

My training in logic calls forth the missing piece. God tells us, "I am holy (and since we are One… yes, your essence is God) then so you too shall be holy." This missing piece of the syllogism – the realization of our identity in God – dawns on us slowly and calls us into the holiness that is our birthright.

LOOKING THROUGH GOD'S EYES, I can see a world that is whole, undivided by class, race, gender, yet exquisitely beautiful in its diversity; each part of the whole uniquely precious. This vision guides me towards justice and opens my arms in embrace of the stranger. My holiness rests on the "I AM" that God speaks from within me.

That "I AM" reverberates through me and also speaks from the center of every moment in time and every molecule in space.

When I chant the *Sh'ma*[1] each day, I am reminded to listen within me for that "I AM" – which is the source of holiness. By listening and paying attention to the holiness at the core of each moment, to the holiness of existence itself, I am sanctifying myself for a life of being holy. This means being true to my own essential nature, which is loving and generous and interdependent.

---

[1] "Listen (Israel)..." this phrase begins the statement that affirms God's unity.

I am blessed with knowing how precious my life is, and through this intimate knowledge I am guided to cherish all life.

The Spiritual Challenge

All my experience combines the perceptions of object and ground. Whatever sensation or sound or shape or color or feeling presents itself in this moment seems to become distinct and separate from the ground of my experience. The ground becomes background and usually is so obscured by my attention to the presenting object, that it all but disappears.

In the pursuit of holiness we are challenged to retain a constant simple awareness of the Ground of our Being (the holiness of God/existence) while at the same time responding in righteousness to the demands of each moment. With our spiritual practice we are building the awareness of that holy ground of pure being as a foundation for our experience.

Some might think that a constant awareness of God might make us "otherworldly" or removed. On the contrary. The amazing paradox is that splitting our awareness between object and ground actually lets us be more present and available to the truth of each moment, as we rise to the spiritual challenge of holiness.

When I have established that holy foundation for my life, then my inner life and outer actions can come into alignment with God's love for all of us. As I move into the world I can become a servant of that love.

And here is the challenge of *Kedoshim*: The divine holiness that is in us must be expressed in the shaping of our lives.

When i am connected to that divine core of holiness, then:

I have reverence for my parents,
where I come from,
I protect and cherish the sacred times of rest,
I leave the corners of the field,
a portion of my earnings for the poor and the stranger,
I do not steal or lie and swear falsely,
I pay my workers fairly and on time.

When i am connected to that divine core of holiness, then:

I do not curse the deaf or
put obstacles before the blind,

I am fair to rich and poor alike,
I don't gossip,
I cannot ignore the violence in my world,
I don't hold grudges or hatred in my heart.

When I am connected to that divine core of holiness, then:

I tell the truth even when it's hard,
I love my neighbor as I would myself,
I keep separate what needs to be
separate for its integrity,
when I eat I am mindful of resources,
I live in awe of the holiness of our world,
and the presence of the stranger
awakens compassion in me.

Kedoshim gives me these measures, so that I can examine my life and see just how connected I am to the divine core of holiness within me. The disconnection from that core will manifest in apathy, mistrust, despair, and destructiveness. The spiritual challenge of *Kedoshim* is to reconnect to the divine perspective within us, to see through God's eyes, hear with Her ears, and open the great heart of compassion that can guide our every thought, word and deed.

Guidance for Practice

Ocean of Being Meditation

Imagine that you are a fish swimming happily in a great sea. The light of the sun shines through to the deep kingdom teeming with life. Your world is beautiful, dangerous and endless, filled with color and adventure. You have a nice school of fish to swim with and everybody gets along pretty well. There's always enough to eat and there are always interesting things to do.

Then one day, you discover the ocean. One day you realize and actually perceive a great spirit that holds everything that you know. You realize that it has been embracing and carrying you all your life, that it is supremely intelligent and loving. You begin to feel its ebb and flow, first very subtly, and then the message of the ocean becomes clearer and more insistent. You realize that the push and pull of the tides are addressing you personally and you want to respond somehow.

You begin to have some doubts so you tell some of your friends at school. The other fish think you are crazy. "There is no ocean," they say. "Where do you see this ocean?"

After a while you have to leave the school and go off on your own, because this sense of the ocean is so mysterious and so beautiful. It is hard at first to do the usual fish things because the sense of the ocean's love is so compelling. But gradually you learn to swim in it and feel its greatness all around you.

After a while you return to your school. Because your heart is overflowing with gratefulness and praise for the ocean, you begin to see how precious this place of the deep is, and you learn how to love all of its creatures.

The practice for this week of Kedoshim is to spend some time each day in meditation imagining and opening to the divine ocean in which we all swim. Let all thoughts and feelings float away, leaving you to encounter the pure presence, which is no-thing, which is the source of all that is holy.

Emor

(Say)

LEVITICUS 21:1 - 24:23

This portion deals with the regulations for the Priests and goes on to legislate the cycles of Shabbat *and the Festivals.*

THE BLESSING

WE ARE COMMANDED to be a nation of priests, each one of us fulfilling the priestly function of mediating between human and divine. In *Emor* we are told that the priest must be unblemished. He must radiate perfection. The offerings that she brings must also be perfect.

As I seek to fulfill my priestly function I look at my life, I look at the physical universe that surrounds me, I look at Nature, I look into the human predicament of every person that I meet. And I cannot find something that is unblemished. The closer I look, the more imperfections I find. Everything and everyone is in process. We are all searching for balance in a world that is in flux. We are all flawed; our physical bodies are slowly or quickly decaying. This is the paradox of *Emor*: I and everything that I offer is likewise flawed, marked with the limitations of my particular perspective and prejudice.

And yet, the truth of perfection permeates the atmosphere of my life, like a tantalizing fragrance.

EMOR IS A PARADOX. To receive the blessing of paradox means that I must expand my embrace. I must create a wider context in which to live and encompass the contradictions that the paradox offers. To live with paradox means I must always be expanding my conceptions of reality. I live in process, continually opening to the wider view. The process itself touches me with its beauty.

THE SPIRITUAL CHALLENGE

THE PARADOX IS THAT WE ARE BOTH PERFECT AND IMPERFECT at the same time. If the priestly function is to mediate between the human and divine... of course it makes sense that we be made of both!

There are times when I look into this world or into the blemishes of my own character, and I am shown the perfection of the Whole. Not only do I see it, I experience that perfection as a "rightness" and I am overcome by its heart-shattering beauty. I celebrate the perfection and let it inspire and empower me. Experiencing that perfection gives me the strength to bear the imperfections. Within the perfection of this dance, we learn and suffer, die and are re-born. Those blemishes that might have disqualified me from the priesthood actually become the doorways into my power as a priest. It is only when I deny those blemishes or hide them from God that my offerings are rejected. When I enter through them, I can touch the perfection within all imperfection.

OUR SPIRITUAL CHALLENGE is to acknowledge with eyes wide open, our flaws and the harm we cause through them, the suffering, injustice and cruelty that pervade our world… AND at the same time to see the absolute perfection of it all.

GUIDANCE FOR PRACTICE

Emor gives us guidance for rising to this challenge. With the celebration of the Holy Days, the Torah gives me a path of continual becoming. During times set aside for holiness, I can dip into the timeless well of perfection and then dive back into the swirling river of change. The cycles of Shabbat *allow me to drink from Edenic streams and taste perfection, and then send me back to face the world of brokenness.*

SACRED RHYTHMS PRACTICE

THE FESTIVALS OF *PESACH, SHAVUOT* AND *SUKKOT* connect me with the cycles of planting and harvest so that I can learn to face death and find there new seeds for planting as the cycle renews itself.

THE HOLY TIMES OF *ROSH HASHANA* AND *YOM KIPPUR* provide me with a cycle of reflection, a time to uncover my blemishes and then turn to God to receive the inheritance of perfection in forgiveness.

THE RHYTHM OF THE SEASONS gets under my skin, flows through my blood. The holy days direct my attention to the swelling and shrinking of the moon. I watch a perfect circle of light disappear into darkness and return again.

I let go of perfection again and again. I live in process, continually opening to the wider view. The process itself touches me with its beauty.

The Torah gives me the practice of contemplating the cycles and flow that lead me to the experience of perfection. Those experiences empower me as a healer, a priest who knows and sees the hidden truth behind our broken world.

Behar

(In the Mountain)

LEVITICUS 25:1 - 26:2

Behar *extends the meaning of* Shabbat *by legislating the* Shemitah, *a resting year for the Land every seventh year. The land is to lie fallow, released from cultivation. After seven times seven years, a Jubilee Year is proclaimed in the fiftieth year. At the time of the Jubilee, slaves are freed and property reverts to its original owner. The laws of Jubilee are instituted to correct the drastic inequality of rich and poor.*

THE BLESSING

AFTER EVERY SEVEN YEARS, *Behar* tells us, the earth itself shall celebrate Shabbat. The land remembers its freedom. And the year after seven times seven years there shall be a proclamation of Freedom. Everyone goes home. Slaves go free. The rigid separations of class and wealth are softened and dissolved. The rich and the poor meet again and remember that they are equal.

The blessing of *Behar* is the lesson that the process of accumulating wealth and of owning property is all an elaborate game. God reminds us, "The land is Mine; it always has been and always will be. You are just passing through." The Sabbatical Year and the Jubilee are God's way of insuring that this game doesn't get out of hand, that we play fair, that no one suffers too much for our ambition, that we remember that it is supposed to be fun.

WHEN THE LAND RESTS, we get to hear its voice. We get to experience its wild restless beauty beneath the surface of our cultivation. When we stop looking at the earth asking what-can-it-do-for-me-how-can-I-use-it? and instead open ourselves to its essential nature, we can begin to know the land and hear its voice. When we hear its voice, we can respond and become responsible stewards. As we respond, the earth becomes responsive to us in return, pouring forth its mystery and abundance.

The blessing of *Behar* is the promise that when we keep these sacred rhythms, we are granted safety, security, a sense of being at home.

The Spiritual Challenge

The security that we are promised contains a spiritual challenge. The word in Hebrew is *la-betach*, which means "security," "safety," or "trust."

So often we try to build a sense of security by acquiring possessions. Our search for security often becomes an impossible drama of "never enough." As we acquire more wealth, nicer clothes, better computers, bigger homes, more knowledge – security continues to elude us. We are conditioned to become consumers as insecurity pushes us to acquire MORE.

Behar teaches us about a different kind of security that comes not from having, but from forging a deep relationship. During the seventh year when we let the land lie fallow and the earth experiences Shabbat, it celebrates its freedom. When the earth is no longer enslaved by our obsession for **MORE**, then we can truly come into relationship with her. We step into mutuality and trust is born.

Once we have heard the voice of the land we will never be the same, even when we begin to play the game of possessions again. Once there is that flash of self-awareness that this **is** a game and all that we see is really God-in-disguise, our playing will be transformed.

And perhaps once, maybe twice in a lifetime, at the time of the Jubilee, all masks, all roles will for a time, fall away. Then we will know that we are loved by God not for the role we play or the work we do, or the knowledge or things we have acquired, but for our true essence alone. Knowing this allows us to see and love each other in the same essential way.

The Jubilee strips us down and teaches us the pure joy of existence. *Behar* challenges us and asks, "Are you ready to sound the shofar and call forth the consciousness of Jubilee? Are you ready to let go of everything and return to your true home in God?"

Guidance for Practice

Conversations with the Land

Choose a small piece of land – it could be your yard, or a wild corner of a county park, or an overgrown city lot, or a piece of woods down the road.

Slowly walk around its perimeter tuning in to the "spirit of the place." Let that spirit begin to speak to you through the soles of your feet as you walk. Open up and fine-tune all of your senses.

Then sit at the center of the delineated space and send your roots down into the depths of the earth.

When you feel rooted and comfortable, begin to speak your words of commitment to the indwelling Presence of God that is in that place.

I always begin by vowing that I will clean up any garbage that I find there. I talk to the rocks, to the plants, to the creatures large and small that call this their home.

I talk to the ancient ones who have walked this land before me and to all future generations. I talk to the birds that fly over and the clouds that float by. I speak to the bedrock and to the underground rivers that flow unseen. To each of these I pledge my loving attention and care.

When you finish speaking, sit quietly, listen and watch for signs. Each breeze, each insect, each cloud, every sound and fragrance holds a message for you to receive and discern.

Take everything personally, knowing that when you do this practice of conversation with the land, it will speak to you in its own language.

Bechukotai

(By My Rules)

LEVITICUS 26:3 - 27:34

This final portion of the Book of Leviticus consists of warnings and admonitions concerning the consequences of our disobedience against God's Word.

THE BLESSING

ON THE SURFACE it seems that the book of Leviticus ends with a stern admonition. If you follow all these commandments that God has given you, then you will be rewarded; and if you do not, you will pay the price. If you are good, then life will go well for you; but if you are bad, you will bring suffering upon yourself.

When I look around at my world, and see good people suffering and people who have acted immorally enjoying the fruits of their crimes, I am sent to find the deeper meaning, the deeper blessing of *Bechukotai.*

When I open to the tone of the text, not just its content, a feeling of familiarity washes over me. I know these places. *Bechukotai* describes two different states of consciousness which may become the lens of perception that mediate our experiences of life's gifts and challenges. I believe we experience Heaven and Hell right here on this Earth.

THE FIRST STATE that *Bechukotai* describes is what might be called "Heaven." In this state we notice the miraculous change of the seasons and really taste the fruit of each moment. There is a sense of "enoughness" in whatever we have, and a feeling of ultimate safety, regardless of changing circumstance.

In our consciousness of Heaven, we are not ruled by fear. Thus we are not overwhelmed by whatever enemy or obstacle we encounter. In this state of consciousness there is a sense of spaciousness and possibility. The Torah awakens us to the possibility of constant grace.

As it says in Deuteronomy 11, "Then you and your children will live out on earth the Divine promise given to your ancestors to live heavenly days right here on this earth."[1]

Once we fully experience this state of Heaven, it can become a seed that we carry within to remind us that the liberation from the slavery of Hell is always possible.

[1] Reb Zalman's translation

Bechukotai goes on to warn us about the other state of consciousness we might call "Hell." When we're in the state of Hell, it seems that God and everyone else is against us. We are ruled by fear, and every challenge we face feels impossible. We are obsessed with a nagging feeling of lack and preoccupied with the sense that something is wrong.

Even when we eat, we are not satisfied. In this state of Hell, even the "sound of a driven leaf"[2] will frighten us and send us running. Here, we feel like strangers, and life itself seems like enemy territory.

In Hell, anxiety causes us to be always on the defensive, and our uncircumcised heart, the heart that is layered over with armor, prevents us from knowing true joy or receiving the Divine Indwelling Presence.

The blessing of *Bechukotai* comes as we begin to recognize these two states in our own experience. This recognition is the beginning of freedom from the tyranny of the Mind. We can learn that Heaven is our true nature, and when we feel lost in Hell we can remember that grace is offered to us and that it is only a matter of time until we find a path that leads us home.

The Spiritual Challenge

It is an incredibly radical realization when we discover that it is the inner state of consciousness, and not outer circumstance, that determines whether our lives are an expression of Heaven or Hell. Personally, this realization stands as the foremost challenge to my own ego, which has struggled for nearly half a century to manipulate my outer circumstances.

The fear-driven ego says, "If only I had these things, this job, that lover, a slimmer body, nicer clothes, a good teacher, friends who were more loyal to me, or more time… then, everything would be OK. The wisdom of my soul says, "I will find Heaven here regardless of circumstances."

I have seen such wisdom at work in the heart of a friend who although suffering through the agonies of cancer, finds himself at long last at the center of a great love. I have seen it in the heart of a woman who is so poor that she barely has enough to eat, yet joyfully shares what little she has. There are those who by all objective measures seem to be suffering in the worst that Hell has to offer, yet they bear witness to the

---

[2] Leviticus 26:36

nobility of the human spirit by radiating a flame of Joy and Love that even great rivers cannot extinguish.

If it is true that only the inner circumstances matter, why do we struggle to change the world, to alleviate outer suffering, to bring peace, to heal the afflicted? The spiritual challenge of *Bechukotai* is to do this work not from fear or anger but from the radiant purity of our compassion. When we are rooted in Heaven consciousness, the fullness of our compassion overflows. It becomes our natural way of being in the world. When we have recognized our own Hell-states, we know the suffering of others. We understand what it's like, so we can reach out and offer a vision of the truth of our inheritance. We can simply radiate that truth and our presence will help transform the world. Steeped in the consciousness of Heaven, it is impossible not to act from compassion.

I ONCE HAD A VERY POWERFUL DREAM in which I experienced the depths of Hell. In this dream, I was in both physical and emotional pain. I was depressed, exhausted and demoralized, and I decided to commit suicide. There was a woman who specialized in assisting people to kill themselves so I went to her for help. She held a pill in her hand and said, "I will give you this drug. It will definitely kill you, but first it will show you the meaning of Life." As I sat before her, I was at first incredulous. "What do you mean?" I shouted. "It'll show me the meaning of Life and then… I'll die?" My astonishment turned to fury and then I became curious. I sat there and tried to imagine what the drug might do, what it would be like to know the meaning of Life, and then die. Something inside me stirred and I decided not to kill myself. I chose instead to live.

GUIDANCE FOR PRACTICE

CULTIVATING THE WIDER PERSPECTIVE OF SOUL

The practice for this week of Bechukotai *is to perceive one state of consciousness from the vantage point of the other. This practice is one of the most powerful keys to mastery, and to breaking the tyranny of the mind. Over time this practice helps us to cultivate a powerful observer within. That observer can slowly teach us the wider perspective of soul.*

WHEN YOU ARE SUFFERING IN A STATE OF HELL, carefully note your feelings. Notice the kinds of thoughts that are manufactured by this state, take note of the memories that arise, notice feelings in the body, rhythms of your breathing, and what the world looks like.

From this difficult Hell-state, call forth the memory of the state of Heaven. Remember what it felt like to see beauty and meaning everywhere. Bring all your curiosity to register the contrast of the state you're in with the one you are remembering.

When you next find yourself in the state of Heaven, take careful note of your feelings, notice the memories that arise, notice feelings in the body, rhythms of your breathing, and what the world looks like.

From this Heaven-state, remember the state of Hell. Remember what it felt like to see the world as meaningless and cruel.

Bring all your curiosity to register the contrast of the state you're in with the one you are remembering.

Awaken your compassion in this place of Heaven to all those who are suffering, and to yourself when you are there in Hell.

Shefa Gold

Numbers
Bamidbar

Journey

Bamidbar

(In the Wilderness)

NUMBERS 1:2 - 4:20

A census is taken and the camp is organized according to Tribes.

THE BLESSING

OUR JOURNEY TAKES US into the Book of Numbers. The Torah, as a guide for our journey, illuminates the process of incarnation in Genesis, and the process of liberation in Exodus. Leviticus concerns itself with maintaining a state of holy connection to God and each other. The Book of Numbers recounts the soul's journey through the wilderness. That spiritual path sets in motion the process of self-awareness, purification, and re-birth.

The Hebrew name for The Book of Numbers is *Bamidbar*, which means "in the wilderness." The wilderness is the place of our journey. We wander for forty years. During this time the generation of slavery dies and a new generation emerges.

The harsh inner reality of the wilderness purifies whatever traces of enslavement we still carry. This wilderness is the midwife of our new life, after long and hard labor. The wilderness forces us to face the resistance, ambivalence and self-delusion that has kept us from whole-heartedly receiving our birthright: the promised flow of milk and honey that is given to us, and through us, with each moment of life. The wilderness will scare out all our old ghosts and send them forth from the shadows into the full light of awareness.

In the wilderness we are stripped of disguises. Defenses fall away. Each part within us is forced to show its true face.

BAMIDBAR BEGINS with the taking of the census. On the spiritual journey it is necessary to look within in order to know, recognize and fully understand the myriad aspects that make up the self, "the parliament of personality."[1]

The census is taken of all those who are able to go forth in battle. The Israelites are counted in order to be deployed. The Levites, those whose job it is to take care of the *Mishkan* and all the holy things in it, are exempted from this counting.

---

[1] This is a phrase I learned from my teacher Paul Ray.

As we take the inner census of the personality, as we list the aspects which comprise the force of our egos, we do so to place their power in service to the soul, to our true essence, to the spark of God within us. Our Levite is the part of us who must guard that essence.

After each tribe is counted and named, it is given a role and a place on the periphery of the camp, surrounding the *Mishkan* and its Levites in the center.

Most indigenous peoples share a keen sensitivity to the compass points. Each direction carries a particular wind or force that can become our ally as we journey. We learn where to stand, where to face and how to open ourselves to those energies.

I look to the East, with Issachar, Judah and Zebulon, to face the rising sun, opening to new beginnings, new possibilities.

I turn to the South, with Gad, Reuben and Simeon, to receive warmth, comfort and constancy.

I look West, with Manasseh, Ephraim and Benjamin, to find a vision of where my path must lead me.

I face the North, with Asher, Dan and Naphtali, and open myself to the wisdom of my ancestors, receiving their guidance and challenges.

I look to the Heavens and open to the wide expanse.

And I look to the Earth beneath me for grounding and support.

The blessing of *Bamidbar* places my soul at the center of the *Mishkan*, guarded and surrounded by the part of me that is mindful of holiness. And that circle is surrounded by the circle of my personality, which places itself in service to the soul. Each aspect stands in its place, knowing that it is the God-spark at the center that is in charge.

The Spiritual Challenge

Every one of the voices that clamor inside me thinks that it is the sole truth. The process of discernment requires great patience, self-compassion and often a good sense of humor.

As we begin to sort out our inner voices, we realize we contain different characters – some of whom would like to take charge of our lives but shouldn't.

An example: My husband and I were in the kitchen making lunch. He was fixing a cheese sandwich for himself. Earlier that day I had told him that I was trying to reduce my dairy intake because of allergies. Suddenly I turned to him and blurted out, "I want cheese!" My husband smiled and asked, "Who was that?"

The voice that had popped out of me was so young and petulant that it made us both laugh. When I examined where the voice came from, I saw that she was about five years old. She was pouting with frustration. Once I identified the voice, I felt compassion for the little girl, even as I let her know firmly and gently that she would not be deciding what was for lunch.

By listening carefully to the voices within, and identifying their source, we avoid becoming victims of that "parliament of personalities" within us which would pull us this way and that. Often their demands are the result of unhealed wounds from the past. Sometimes, the decisions made by the wrong aspect of our personality are more serious than what to eat for lunch. Great harm can be done to ourselves and others. An even more serious consequence is that we may never allow the holy and wise one within us a chance to be heard.

Guidance for Practice

There are two practices for this week of Bamidbar. *The first is a meditation to help you observe your thoughts.*

Noticing Thoughts

Find a comfortable place to sit, close your eyes, and allow your mind to settle down.

Pay attention to the tone and feeling of each thought rather than to its content.

Set a timer and sit for ten minutes. Notice each thought, label it and gently let it go, waiting for the next thought to emerge.

For example, as I sit quietly a thought pops into my head about someone I need to call today. I notice that the tone of this thought is anxious. I recognize the worrier who feels like she's juggling too many things.

The thought of breakfast triggers a whole series of thoughts about what I might cook for dinner tonight. I recognize the planner, who always likes to be one step ahead of the game. The practice of meditation helps us get to know the voices inside our heads. With recognition comes compassion, and with compassion comes freedom. I can choose which thoughts to act on, which thoughts to release.

Identifying Inner Voices—a week long practice

The second practice for this week of Bamidbar *is to identify and name at least three of the voices that sit in the parliament of your personality.*

Focus on this practice throughout the week. Pay attention for the moments when you hear one of those voices rise up within you.

When you hear a voice, stop and identify it. Give it a name. Ask her how old she is. Find out what she is really afraid of, then comfort her and send her to her proper place at the edge of the camp.

Then you can turn within and call forth the Levite, the one who guards the Holy of Holies inside you. Ask her to take charge, to bring her wisdom to your life.

Turn fully towards that holy center and listen.

Naso
(Lift/Add)

NUMBERS 4:21 - 7:89

This portion gives us the ancient Priestly Blessing. It also describes the ordeal of the woman who is accused of unfaithfulness by her jealous husband.

THE BLESSING

AT THIS TIME OF *NASO* we give and receive the great and ancient Priestly Blessing. Our arms are outstretched above the tumult of our lives and our hands imitate cloven hooves, invoking the power of the animals of our shepherding ancestors who bless this world through us.

God commands the priests (and the priest or priestess within each of us) to bless each other with these words:

"May God bless you and guard you.
May God shine his faces upon you and grace you.
May God lift up his face to you and give you peace."[1]

May you be filled with the Divine Flow
and may its essence transform you
so that you are protected from your habits of distortion.

May the fierce and loving light of God shine
through all illusions of self, dissolving the walls
that seem to keep out the miracle of grace.

May the face of God that is hidden in everything
remove its mask and reveal the truth
of our inter-connectedness.
And may the love that shines through
the face-of-all-things give you peace.

The Divine command concludes: "So shall they put my name upon the Israelites and I will bless them."[2]

---

[1] Numbers 6:24-26
[2] Numbers 6:27

Through this blessing, God's name – the Divine Essence – rests upon us.

The privilege of carrying the Name/Essence of God into the world is the greatest blessing we can bear. It is giving and receiving at once. It is the pure state of becoming and being a blessing. When I carry that essence consciously, every moment begins to sparkle with meaning— even moments of suffering, moments of terror, even the moment of my death....

Each moment is received by a heart that is as vast as the sea and alive with compassion. Carrying that Divine Essence is like being a drop that knows the ocean within it. The Divine Name/Essence makes us infinitely large, certainly big enough to absorb and endure the events of our lives.

The Spiritual Challenge

Naso describes a spiritual challenge that all of us must at some point endure. This challenge is symbolized by a woman who is accused of adultery by her jealous husband. She undergoes a test to determine if she has indeed been unfaithful.

That woman is each of us, married to the Divine Essential Mystery. Our relationship to that mystery is dynamic and complex: dynamic, because we are always moving in and out of connection – remembering, forgetting and remembering again; complex, because the ego is oftentimes engaged in a subtle (or not-so-subtle) practice of deception.

In the ordeal that *Naso* describes, we ask the truth to make itself known, even if it will make us uncomfortable. We ask to cut through the web of self-deception in order to discover if we have truly "gone astray."

When I was a child I had frequent stomach-aches. I was outwardly very shy, but had an active inner life. As a teenager, I began to notice a pattern to my stomach-aches. Whenever I had something to say and didn't say it, the unsaid words would immediately go to my stomach. My body would not let me withhold my truth without paying the price. My body became a strict teacher, and I listened to its signals in order to find my voice. I was the woman who had gone astray, set back on my path through the power of a fierce love.

When the woman who is tested in *Naso* proves her innocence, her loyalty to Truth, she is made fruitful; failing the test, she is left barren.

So too, our creative lives depend on the unwavering commitment to our essential wholeness and integrity, and we betray that integrity at our peril.

The spiritual challenge of *Naso* is to receive the ordeals of our own lives as agents of Truth. Through them we are tested, humbled and refined. Our defenses are stripped away. We are distilled to our essence. In response to this challenge, I vow to use everything in my life, in service to the Truth – to let life's bitter waters dissolve the web of self-deception that I weave. If I have been led astray by my fears or delusions, I ask that the flow of my life lead me back to the Truth.

This is no small request. Making such a request of life requires that we pay close attention and be prepared to receive the response in the language in which life speaks to us: that of everyday circumstances.

I have learned that this perspective on life must be limited to the personal. I do not have permission to see someone else's life this way or to interpret their hardship as a gift. Compassion is the correct response to the suffering of others. The perception of my own ordeal, however, may be transformed into a force of healing and truth.

Guidance for Practice

Blessing our own Ordeal

Sit quietly for a few minutes and quiet the mind by focusing on the breath.

Close your eyes and see the pathway of your own life's journey, spiraling up a great mountain. Stand at the summit and look down on the landscape of your life. Find the path that you have traveled. Trace it from birth through childhood, adolescence into adulthood, imagining what the landscape looks and feels like viewed from a long perspective.

Let your attention be drawn to a particular point on the path, a place of ordeal.

Call up an image of yourself at that point of ordeal and pour out your compassion on the one who you were.

Slowly and clearly speak to her the words of the Priestly Blessing:

May God bless you and guard you.
May God shine his faces upon you and grace you.
May God lift up his face to you and give you peace.

Return now to the summit and say a prayer of gratefulness for your path. The most powerful and transformative prayer you can say is simply, "Thank you." At first the words might ring hollow, but as you keep saying, "Thank you," the sound in your voice will begin to change and the words will be filled up with the hidden meaning which emerges from that point of ordeal on your journey.

Stay at that summit of gratefulness for a few minutes, noticing the feelings in your body.

Return your attention to the breath.

Beha'alotekha

(When You Raise Up)

NUMBERS 8:1 - 12:16

Beha'alotekha *describes the Israelites' departure from Sinai, beginning with directions for lighting of the Menorah. God also commands the making of two silver trumpets which are to be sounded at the time of setting forth on the journey.*

THE BLESSING

BEHA'ALOTEKHA DESCRIBES THE INNER GESTURE of "setting forth" as we continue to move through the wilderness. Our journeys are in some sense always just beginning. Wherever we stand in our lives can be perceived as the place of infinite potential, the intersection of Being and Becoming, the threshold of the beyond. From this vast potential of "here and now" we are either sent to who we are becoming or we get stuck in the traps of illusion or fear.

The blessings of Light and Sound are given to us to help us break through these obstacles and move forward on our path.

The blessing of Light and the blessing of Sound can inspire us forward. They are the tools we use to release ourselves from the slavery we carry within.

The name *Beha'alotekha* refers to the "lighting" of the *menorah*, the golden candelabra in the *Mishkan*. This is the fire that lights our way forward. The gold of the sun is awakened in us through the service of the *menorah*.

The silver trumpet is a priestly instrument. The silver of the moon is awakened in us through the service of the trumpet. Its tones serve two purposes: first to call us to our center, and then to send us on our journey.

We journey by stages. When we are ready to move to the next stage of our journey we must open ourselves to the call of the silver trumpets. Their sounding will help to gather us – giving us access to both inner and outer resources. And their sounding will reveal the obstacles before us – clearing the way forward and sending us newly inspired to our destiny.

The Spiritual Challenge

We embark upon this journey of purification without knowing how far or how long it will be. Obstacles arise in the form of resistance. Resistance arises in the form of cravings, doubts, weariness, restlessness, or aversion.

I used to think, "If only I didn't have such resistance I could really do my spiritual work." Then I realized that recognizing and confronting resistance IS my spiritual work. The very obstacles that arise to block my way home serve to show me the face of my own enslavement. Looking into that face I will know where my work lies. The face of resistance always wears a mask. It masquerades as THE TRUTH. My work is in unmasking resistance and freeing myself from its compelling power so that as I stand at the crossroads of this moment, I can choose my path in conscious, loving clarity.

Having left Sinai to renew their journey, we hear the story of the Israelites' murmuring and rebellion in the wilderness. Their behavior is a merciless mirror which reflects our own tendencies towards resistance on the spiritual path.

The spiritual challenge of *Beha'alotekha* is to hear the murmurings and rebellions of our ancestors and recognize them as our own places of enslavement calling for freedom and healing.

When I witness my ancestors' complaints, I must listen to my own bitter whining. Listening deeply with compassion, I hear the fear inside my voice and I remember when that fear was born. Then I know that my spiritual work will be to heal the wounds that gave birth to that fear and to work at cultivating trust.

When I witness my ancestors' lust for meat and for the food of Egypt, I turn to investigate my own cravings. When I discover a hunger that seems never to be satisfied; a thirst that is never quenched; a hole inside me that can never be filled; then my spiritual work consists of investigating that craving by entering into that "hole" and experiencing the emptiness within. This will lead me to Truth.

When I witness my ancestors' weariness with their journey, I turn to examine my own lack of energy for practice. When I hear their expressions of doubt in the leadership of Moses, my work becomes that of unmasking the face of my own doubt and coming to understand how and why I sometimes silence the voice of the prophet within me.

Guidance for Practice

Resistance Meditation

When taking on a spiritual practice it is important to recognize and identify the voices of resistance. Some people sit down to meditate and soon begin to fall asleep. All the energy seems to drain out of them the moment they become relaxed enough to meditate. Others feel so restless that they want to jump out of their skin and they find it difficult to sit still. For some people, resistance wears the mask of longing or craving or ambition. Their mind reaches out for what's next. Others find themselves caught in aversion. Nothing seems quite right. The mind finds something wrong with the teacher, the practice, the pillow, the temperature or the place. And for some people, the voice of doubt sabotages their practice, never letting them completely surrender.

The more you can recognize the voice of your resistance, the less you will find yourself at its mercy. Once identified, it loses the power to call itself THE TRUTH. *And you can then begin to call on the blessing of Light and the blessing of Sound in clearing the way, gathering your attention and setting forth on the path that is before you.*

Identify a voice or force of resistance. It may be disguised as sleepiness, restlessness, craving, aversion or doubt. You might recognize yourself in the complaining and rebelliousness of our ancestors. Unmask those voices with great compassion.

Close your eyes and light the golden *menorah* inside you. Imagine its light shining forward dissolving all obstacles, melting all resistance and renewing your resolve.

Find the two silver trumpets and let the priest or priestess within you blow them with enough force and beauty to energize, calm, and inspire your way forward.

(Thank you to Sylvia Boorstein for her teachings on the hindrances.)

Shelach Lekha
(Send for Yourself)

NUMBERS 13:1 - 15:41

This Torah portion tells the story of the spies that are sent forth to survey the Land of Canaan in preparation for its conquest. They return with a mixed message. The Land is superb but too well-fortified to be conquered. Moses is bitterly disappointed with their fearful report and so decides that the people must wander another 40 years (until the generation of slavery has died out) before they can enter the Land.

Shelach Lekha *concludes with the instruction to wear fringes of blue as reminders of holiness.*

THE BLESSING

GOD SAYS TO MOSES: "*Shelach Lekha*" (send for yourself) spies to scout out the Land. The spies sent by Moses return both enraptured by the land and terrified at the prospect of making their permanent home in that elevated state of consciousness.

So too, this portion blesses us with a mission: Spy out the Land of our Inheritance, taste the milk and honey that flows from the Land of Promise, and let that taste guide us on your journey. The blessing we receive is a glimpse. What we do with that glimpse becomes the challenge.

Over a lifetime we are given glimpses, flashes, and hints that open our awareness to the Reality of paradise and unity that underlies this world of constant flux. We are graced with a timeless moment in which the infinite is revealed as the source of our finite world. We are sent to that land of expanded consciousness through imagination, practice and grace. We return from this taste of enlightenment either empowered to receive and integrate the supreme blessing into our lives, or completely terrorized by the incomprehensible immensity of what we feel is beyond our grasp.

"The land eats up its inhabitants," report the spies. And they are correct. The small ego-driven separate self cannot survive in the pure air of that land. The "I" will be dissolved, called beyond itself, merging with the beauty and the mystery of that place.

The spies return from their mission divided.

AFTER A PEAK EXPERIENCE, we return to our life shaken. Whatever negativity is in us, born of grief or conditioning, is still there. Yet some part of us remembers that immensity, that taste of the infinite... or tries to remember.

That is our work: to remember what we have glimpsed and to plant the glimpse like a seed in the soil of our lives.

Shelach Lekha blesses us with both the mitzvah of remembering and a technology for fulfilling that mitzvah. We are instructed to put "*tzitzit*" (fringes) on the corners of our garments and to place at each corner a thread of the purest blue. Looking upon that color we will be reminded of the Sea, and the Sea will remind us of the Heavens, and the Heavens will remind us of the Throne of Glory that we glimpsed in a moment of clarity.[1]

The Spiritual Challenge

The blessing we receive is a glimpse. What we do with that glimpse becomes the challenge.

When I was in my twenties, I read *Be Here Now* by Ram Dass and I thought, "How simple! And how wonderful! That is how I will live my life."

And then I had a dream. The dream gave me a glimpse into the state of consciousness that I was asking for – one of complete openness and presence. The dream showed me just a few minutes of that state. I saw the brilliance of every color, the symphony in every sound; each breath was breathed as a miracle; each moment held a lifetime of experience. I woke up totally overwhelmed... and sobered.

I knew for sure that I was not ready to enter the Land. I understood how naïve I had been to think I could attain that state without preparation. And I began to get a sense of the work that would have to be done in the wilderness during the next 40 years. I would need to build the strength of the container that might receive my inheritance: the fullness, the richness, the beauty, the mystery of each moment.

We glimpse the Promised Land, the place that is flowing with milk and honey, and then must return to the wilderness of our lives. This circuitous journey sets up a tension within us. We know the taste of perfection and yet the urge to reach for it calls us to battle again and again. We know that beneath the mask of suffering, there is grace. We have seen the light that is imprisoned within the shell of the world, the shell whose stubborn opacity shields us from the power of the truth within. The memory of our glimpse fuels our journey and keeps us from suc-

[1] Talmud *Menachot* 43b

cumbing to the illusion and tyranny of this-is-all-there-is physical reality. That memory guides us through the wilderness.

SHELACH LEKHA GIVES ME THIS SPIRITUAL CHALLENGE: to remember what I have glimpsed and to plant the glimpse, like a seed, in the soil of my life. And *Shelach Lekha* warns me that if I deny that glimpse – if I doubt its validity – then I will be denied entrance to the Land of Promise – the state of consciousness that witnesses Divine Presence filling the whole world. To plant the seed of that glimpse requires that I acknowledge and celebrate it, and that I nurture its growth with my loving attention.

Guidance for Practice

Planting the Memory of the Glimpse

OUR PRACTICE FOR THIS WEEK of *Shelach Lekha* is to remember and honor a moment of glimpse. It may have happened last week or 40 years ago. In that moment you experienced the perfection of the universe; you drank from the flow of milk and honey that is your inheritance. (If you cannot remember such a moment, then imagine one. Trust your imagination to lead you to the memory.)

TAKE A MENTAL PICTURE of the scene of that memory and put a frame around it.

NOW OPEN UP A HOLE at the right bottom corner of the picture and drain out all the color from it. Replace the plug.

OPEN UP A HOLE at the left top corner of your picture and pour in the purest blue light that you can imagine. Stay with that picture filled with blue light and feel the glory of that moment within you.

NOTICE THE FEELINGS in your body.

NOW WHEN YOU LOOK AT THE BLUE of the *tzitzit* or the blue of the sky or the sea, you can be reminded of the glimpse of promise that you were given.

LET THE FORCE OF THAT GLIMPSE guide you through the wilderness.

Korach
(The Rebel)

NUMBERS 16:1 - 18:32

This Torah portion tells the story of Korach who led a rebellion against Moses during the journey through the wilderness. Moses accepts the challenge. The earth opens up and swallows the rebels whose firepans are beaten into coverings for the altar. Each of the twelve tribes sets up a rod marked with their name before the Tent of Meeting. In the morning Aaron's rod has budded, blossomed, and produced ripe almonds.

The Blessing

What is the blessing that comes from full-out rebellion? Whining, complaining, foot-dragging, depression, and debilitating exhaustion are pushed aside as Doubt stands up and cries aloud, "Let's put my truth to the test!"

Korach airs all the doubt that has been festering within us. He stirs it up and lets it be heard. Hidden doubt eats us up from the inside, draining strength that we need for the journey. When our righteous indignation mixes with fear and greed and envy and ambition, and brings all those feelings out into the open, then all those deep-seated places of slavery can be transmuted by compassion and wise perspective. We can then embark on a path of healing.

Korach forces the hand of Truth. Without Korach, we grumble along, swallowing our bitter questions and doubt, and gradually lose our vision and power. Korach represents a stage of development that is crucial to finding our voice. Korach's fate is ambiguous; it is not clear whether this quintessential rebel is punished or dies. In our tradition, Korach, the apparent villain of the story, is nevertheless tendered the great honor of having his name associated with twelve of the most beautiful psalms. Clearly, the one who found his voice passed this facility on to his children who became great singers in the Temple.

Korach is the power in us that has not yet matured, which has not yet been tempered by humility. In one of those psalms, Korach's children describe the nature of power that has finally matured. "Kindness and Truth are met together," they sing. "Justice and Peace have kissed."[1]

---

[1] Psalm 85:11

As a young rebel, my truth sometimes lacked kindness. My passion for justice sometimes shattered peace. Yet what a blessing it was for the power of Korach to rise in me and teach me that my pointed challenges and questions were holy. Over a lifetime of mistakes and repentance, wisdom gradually emerges to call together kindness and truth and to kindle the love between justice and peace.

The firepans, used for offering by those who joined Korach and who died in the fire of rebellion, were later hammered into plating for the altar of sacrifice. Gathered from the charred remains of confrontation, the firepans had become holy. Searching through the rubble of my own rebellions, I find that a great deal of my arrogance has been burned up in the fires of experience, but there in the ruins I also find treasures: my passion for truth, my holy questions.

The Spiritual Challenge

Our challenge is to allow our Korach voice to emerge in its time and to listen carefully to its nascent power. Be aware of what danger you unleash, as well as the potential for refinement and maturity. Listen to the sound of your impatience, your ambition, your jealousy, your greed. Also hear its passionate life-force.

"Korach took..."[2] are the first words of this portion. Grammatically, the "taking" in this verse has no object. Taking, here, is a description of Korach consciousness – power that has not yet matured. Korach's untempered drive is the slavery from which he must free himself.

In his book *Ishmael*, Daniel Quinn divides the world into Takers and Leavers. Takers base their power on the fundamental misconception that they are separate from the world and that the world was created for them. Takers exert their power by consuming the world.

Our spiritual challenge then, is to call forth our raw power and engage in the process of its maturation. To do this we must shatter the myth of our separateness and begin to know ourselves in connection. And we must be able to discern the damage that our "taking" has done.

In the aftermath of Korach's rebellion, Aaron, as High Priest, takes his stand between the dead and the living, and thus ends the plague. The plague of our own time is the unchecked immature power that threatens to consume the world. To stand as High Priest between the dead and the living is to know clearly the destructive aspect of our power and to take a stand in fierce loving protection of the sacredness of all life.

---

[2] Numbers 16:1

The final test of power is whether it is life-giving. In the story of Korach, God devises a test to discern the face of mature power. Each of the twelve tribes places its own staff, a symbol of its power, into the holy center of the community. The next day it is revealed that Aaron's staff has sprouted, blossomed, and produced almonds.

This is how we know when our own power has matured. We look for the sprout, the blossom, and the fruit. What have we grown by our power? What beauty have we brought into the world? And how, with our power, have we nurtured ourselves and others?

Guidance for Practice

Refining the Rebel Within

This week of Korach sends me to memories of those times I was called rebellious. I remember my confusion; my only aim was to speak my truth and fight against what I perceived as hypocrisy. Now I see that I lacked patience, compassion and humility, but my intentions were good and the passion that moved me came from the sacred core of Divine Essence within me.

The practice for this week of Korach is to dig up the rebel buried within you and combine her essence with the specific qualities that you have worked long and hard to develop.

Remember your own passion which may have, over time, been dampened by life's disappointments.

Remember the rebel you once were and the energy that moved through you at that time. In the portion of *Korach,* the earth opens her mouth and swallows the rebels. They are planted in the ground like seeds, waiting for just the right conditions to grow into their fullness.

Imagine the rebel you once were as a seed planted deep in the ground. Now you can bring to that seed exactly the qualities that would help it grow.

You can water it with patience, shine on it the light of compassion, and fertilize the soil with all the shit you've been through.

Chukat

(Rule)

NUMBERS 19:1 - 22:1

Chukat *begins by describing one of the most mysterious rituals described in Torah - the rite of the Red Heifer. The ashes of the Red Heifer are mixed with certain specific ingredients and mixed with water to create special waters of purification. This mixture is used to purify anyone who has contact with Death.*

Chukat *recounts the deaths of both Aaron and Miriam. After Miriam dies, the people are thirsty and complain to Moses. God tells Moses to speak to the rock in order to draw forth water, but instead of speaking to the rock he hits it.*

THE BLESSING

DURING OUR TORAH JOURNEY THIS WEEK, both Miriam and Aaron will die. The Torah portion *Chukat* prepares us by beginning with a ritual that purifies us at those times when we come into contact with death. It is one of the most mysterious and powerful rituals of Torah. The great blessing of *Chukat* is the knowledge that whatever our defilement and whatever our mistakes, we can always return to our essential purity.

Whenever I seek to learn from mistakes I have made, I look for a pattern and then try to understand the source of that pattern. It is understood by our Tradition that the quintessential mistake of our ancestors as they wandered through the wilderness was the sin of the Golden Calf. This portion begins by discussing the great ritual for purification. The first and major ingredient required for this ritual is the Red Heifer. (The heifer is a mother cow that has never been yoked.) To know the source of sin, I must lay the Red Heifer on the fires of Truth. Because she is the mother of the Golden Calf, the source for the pattern of sin, her ashes are the first ingredient that I will need for purification.

ON THESE FIRES OF TRUTH I will also place just the right proportions of pride and humility, represented by tall Cedar and low-growing Hyssop. I will need both pride and humility in order to accomplish my journey of purification. Pride allows me to stand tall enough to see the path ahead, and humility connects me to the earth beneath my feet. The last element the Torah requires for this ritual is Crimson, my passion, which adds my own holy fire to these fires of purification. Thus, the recipe includes Insight, pride, humility and passion, mixed with living waters, the compassionate flow of Life, combining to provide the perfect alchemical formula for our renewal.

The Golden Calf is built when we lose faith in an invisible, unnameable God who may have abandoned us to die in the wilderness. We are tempted to build a life around this Golden Calf, thereby placing something other than God-the-essential-mystery at the center of our attention. That life built around the worship of security or happiness or wealth or fame obscures the root fear of Death that has unconsciously driven us.

When we are ready to identify our Golden Calf, then we must trace its roots to find the Red Heifer, the impetus for our own idolatry, the clue to our own pattern of sin. Then, we are able to offer up the ashes of the Red Heifer, the insight into the nature of our root fear. When death touches our lives, we can be protected from our own tendency towards fear, by the blessing of this insight. Having faced our fear, we need not live in its shadow.

The Spiritual Challenge

Chukat tells us of Miriam's death, and immediately afterward the text notes that the people are thirsty. Their thirst drains them of strength for the journey and fills them with despair. They complain to Moses and Aaron who ask God for help. God tells Miriam's grieving brothers to speak to the rock before the assembled community, promising that it will yield water for everyone. Moses speaks sharply to the thirsty masses and then hits the rock twice instead of speaking to it.

Miriam had a way with water. She could touch the depths with her song and call forth spiritual nourishment. No matter how difficult the journey, Miriam's dance would bring ease and beauty to the process itself. She carried with her the feminine wisdom that could not be written down. Upon her death we are given a spiritual challenge: to reclaim the source of her wisdom, to discover the song in our voice and the dance in our step.

Moses was given this challenge, and he failed in order that we might learn from his mistake. Moses blamed the thirsty people for their complaint and then took credit for the life-giving power that was God's alone. When he struck the rock twice, it did pour forth water, but it also exacted a great price. Until we learn to speak to the rock, we will be denied entrance to the Land of Promise.

To speak to the rock means to be in conversation with the natural world; hitting it is an attempt to subjugate nature. Miriam knew the words and she knew the music that would open the deep and secret places of earth-wisdom. The spiritual challenge of *Chukat* is to call Miriam's wisdom back to us, to re-open the conversation with the rock that was interrupted by Moses' mistake.

Guidance for Practice

The Ritual of the Red Heifer

Look into your experience and find a mistake made in the recent past. It might be a misspoken word that hurt a friend, or a bitter feeling that spilled out unconsciously in a look or gesture.

Examine the mistake and see if it fits any pattern in your life. Have you ever done or said or felt this before?

When you have discerned a pattern in your behavior, hold it in your heart with the utmost compassion for yourself and ask the question, "What am I really afraid of?"

Keep digging deeper beneath each layer of fear until you reach the root fear.

Name it and write its name down on a slip of paper.

Make a fire and burn that slip of paper in it.

Sing three songs into the fire.

For Cedar, sing a song that expresses
your pride and dignity and nobility.

For Hyssop, sing a song that expresses
your humility and remorse for your mistakes.

For Crimson sing a song that expresses
your passion and joy.

Take the ashes from the fire and mix them with fresh water from a stream or pond or sea.

Set this purifying compound, these waters of lustration, in a special place so that when your root fear is triggered you can look upon it and touch it and remember your essential purity.

Balak

NUMBERS 22:2 - 25:9

This Torah portion tells the story of a prophet named Bil'am hired by King Balak to curse the Israelites. This prophet-for-hire has an amazing adventure which includes listening to his talking donkey and encountering angels. In the end Bil'am blesses the Israelites with the words 'Mah Tovu.'

THE BLESSING

HERE IS THE STORY of our evolution as prophets. The blessing of Balak expands and deepens the place of prophecy in our lives.

In our story, Balak tries to hire the prophet Bil'am to take a journey to curse the people Israel. Bil'am follows Divine guidance and refuses at first, but then after a second delegation implores him, God advises the prophet to go, but reminds him that on this journey of prophecy, he must listen and respond to the word of God. When Bil'am sets out, God immediately becomes angry.

To receive the blessing of the portion of *Balak*, we must first solve this mystery. Why would God be angry with Bil'am for promptly fulfilling a Divine request?

The answer unfolds in the amazing story of his journey during which the true meaning of prophecy is revealed. Three times a Divine angel with sword in hand appears to Bil'am's donkey who obediently changes her course in response. Each time Bil'am, losing his temper, beats the poor donkey with a stick. Finally she speaks to him saying, "What have I done to you that you should treat me this way?" Only then are Bil'am's eyes opened. He sees the angel his donkey had seen all along, and he bows to the ground. Again Bil'am is told to continue on his journey, but is reminded again to pay careful attention to the word of God.

And now the mystery of God's "anger" is revealed. God is saying, "You must pay attention to my word as it appears in each step of your journey. My word comes to you through the wisdom of your body (the donkey that has carried you so loyally all these years), through the details of your embodied life, and through all your worldly senses. Here is how I address you now, and not only in dreams or visions." Through the story of Bil'am and his talking donkey, God expands for us the meaning of prophecy.

WHEN BIL'AM'S EYES ARE OPEN he can really pay attention – and profound words of blessing can flow through him. Three times the flow of blessing and prophecy pours forth, as if to atone for the sin of beating the donkey three times – ignoring the Divine wisdom of the body.

As the flow of prophesy begins, Bil'am falls to the ground, his eyes unveiled. As we touch the earth, honoring our earthiness, and stay true to the word of God as it is spoken through the donkey part of us, then we will be able to transmit visions of goodness and victory to the world.

The Spiritual Challenge

All of us are burdened in some measure with the belief that body and spirit exist as two separate realms. Because this belief is buried so deeply, we may not even know it is there. But it is a lie that exacts a steep price and bars us from touching the fullness of what it means to be human which is to be a "holy animal."

Often our journey of spirit removes us from the holiness of the body… or our journey of embodiment disconnects us from the vastness of our spiritual reality. Behind these tragic journeys is the lie that body and spirit are distinct and separate worlds. The lie is: if you yearn for one, then the other must be sacrificed.

Through the marriage of body and spirit, prophecy is born. The spiritual challenge of the Torah portion *Balak* is to listen to the word of God through the voice of the body, through the voice of an embodied divinity that surrounds us in each moment, that permeates our world at each step of our journey. Psalm 95 says, "*Hayom: Im b'kolo tishma-u*!" Today: If only you would hear His voice! God's voice is manifest in the Here and Now of the ordinary details of our lives… and we will hear it, *if* we pay attention.

We are challenged to receive God's voice in the sound of this world – in the voice of a friend, an animal, the wind, or the body that has been carrying us so loyally all these years. We are challenged to wake up to whatever has been occurring below our range of awareness, whatever we have dismissed as unworthy or undeserving of our attention. It is there that the word of God must be discerned.

Guidance for Practice

Our practices for this week of Balak are designed to expand our awareness of the body, to learn to hear its voice, and to receive its wisdom.

Expanded Awareness Practice

The first practice is dedicated to cultivating an attention for detail. It was given to me by Shoshana Cooper. Since she is a teacher of Tea Ceremony, Shoshana instructed me to make my tea each morning with a special awareness. "Just pay attention to the hand that is NOT making tea." By bringing our attention to the "other" hand we begin to expand our awareness to include a wider field. It changes the way we move and opens us up to what we would normally miss.

Choose one simple action that you do every day (like making tea).

Pay attention to your non-dominant hand. Just watch what it does.

Notice how this awareness changes the quality of the action.

Articulate with a spirit-buddy[1] just how that change manifests in your experience.

Body Wisdom Awareness Practice

Become aware whenever you experience a strong emotional trigger (sadness, anxiety, anger, fear).

Take a moment to ask the question, "Where do I feel this in my body?"

Instead of just reacting to that feeling, stop and investigate its source in the body.

Imagine breathing in to the place in the body where the emotion is found.

Let the emotion form into a shape, color, texture or image. Ask the body to reveal its truth and wisdom to you through the power of imagination and association while paying close attention to the physical sensations that are triggered by a thought or feeling.

We become prophets by paying attention, integrating the wisdom of body and spirit, and then dedicating our wholeness in service to the whole and holy.

---

[1] see Appendix p.232 for an explanation of this aspect of practice.

Pinchas

(The Zealot)

NUMBERS 25:10 - 30:1

Pinchas is a zealous priest who kills a Midianite woman and her Israelite lover at the entranceway to the Tent of Meeting. In this portion, Pinchas is rewarded for his actions and is given the covenant of Peace and eternal Priesthood for his descendants. Afterwards, a second census is taken of the Israelites. A group of women, the daughters of Zelephechad, demand from Moses the right to inherit land. Moses consults with God and God agrees with the women.

The portion concludes with a description of our daily and festival offerings.

THE BLESSING

AFTER PINCHAS kills the lovers in the act of defiling the Holy Sanctuary, God rewards him for his zeal. He is given the Divine Covenant of Peace and the gift of eternal priesthood. These are our blessings as well, when we acknowledge and integrate the archetype of the Zealot within us.

The zealot is the one who acts fearlessly, without hesitation, without stopping to ask permission. He translates the yearnings and guidance of the heart into bold decisive action. When the zealot inside us is not honored and given a place of respect within us, we fall into complacency, ambivalence or paralysis. We become the woman of the Song of Songs who hears her beloved knocking and hesitates, saying, "I have taken off my clothes, how can I dress again? I have bathed my feet, must I dirty them?"[1] When finally she answers the door, he is gone. Our hesitation results in the tragic loss of the opportunity to meet Life, face to face, right now!

THE TORAH TELLS US that with his deliberate and powerful actions, Pinchas ended a plague. As this is the text's first mention of this plague, we must conclude that it is a plague we didn't even know we had (or that we suffered unawares).

The plague that Pinchas ends is the tragedy of our perceived powerlessness. This plague takes the form of an inability to act deliberately and decisively in the name of the love and righteousness inside us. As this plague ends, the blessing of eternal priesthood is bestowed upon us and with it, the Covenant of Peace.

[1] Song of Songs 5:3

Our priesthood gives us the power to stand courageously between Life and Death and embody the yearnings of the heart for the good of all. In overcoming our powerlessness and paralysis we receive the blessing of wholeness, which is the Covenant of Peace.

When our inner guidance and yearnings are connected with our outer actions, we breathe a sigh of relief, ending the plague of powerlessness, hypocrisy, ambivalence, and complicity. Opening to the blessing of this covenant, we receive the benefits of "*Shalom*," which means both "peace" and "wholeness."

The Spiritual Challenge

Just as soon as the archetype of the Zealot emerges in our story, God commands that we take a census. Our spiritual challenge is to locate and integrate this powerful archetypal energy in the context of the whole. For when it is split off from the whole, the zealot becomes a dangerous and destabilizing force in the personality or in the community.

As focused, directed power emerges and is acknowledged, we must respond immediately by taking stock, widening the perspective and integrating that force of zealotry into the whole. As the voice of truth breaks forth, we call forth a memory of the whole, so that truth can be married to kindness, and its force can be turned to healing rather than destruction.

When we surround that force with values of compassion, mercy, tolerance and understanding, then the power of zealotry confers vitality and clarity upon those that experience it.

The census that follows our acknowledgement of Pinchas, the power of zealotry within us, gives us the opportunity to refine that power in the context of the whole. The results of the census show us that we have changed since leaving Egypt. The journey has transformed us.

As the census proceeds we can also begin to notice the parts of us that have been unfairly ignored or pushed aside. We can begin to challenge the accepted ways in which power has been distributed. Certain parts of myself have swollen in importance, while other parts have become all but invisible.

This challenge comes forth in this portion of *Pinchas* in the form of the daughters of Zelephechad who demand to be noticed. The women challenge the laws of inheritance that favor sons over daughters and in doing so, they plant the seeds of challenge under the hardened soil of the status quo.

Our spiritual challenge is to give voice to the parts of us that have been denied and ignored. (Perhaps the power and *chutzpah* of Pinchas will inspire us as we step up to this challenge.)

To UNDERSTAND THE CHALLENGE of integrating this aspect of *Pinchas*, I would share a vision I had.

> **In this vision I met a great, beautiful and powerful tiger.**
>
> **I asked the tiger, "What is the secret of your power?"**
>
> **"I have three," the tiger said.**
>
> **First, I do not cherish anyone else's opinion of me. Second, I attune myself to the cycles and rhythms of Nature. And third, when I need to act, I do so without fear or anger."**

These secrets of power, given to me by the tiger, are also the secrets of *Pinchas*. In this instruction we find the ideal by which to measure our own integration of the Zealot archetype.

Guidance for Practice

This portion concludes with a detailed description of our daily and festival offerings. God describes these offerings as,"my food."[2] *These are offerings of awareness – surrendered to the fire of our lives in order to feed that God-place within us. That God-place within us hungers for this "food" of awareness that we offer each day. Awareness, made manifest in our spiritual practice, is received by God (and the God-sense within us) as a sweet savor.*

God, the Subtle-Reality-Underlying-Everything, revels in our attention and in our attunement with the seasons. We nurture the Divine Reality by paying loving attention to the turn of day and night, and to the renewal of the week with Shabbat. *We nurture and pleasure the Divine Reality by honoring the cycles of the moon and sun, and by celebrating the seasons of planting and harvest.*

Consecration Practice

[2] Numbers 28:2

During this week of *Pinchas*, take a moment before each prayer, each blessing, each conscious practice you perform, and consecrate your intention as the food of God. Make your practice into an offering that sustains, nurtures and brings pleasure to the spark of God within you and to the energy that connects and enlivens all of Creation.

I suggest writing some notes to yourself affirming this consecration to post around the house in the places where you do your practice – at your altar, on your kitchen table, or wherever blessings are said. It might read:

I dedicate the power of my spiritual practice
to nurturing the Divine spark in me and in the world.

Mattot
(Tribes)

NUMBERS 30:2 - 32:42

This portion describes the Israelite's war against the Midianites.

THE BLESSING

THE BLESSING OF *MATTOT* is well-hidden beneath a dark and terrible story of vengeance. "The last thing you will do before you die," God whispers to Moses, "is to manifest the battle that has been raging within you."

When Mohammed talked of Jihad, Holy War, he described the "Lesser Jihad," the battle that we wage *outside* of ourselves, and the "Greater Jihad," the battle that we must face *within*. All the holy wars that we fight, all our enmity and fierce devotion to the cause of destroying one another, can be traced back to the true battle raging within us. That inner battle rages on beneath our awareness, yet its power, projected out on the "other," fuels the injustices of the world. When those injustices become so dramatically evident and painfully obvious, it is possible to have a blessed moment of stunned awareness that sends us within, in search of the source of this madness. It is at this moment that the blood that is on our own hands shocks us awake. It is when the furious words that come out of our mouths are so clearly contradictory to our professed values, that we are forced to acknowledge our "Greater Jihad," the war that rages inside us.

MOSES RAISES AN ARMY and launches a war of revenge against the Midianites. After killing all the Midianite men, taking the women and infants prisoner, burning the Midianite cities and seizing the Midianite wealth, the army returns. They are greeted by Moses who is furious. "What! You let the women live?!" he demands. And then he commands the army to murder all the mature women and the male infants.

In this terrible moment, that contradicts all the laws of mercy and kindness, that overturns even the laws of warfare; in this moment of witnessing the awful cruelty unleashed by unrestrained power, even the most callous among us must begin to wonder, "What is the source of this hatred? What is fueling this obsession? How can it be stopped?"

We look to the life-story of Moses for answers. The name of this portion means "Tribes." Where do we find our identity? How is that identity sustained? How is it threatened?

MOSES GREW UP WITH TWO IDENTITIES: Egyptian prince, and child of Hebrew slaves. When he left Egypt, for all intents and purposes he himself became a Midianite. Moses married Tzippora, a Midianite woman. And his father-in-law Yitro became his teacher. The Midianite tribe became his family. Legend has it that he lived there as a shepherd for 40 years, learning and growing into his calling as prophet.

Whenever we try to reject a part of ourselves, that part becomes our shadow. The shadow is the part of us that is hidden from the light of consciousness. In that moment when blind fury unfolds into hatred against the other, we can be sent from the Lesser Jihad, from the battle in the world, to the Greater Jihad – the battle within. We are jarred into the realization that the external battle is only a dim reflection of the inner battle that has been raging all along. Once exposed, the shadow can be healed.

Only when we acknowledge the warring tribes within us, can we begin to make peace, first in ourselves and then in the world. A moment of tragic cruelty, illuminated by the light of humility and wisdom, becomes a hard-earned blessing. In that moment, our identity expands from tribal to universal. In that moment, our tribal identity becomes transparent. The structure of that identity still gives us meaning and comfort, but we can also see right through it and celebrate the many tribes that constitute the human family, all of us interconnected, bound to each other through our shared humanity.

The moment when Moses' cruelty is unmasked, and we see a man at war with himself, is a moment of blessing. The moment when Moses' violent turmoil is revealed, we see a man who has rejected a part of himself. This is a moment of blessing. In this moment the spiritual work of healing begins.

LET US REMEMBER that the Torah is not a story about someone *else* and it is not about some *other* time. It is a map of the inner landscape. It is a revelation, shining the light of awareness on all the myriad facets of human experience. AND IT IS HAPPENING IN THIS PRESENT MOMENT. If we are to truly receive the blessing of Torah, we must take the opportunity of our shock at Moses' cruelty to unmask and face our *own* capacity to dehumanize the other. The story of *Mattot* shows us that our own cruelty is the result of an inner struggle long buried by our defenses and denial. In that struggle, our tribal identity is rendered opaque. Our identity becomes a shield and a weapon; a shield against the truth of our human vulnerability, and a weapon against the "stranger."

We find the blessing of *Mattot* in the fact that although the Torah tells us of Moses' command to kill the women and children, it doesn't tell us whether this order was ever carried out. Each of us must search within and discern our own capacity for cruelty born of our personal confusions, conditioned misperceptions and brokenness. Yet ultimately, it is up to us whether those shadows will birth tragedy. It is up to us to decide whether or not their orders will be carried out.

When I listen for the negativity of my shadow side and encounter a voice of hatred or jealousy or an urge for revenge, I must avoid reacting with blame, shame or recrimination. My response must be compassion for myself. Only when my remorse is healthy can it become a blessing. For only then will I have the reserve of compassion to annul the command of cruelty.

The Spiritual Challenge

I once taught a weeklong retreat called "The Path of Devotion." People from many different tribes attended. Though every one had a different religious practice, and came from a different culture, by the end of the week we had fallen in love with each other. We were amazed to feel so close to people from different faith traditions. What connected us was a shared experience of devotion, surrender, gratefulness and service to the Great Mystery around which all our traditions revolve. Because we did not have a shared language, we entered into the place beyond language. Because we did not have a shared practice, we stepped into each others practices looking for beauty, looking for the familiar essence that transcends form. Because we had no shared history, we stepped into the sacred now. Many of the participants remarked that they actually felt a closer connection to others on the Path of Devotion than they did to those of their own tribe.

I left that retreat and went directly to a Jewish retreat center to teach a Jewish workshop. I felt at first as if my world had suddenly gotten much smaller. I felt a terrible sense of claustrophobia. It was depressing to feel so cramped and confined, compared to the expansiveness I had experienced the week before. I spent a couple days in crisis, feeling the spiritual challenge of *Mattot*, of "Tribe."

Then something wonderful happened. I had a vision of my tribe as a crystal palace. I could see its complex and beautiful structures, feel its strength surround me and glory in its form. In the next moment I shifted my gaze just ever so slightly and could suddenly see through the form to the dazzling expanse beyond it. I saw the sky filled with stars, each star shining its unique light. My own tribal structures became windows through which my consciousness could soar. And with another slight shift of my gaze I could focus again on the magnificent forms that held and supported me.

After this vision I returned to my Jewish teaching, to my tribal exploration, with a sense of gratefulness and renewed inspiration.

WITH SOME PRACTICE we can become aware of both perspectives at once, both the Tribal and the Universal.

I sometimes get letters from people who have had experiences in which they discovered their true nature as infinite beings connected to everything and everyone. After seeing this truth, they wonder, "How can I return to my tribe of origin? Why should I return? Haven't I grown beyond the pettiness of Religion and tribal consciousness?"

I share my own experience of this dilemma. As members of a tribe, we have to face the accumulated shadow of our people, built up over millennia. It's very messy work. Stepping outside the tribe we may feel suddenly free of the burden of history, guilt, expectation, neurosis. Yet I suspect that this "freedom" is shallow. Underneath our newly universal perspective, the tribal consciousness lays buried, unhealed, waiting for a crisis to trigger it. Then it will emerge unbidden, turning us inside out, revealing whatever it is inside us that we have been trying to avoid.

To accept oneself as a member of a tribe is to step onto the path of the particular. Traveling that path inward with eyes and heart wide open, you will eventually find yourself in the garden of universal consciousness. There, the truth of our oneness and connection is made unquestionably apparent. I don't have a lot of faith in short-cuts. It is the journey itself that heals us.

There is no other way to reach God's perfection except through the shattered flaws and brokenness of our individual Human experience. There is no way to our Divinity except through our Humanity. And our Humanity consists of layers of identity – an inheritance of both blessing and challenge.

AS I RISE TO THE CHALLENGE OF *MATTOT*, I must accept my place in a particular body, family, tribe, and nation, with the responsibility of healing their particular distortions and uncovering their distinct treasures.

We engage in this work for ourselves, for our ancestors, and for our descendants.

The other side of *Mattot*'s challenge is to remember the Oneness and interconnectivity that is our true nature. This remembrance of the Universal must inform each step we take on the path of the Particular. This remembrance ensures that the values of the Tribe will be continually refined, until the good of the Tribe becomes the good of All.

Guidance for Practice

There are two practices for this week of Mattot.

Layers of Identity Practice

Explore the many layers of identity that may lay buried beneath the ground of your personality.

This may be accomplished through journaling, or better yet, find a Spirit-Buddy,[1] preferably someone who knows you well and can reflect back to you some of your blind spots. One by one, investigate the layers of your identity.

Ask some questions, such as: "How has this identification affected my perception of others? What baggage does this identification carry with it? What beliefs about myself grow from this aspect of my identity?

Layers of identity include race, gender, religion, nationality, class, region or lifestyle. And there may be other more subtle identifications that affect our perceptions of self and other. I may see myself as an outsider, or an artist, or an intellectual, or a rebel, as a liberal, or an environmentalist, or a feminist... All these definitions delineate a particular "Tribe" with boundaries, qualifications and expectations that determine who is included and who is excluded.

The goal of this exploration is to become of aware of the many facets of your identity and understand the influence of the Tribe in shaping your attitudes, behavior, and self-image.

---

[1] see Appendix page 232 for an explanation of this aspect of practice.

The Bowing Out of Names Practice.

This is a very powerful practice of surrender that I learned from my teacher, Paul Ray. With this practice we can reach beneath the layers of identity that we have accumulated over a lifetime of tribal living. It is a temporary disrobing of the garments of our identity so that we may experience our bare-naked existence.

This is a bowing exercise. We will be reciting names for ourselves as we bow.

Begin by sitting in a chair or kneeling on the floor.

When you bow down, let the force of gravity move you and when you lift yourself up, be careful to roll up from the bottom of your spine to the top, so that you don't hurt your back.

With each downward bow, you exhale and say, out-loud, one of your names that represents a layer of your identity or a name that you've been called. There are so many names and roles and identities that we've internalized over the years, and this is an opportunity to surrender all of them, one by one.

As you come up, you can inhale and breathe in the pure content-less Presence of God that fills the empty space within you.

I might start by bowing out: Shefa… Jew… American… rabbi… writer… musician… wife… sister…. I would also include adjectives, some of them might even contradict each other: smart... not smart enough... open... compassionate... tumultuous... silly... too serious, etc.

When you run out of names, (and it may take a while), sit in the silence and emptiness of just being.

Massei
(Journeys)

NUMBERS 33:1-36:13

Massei outlines the forty-two stops along the way on our wilderness journey.

THE BLESSING

SOMETIMES I THINK OF MY LIFE as one long interesting journey. *Massei* reminds me that every journey takes place in stages and each stage carries its own distinct blessing to be unwrapped and savored, its own messages to be gleaned and digested. The word *Massei* really refers to the "setting forths" we do. As each stage of a journey comes to an end, we pull up our stakes and move on, initiating a new adventure. At each stage of the journey I become aware of my own transformation. I'm never the same adventurer who set forth the last time.

Forty-two stops or stages along the Israelites path are enumerated and named. Each stopping point on the journey holds a blessing for us. The Ba'al Shem Tov reminds us, "Whatever happened to the people as a whole will happen to each individual. All the forty-two journeys of the children of Israel will occur to each person between the time he is born and the time he dies."

We recount the itinerary of our wanderings in order to receive the lessons and blessings of each stage of our journey. As we become aware of the significance of each stage, we can receive its benefit. It is our awareness and appreciation that transform our story into a blessing.

THE SPIRITUAL CHALLENGE

IT IS IMPORTANT TO REMEMBER at each stage of our journey that we will encounter some obstacle or resistance. However annoying, difficult or devastating that obstacle is, its presence can call forth a particular power that lies hidden within us. The way in which the obstacle compels us to transform demonstrates the exact transformation our soul needs for its growth. In fact, the potentials that lie buried within us often require an appropriate challenge in order to be released and manifested.

It is more than a strange coincidence that the secret, unpronounceable name of God that can dissolve the obstacles in our lives has forty-two letters. Perhaps each letter represents one stage in our journey and the magic power of this name lies in its potential to embrace all the stages at once.

Rabbi Nechuniah ben Hakanah, who lived in the second half of the first century C.E., wrote a special prayer with forty-two words, the initials of which comprise the forty-two letter Divine name. The first line is: "*Ana B'choach Gedulat Y'mincha Tatir Tz'rurah*" (Please, with the strength of your right hand, untie our tangles). Rabbi Nechuniah wanted to be able to pronounce the unpronounceable, to call out and call forth the reality of the whole in order to deal with the stubborn tangles that keep us stuck.

We move through our obstacles by knowing them in the context of our life's journey. The spiritual challenge of *Massei* lies in seeing the big picture, even as we are stopped along the way by seemingly insurmountable resistances or difficulties. Those "impossible" challenges that we face represent the work of our soul's growth. Understanding that the obstacles are the point of the journey may help us to manage the pain or despair that we may experience as we encounter these inevitable difficulties along the way.

At the time of my divorce years ago, the pain of my broken heart seemed unbearable. My tears filled up every crevice of my being and overflowed until I could barely imagine ever feeling happy again. At some point, a small wise voice spoke inside me and said, "In a year you'll feel just fine, maybe even better than fine." I believed that voice, embraced its promise and had a moment's vision of myself a year from then, filled with joy. Then I saw the year ahead during which I knew I would be doing the hard work of grieving and healing from not only this divorce, but from every loss I had ever suffered. "Can't I just skip this year?" I whined.

We learn from *Massei* that every stage is essential to the journey. There are no short-cuts; no way to skip over the challenges. Even what seem like mistakes or dead-ends or wrong turns along the way can provide us with the necessary raw ingredients for wisdom. Those ingredients must be prepared with self-compassion and unwavering attention, cooked with patience and humility, and served up with a sense of humor.

Guidance for Practice

A Ritual for Honoring the Journey

I originally conceived this ritual to honor a friend's 50th birthday, that she might look back and receive the blessings and lessons of her journey thus far, and release whatever might be weighing her down from the past.

Preparation: Invite friends and loved ones and set a beautiful table. Prepare a special cup for each decade of life and fill each cup with your most favorite drink from that era. For example you might fill your 0-10 cup with chocolate milk, your 10-20 cup with root beer, your 20-30 cup with coffee, your 30-40 cup with fine brandy, etc.

Begin the ritual by welcoming everyone and chanting:

"*Kosi R'vaya*" [1]
My cup overflows

The cup of the first decade is then passed around the table. Each person reflects on that decade of their own life and shares what it is they learned from that stage of the journey. If the ritual is honoring a specific person's passage, he or she receives the cup last to drink in the blessings of wisdom that the others have gathered. The cup can then be passed around once more, and if someone would like to let go of a shame or blame or regret that they may yet be carrying from that time in their life, they can release it into the cup, either aloud or silently.

After each cup, everyone chants, *Kosi R'vaya.* As you pass from decade to decade, only those who have lived in that decade can take the cup and share ... so gradually the younger people become silent and may benefit from listening to the wisdom and experience of their elders.

At the end of the ritual each person can choose to sip from the cup that represents a time from their life that holds a lesson they need to remember and integrate right now.

[1] From Psalm 23

DEUTERONOMY

D'varim

PRACTICE

D'varim

(Words/Things)

DEUTERONOMY 1:1 - 3:22

This portion begins Moses' historical review of the long desert journey.

THE BLESSING

THE BEGINNING of the Book of Deuteronomy places us at the border of The Land of Promise after a lifetime of journeying. We pause now to look back at the path we have traveled thus far in order to understand its meaning, receive its lessons, and embrace the wisdom and love that we have received through grace and diligent practice. It is indeed a blessing to come to this place of such wide perspective and calm discernment.

The Torah tells us that by linear calculations our journey should have taken but eleven days. How did it take a lifetime – forty years – to arrive here? Our calculations must rely on a different kind of sense.

Our journey through the wilderness has not taken the form of a straight line, but rather a series of breath-taking spirals that drop us again and again at the same point in a cycle, each time at a new level, with an added dimension of awareness. The blessing of *D'varim* is the expanded awareness that comes from the attainment of a wide perspective – the ability to see our own lives from the vantage point of dispassionate clarity. From here we look back on our defeats and our victories, gleaning the blessings of both.

THE SPIRITUAL CHALLENGE

AS WE SURVEY THE PATH WE HAVE TAKEN and remember our times of humiliating defeat as well as those of jubilant victory, we can look within and see how we have been shaped by these experiences. We carry our defeats and victories in our bodies and psyches. If we do not take opportunities to examine how these experiences have affected us, our defeats and victories will continue to exert their power over us and determine how we respond to each present moment. We will be enslaved to the past. This enslavement will prevent us from entering the Land of Promise that is before us.

The spiritual challenge of *D'varim* is to attain an expansive perspective on our lives in order to investigate the imprint of each defeat and each victory. It is then possible to learn from those experiences and turn them into wisdom for the journey.

In rising to this challenge, we first remember our moments of disappointment, shame, loss or hopelessness that we have accumulated on our journey. How do we wear our defeats? Do they weigh us down? Embitter us? Armor us? Shame us? Immobilize us?

Or can we be pruned by them? Learn from them? Be humbled and lifted up? Find compassion for others and ourselves through them? Every defeat can be either a destructive force or a fertilizer for growth and heart-wisdom. The spiritual challenge is to mitigate the destructive force of our defeats through self-compassion and to turn that force instead towards ultimate goodness as we build the strength of our character.

In rising to the challenge of *D'varim*, we next turn to our moments of accomplishment, celebration, and fulfillment. How do we wear our victories? Do they make us arrogant? Do they separate us? Make us complacent? Dull? Judgmental? Forgetful of others' suffering? Or can we learn instead to overflow in gratefulness, channeling that overflow into acts of compassion and justice?

The spiritual challenge of success is to give credit to the God-Source of all blessing and to respond to our abundance through expressions of generosity. The danger posed by victory is that its force may be seized by the false self to build itself up. The result is an expense of vital energy diverted to the ego in further protection of its defenses. Victory can offer both the possibility of expansion into the sweetness of knowing we are worthy; or contraction, in our compulsion to rigidly defend the turf we have conquered.

Guidance for Practice

Body Teaching

Our practice for this week of D'varim *is first to use the body as a vehicle for entering your places of defeat and victory, and then to allow a physical expression to emerge that can lead to the liberation of self-knowledge. Our bodies never lie. They become our teachers when we learn to release past experiences that have been locked up inside flesh.*

WATCH YOURSELF THIS WEEK AND NOTICE A GESTURE that is expressive of defeat. It could be a droop of the shoulder curving protectively around the heart, the shuffling of your step, a dull expression on your face that you catch as you pass a mirror. Whatever you find, remember it for your practice.

ALSO WATCH YOURSELF THIS WEEK AND NOTICE A GESTURE OF VICTORY. You might find it in the tilt of your head or in a knowing smile, in the spring of your step or in the rigidity of your shoulder. Whatever you find, remember it for your practice.

WHEN YOU SIT DOWN TO PRACTICE, BEGIN BY BLESSING the path you have traveled and vowing to use the force of all your defeats and victories towards the attainment of complete freedom, unfettered by the past, so that you might enter the Land of your Inheritance.

LET YOUR BODY EXPRESS THE GESTURE OF DEFEAT and exaggerate it. Breathe into that exaggerated gesture and allow your mind to free-associate images, memories, beliefs or words that that gesture engenders.

SHARE OR WRITE OR DRAW OR DANCE what emerges.

REPEAT THE SAME PROCESS with your gesture of victory.

By listening to our bodies, we learn from our experiences of victory and defeat. We can release ourselves from the burdens of the past and move forward in freedom.

V'Etchanan
(And I implored)

DEUTERONOMY 3:23 - 7:11

V'Etchanan *tells the story of Moses' plea to enter the Promised Land. It goes on to recount the Ten Commandments, and also gives us the* Sh'ma, *our central prayer that affirms the Unity of God.*

THE BLESSING

THE DRAMA OF *V'ETCHANAN* recounts Moses' plea for grace. As our story unfolds, Moses implores God to allow him to enter the Promised Land. God's response is interpreted by Moses as an angry and terrible "NO!"... as a withholding of grace.

God says, "*Rav lakh!*" You have so much! Stop fixating on your idea of what you want! And then God instructs Moses to climb to the top of the mountain and get a clear view in all directions so that he might see and know that he has already arrived. The promise has already been fulfilled.

As we search for Grace in our own lives, we often come to that search with a preconceived notion of what our success must look like. We look towards the Promised Land – the right partner, perfect health, enough money, the right places to live and work. Our time and culture condition our goals; they drive us onward in our journeys, blinding us to the destination beneath our feet. As Grace pours into our lives from within or without, we will not recognize or receive its flow if we are fixated on a certain picture, on a particular outcome, a specific idea of success. Our expectations will blind us to the Promised Land that is before us and within us.

THE BLESSING of *V'Etchanan* is the opportunity to hear God's words again, "*Rav lakh*," You have *so* much! I am answering your request in this very moment, but you must open your eyes to receive it. You must lift your eyes beyond your own limited expectations. You must climb the mountain to take in the wide expanse. You don't need to cross the Jordan. You are already Home.

We take this journey in order to be strengthened, purified, transformed, refined. We journey so that our eyes may be opened.

V'Etchanan blesses us with a map for that path of awakening in the form of the Ten Commandments and the *Sh'ma*.

The Ten Commandments, written on the tablets, represent the Covenant. This covenant is the Truth of our connection to the ultimate reality hidden beneath the apparent surface of things. *V'Etchanan* blesses us with a path of attunement to the essential truth of our existence. Ignoring or contradicting the guidelines carved on the tablets of covenant, will serve to keep us from knowing and experiencing that connection to God and to the whole of Life. If the line of connection to our Source is broken, then awakening becomes impossible and our relationship to Reality becomes distorted.

But what kind of blessing is this? Haven't we already received the blessing of this gift earlier in our journey in the Book of Exodus? How can it be given again? Here is the secret of Deuteronomy; its earliest title being *Mishneh Torah*, the "repetition of the Torah."

What looks like repetition is actually the journey spiraling to a deeper level. When the Ten Commandments are given a second time, they are not accompanied by fire and thunder as they were at first. Instead they are given in the quiet of our practice, and they open us to an even deeper mystery, which is the *Sh'ma*. "Listen God-wrestler, YHVH is your God, YHVH is One." The words of the *Sh'ma* pierce through the veils of illusion. These words have the power to awaken us from our trance of separation that obscures the truth that there is Only God.

I first experienced the power of the *Sh'ma* in a Native American Sweat Lodge. This happened one moonlit night more than twenty years ago in a lush New York forest. The ceremony was being led by a very learned and devout man, Jewish by birth, who had been adopted into the Lakota tribe. He chanted in their holy language and followed their rules and traditions with respect and reverence.

Sweat Lodges are designed to facilitate our deepest prayer. Volcanic rocks are heated all day in a fire and then ceremoniously placed in to a hole at the center of the lodge. The door is closed and the circle sits in complete darkness except for the glow of the red-hot rocks. As sacred herbs touch the rocks, the lodge fills with smoke. As water is poured onto the rocks, the lodge fills with fragrant steam. As our artifice is burned away, the lodge fills up with prayer.

This particular lodge was hotter than any I had ever experienced before. The heat, smoke, and chanting seemed to strip away everything – ideas, memories, hopes, will, my very identity felt as if it was burning away. I felt like I was going to die. Suddenly we all cried out the *Sh'ma*. (In truth, I didn't even know these people were Jewish.) As the sound of this ancient prayer poured through us, ten spiritual seekers – all born Jewish – none of us connected to a Jewish path, were all startled awake. Completely cleansed of fear, we were all suddenly open to a Love that was at once given and received.

I still call on the memory of that *Sh'ma* in the Sweat Lodge to inspire me in my prayers. It inspired in us the power to transcend our fear of Death – a fear that is rooted in our identification with Duality – the mistaken conception that anything is separate from God.

When God tells Moses to climb the mountain and lift his eyes, we are being invited to receive a glimpse of Unity. From the summit of this mountain, everything that we thought separate, all of the opposites that have warred within us, are suddenly united. It is all *Echad* – "One." Then the fullness of Love can flow. Then, "You shall love God with all your heart and all your soul and all your might." When we experience the knowledge of the Unity beyond Duality, it takes root inside us, and we become lovers of the highest order.

The Spiritual Challenge

V'etchanan offers us the challenge of transforming the power of Desire from a potential prison into a vehicle for Enlightenment. Each of us must climb the mountain of our own desires and lift our eyes to see beyond what we have come to expect or imagine.

Sometimes our spiritual challenge comes to us in the form of a koan. In the tradition of Zen Buddhism, a koan is a question that can't be answered by linear thinking. Instead we must embrace the question itself, by taking it into our meditation and into our lives. The apparent contradictions that emerge on the path of our Torah Journey require that we open ourselves to living with and being with the Mystery until the answer breaks forth from a place beyond rational thought, a place of knowing and experience.

V'Etchanan teaches us that our very lives depend upon developing the practice of *D'vekut*, cleaving to God through the fullness of loving desire.[1] Twenty verses later, God defines Herself as "a consuming fire."[2]

The Talmud asks: "How do we cleave to a God who is a consuming fire?"[3]

---

[1] Deuteronomy 4:4

[2] Deuteronomy 4:24

[3] Talmud Bavli, *Ketubot* 111b

This koan leads us to the edge of a great abyss. Every step of our journey has been fueled by a profound longing for *D'vekut*, the experience of Oneness. Yet the self who desires must be annihilated in the process. "How *do* we cleave to a God who is a consuming fire?"

Guidance for Practice

Our Holiday of Fulfillment

Our Holiday cycle celebrates the steps along the way of the Journey from Egypt to the Promised Land. Passover commemorates the Exodus from Egypt; Shavuot *remembers the giving of the Torah at Mount Sinai; Sukkot celebrates our journey through the wilderness. So it was perplexing to me that there is no holiday that celebrates the longed-for arrival in the Promised Land. After all, that was the point of the journey, wasn't it? A celebration would seem to be in order. When do we celebrate the completion of our journey?*

I put this question to Rabbi Lawrence Kushner, and he suggested that Shabbat was our holiday of arrival in the Promised Land.

Shabbat is the time of experiencing the truth of "coming home." We expand our consciousness wide enough to embrace the paradox that our lives are a difficult and harrowing journey filled with struggle, tragic loss and suffering… AND YET, we have already arrived, and each moment offers us its absolute perfection. All week long we may long for Messiah – an era of Freedom – when we come to Shabbat we know that we are already redeemed.

After lighting the Shabbat candles this week of *V'Etchanan*, take some time to gaze into the flames.

Receive the Divine words, *"Rav lakh"* – You have SO much! Stop fixating on your idea of what you want.

Then send your stories, your tragedy, your questions, your unquenchable desire into the flame. Let the power of God-Who-Is-a-Consuming-Fire burn away regrets and pride for the past; let it burn away worries and hopes for the future.

Let God-who-is-a-consuming-fire reveal this present expanded moment of Shabbat. Let these Shabbat flames illuminate the expanse of the Promised Land within you.

Rest in the knowledge and pleasure of coming Home at last.

(I used to perceive Judaism as enormously depressing, always remembering the destruction of the Temple, mourning a terrible history of oppression, and yearning for an impossible future. Yet now I see that Shabbat, *the holiday of arrival and fulfillment, is our most nurturing, most accessible, most important holiday. And it happens every week!)*

Ekev

(Because)

DEUTERONOMY 7:12 - 11:25

Moses warns the people about the spiritual dangers that will face them when they enter the Land and cautions them to remember God who is the source of all blessing.

THE BLESSING

EKEV MEANS "because." Our covenantal obligation binds us to pay careful attention to the details of service to Life and Love. It is BECAUSE of that attention that we become present and receptive to the Great Flow of blessing. It is BECAUSE of our remembrance of God-Shining-Out-From-the-Center-of-All-Things, that we can truly experience this blessing. As we receive the blessing of *Ekev*, the blessing is expanded to include an understanding of just how and why this blessing comes to us.

Blessing is such a subjective thing. I once suffered a bad case of food poisoning. Even after recovering from the worst of it, I didn't have an appetite for a week. When my hunger and ability to enjoy food finally returned, it felt like such a miracle. I have not taken the blessing of my appetite for granted since. Without the affliction of food poisoning, would I have ever understood the blessing of appetite?

The Torah portion *Ekev* gives meaning to the difficulties of our journey. We are afflicted and tested so that God will know what is in our heart, which means that we will come to know the depths of our own hearts and there find the gift of being human. Our hearts hold the key to making all of our life into a blessing. The Blessing of *Ekev* can be found in its words that say "You shall eat and you shall bless, and you shall be satisfied."[1] From this text we derive the *mitzvah* of *Birkat Hamazon*, the blessing after the Meal.

YOU SHALL EAT: Open yourself wide to receive all the goodness and beauty of the world. Take in with pleasure the fullness of its nourishment.

YOU SHALL BLESS: When you eat, remember the Source of all Goodness. Taste God in every bite and acknowledge the gift you are receiving.

[1] Deuteronomy 8:10

AND YOU SHALL BE SATISFIED: Instead of immediately reaching out for more or for what's next, rest consciously in the fullness of this moment, this bite, this morsel of life.

THE ADDICTIONS AND HABITS that keep us unsatisfied also prevent us from the passionate fulfillment of our relationship to God. The prophet Jeremiah quotes the Divine Lover's lament, "They have forsaken Me, the fountain of living waters and hewed them out cisterns, broken cisterns, that can hold no water."[2] (God brought us out of slavery to be in loving relationship with the Divine spark in all things. That relationship is fulfilled through the blessing of satisfaction.)

True satisfaction grows into gratefulness and thus makes our eating holy. When we experience true satisfaction, we are filled with energy rather than complacency. True satisfaction prevents over-consumption, because it slows down the process and lets us savor each bite. Experiencing satisfaction, we are cured of addiction, and the chain of habit is broken.

THE SPIRITUAL CHALLENGE

IT IS POSSIBLE to eat everything in sight and to say 100 blessings a day in perfect Hebrew, and yet remain unsatisfied. The spiritual challenge of *Ekev* is to break the spell of consumerism whose power rests in our continual dissatisfaction.

As you enter the Land of your life: a land of fountains and depths, valleys and hills, shopping malls and glossy catalogues, a land of wheat and barley, television commercials and billboards and vines and fig-trees and pomegranates, a land of olive trees and honey, a place of comforts and the illusion of security... you are in mortal danger of forgetting where all of these gifts come from. It will seem that you made this life for yourself, that *you* are the Creator.

As I go in to conquer the land and make a life for myself, the force of my ambition begins to rise. Each success feeds that ambition; each failure pushes me into exerting more force. Here is the spiritual challenge of *Ekev.* How do I protect myself from the corrupting power of my own ambition? How do I discern between self-destructive greed and a true, healthy appetite for pleasure that allows the blessing of satisfaction to manifest?

---

[2] Jeremiah 2:13

Ekev teaches us that as you enter the Land of your life, you need not be afraid of anyone, for the great and awesome force of divinity resides within you. That is the key. I must recognize the force of my ambition to be, in reality, the God-force that moves through me. The moment I mistake that power as my own, I am in danger of corruption. If my attention leaps to the next possibility for satisfaction without resting in this present moment and savoring its richness, it is a sign that I have succumbed to the momentum of my own greed.

WHEN WE CROSS from the place of our spiritual practice into the Land of our everyday lives, *Ekev* tells us that we must circumcise the foreskin of our hearts, and be no more stiff-necked.

The layers of defense built up around my heart will actually prevent me from tasting and receiving the subtleties and richness of this world. With my senses I receive the color and fragrance, taste and texture of Creation. But then the foreskin of the uncircumcised heart will prevent me from benefiting from those riches. It will deflect the fullness of pleasure, beauty, and nourishment that my soul requires. Feeling deprived, I will always want MORE. The uncircumcised heart keeps me forever hungry, forever unsatisfied.

So what is the foreskin of my heart?
And how does this circumcision happen?

TONIGHT I WATCH as moonlight dances on the water. I stop my worrying, let go of my plans, and surrender to the simplicity of light and water and a cool breeze against my face. I look up at the stars and feel my place among them as all the petty dramas of the day dissolve in this vast expanse. My body opens to the pleasure of just being. My spine lengthens, shoulders drop, belly softens, and breath deepens. The whole world seems to breathe with me.

And what does it mean to be stiff-necked?
How do I recover my full range of motion?

I HAVE BEEN rushing around all day, trying to get things done. I have been focused on my "To Do" list, trying to do as much as possible, trying to accumulate power and knowledge. I lift my head from the list, from my accomplishments and I notice the world. Suddenly the world lifts me up above the smallness of my life. The panorama of Creation spreads out before me. In a flash I am the primordial human seeing from one end of the world to the other. I see everything. And I know absolutely nothing.

Guidance for Practice

Lifting up the Holy Sparks in Our Food

"You shall eat and you shall bless and you shall be satisfied." Our practice for this week of Ekev *is to fulfill this commandment in the dangerous land of our everyday lives. So many Jewish spiritual practices are about eating, because it's a fragile time for consciousness. There is a tendency to lose awareness, go on automatic. When our level of awareness drops, we don't notice the subtleties of satisfaction. We may eat to try to fill some other unacknowledged hunger that has nothing to do with food.*

Spiritual practices that surround eating are designed to open our eyes to the miracle of appetite, taste, nourishment, and satisfaction. When we eat, we are transforming matter into energy. In Hasidic language, we are "lifting up the holy sparks" that are in the food.

The Ba'al Shem Tov teaches,[3] "When you are eating or drinking something, have it in your mind that the taste you feel in your mouth when you are chewing or swallowing is the innermost holiness of the food, the holy spark that is in the food or drink."

As we lift the holy sparks up to their source, so may we be lifted through our enjoyment of them.

Prepare a sacred meal and set the table beautifully with candles, flowers and your best dishes. When you sit down to eat, imagine that your table is the holy altar in the Temple. Say a blessing. Savor the fragrance of the food. (No TV or reading during this meal.) Eat slowly, enjoying each bite, knowing that the taste of the food holds its innermost holiness. After your meal, take a few minutes to experience satisfaction.

The traditional *Birkat Hamazon* (Grace After Meals) is composed of four main blessings. Create your own blessing in four parts by meditating on each of these four themes. Take a few moments to commit your new blessing to paper.

[3] *Derech ha-Tovah veha-Yeshara, Seudah*, p.27b. Quoted in Buxbaum, Yitzchak, *Jewish Spiritual Practices* (Jason Aronson, 1999)

The food – Gratefulness and wonder at its taste and texture and fragrance and nourishment.

The land from which the food grew – Gratefulness and wonder at the process of growth (from sun and seed and water) through harvest.

Jerusalem – Find the center of holiness within yourself. Bless the place within that allows you to experience the miracle of this meal.

Goodness itself – Through the pleasure and energy of this food we are reminded of the essential Goodness of life.

Place the blessing you have written on your table to keep it handy during this week of *Ekev.*

Recite your prayer at least once each day after you have eaten.

Re'eh

(See)

DEUTERONOMY 11:26 - 16:17

Re'eh begins by exhorting us to see clearly the choices that are laid out before us, and to choose the way of blessing. This portion ends with a detailed description of the three festivals of pilgrimage.

THE BLESSING

RE'EH BEGINS BY COMMANDING each of us to "See!" – to open the eyes of our hearts and behold the world that has been set before us. This clear seeing is both our redemption and our blessing. Only when our vision is no longer obscured by false beliefs, fear, or the illusion of separateness, can we experience the freedom to choose the Blessing that is being offered to us. We are commanded first to SEE, because without that clear vision, it may not be possible to discern blessing from curse.

The vantage point of Deuteronomy allows us to see where we have been – "the long strange trip it's been,"[1] – and the doors of possibility that open before us in response to our "seeing." If we believe that we are powerless, if we believe that the Land of Milk and Honey is beyond our reach, then we will not see those doors of possibility. We will be stuck forever at the threshold.

WHEN I WAS a wild, imaginative youngster, passionately trying to express my visions of possibility, the grown-ups around me often responded by saying, "I'll believe it when I see it." Intuitively, I understood that the process works the other way around. We usually see only what we already believe. And our beliefs are determined by the particular mind-state of the moment and our collective conditioning.

Re'eh tells us that at every moment, with eyes wide open, we can choose between Blessing and Curse. The blessing appears when we are attentive to the flow of God that pours through us. And the curse befalls us when we ignore that flow and instead "go after other gods that we did not know."[2] The word for Knowledge, "*da'at*," refers to the kind of knowing that is intimate. The same word is used to denote "sex." (To know someone in the "Biblical sense") That God-force, which will open the

[1] "Truckin'," from the Grateful Dead album, *American Beauty*, 1970, lyrics by Robert Hunter

[2] Deuteronomy 13:3

possibility of blessing, is so close to us. (Mohammed says that God is as close as your jugular vein.)

The gods that we pursue, the ones that are not intimately flowing through us and interpenetrating our essential self, distract us constantly. This predicament of feeling compelled to "go after other gods that we did not know" describes the mind-state of disconnection from Source. That state which sometimes manifests as addiction, despair, or cynicism (or just a diminished vitality), obscures the choice that is set before us. Instead of making that choice for blessing in each moment, we are compelled by an unnamed desperate hunger to be made whole, and then we make blind, false choices.

The freedom to choose between Blessing and Curse depends on our clear seeing, and our clear seeing depends on the mind-state that we're in. Our mind-state is dependent upon how connected we are to Source in each moment.

The blessing of *Re'eh* is a vision of the reality that is set before us that encompasses and transcends all Duality. When we have accessed that clear vision, our choice is evident.

The Spiritual Challenge

There is a grammatical inconsistency in the first sentence of *Re'eh* that may hold the secret to our exploration of vision. The text says, "See, I have set before you this day..."[3] The imperative verb "see" is in the singular in the Hebrew phrasing, yet the "before you" is in the plural. In the journey of Torah, a mistake like this becomes a doorway. In the journey of Torah, a mistake like this calls us to face a spiritual challenge. What is the relationship between my personal awakening and our collective awakening?

We live at a time when our collective awakening, as communities, as nations, as a species has become crucial. As we confront the growing disruption of the global climate, the depletion of vital resources, the growing disparity between rich and poor, the rapid extinction of plant and animal species, and the spread of devastating weapons on our planet, it is clear that the human family must wake up and make fundamental changes in the way we treat each other and our environment. God sets before us (as a collective consciousness) the choice for blessing or curse. Yet, in approaching that collective awakening we are each addressed per-

[3] Deuteronomy 11:26

sonally, in the singular. You personally must open your eyes. You personally are challenged to see.

When I first moved in to my home, which is quite isolated high up in the mountains of New Mexico, I did not know a soul in the area. So one snowy morning soon after I had moved in, I was very surprised and delighted to hear the doorbell ring. At the door were two tenacious Jehovah's Witnesses who were quoting from Isaiah and vigorously informing me about the rewards of Heaven, and the punishments of Hell.

I invited them inside, took out my Bible and happily began correcting their translation and interpretation of scripture. I felt blessed to have company and conversation about what mattered most. Together we surveyed the blessing and curse that was set before us.

Then something happened.

As I listened to their talk of Heaven as some far-off place, I felt as if a veil across my eyes were suddenly dropping away, and all at once I could "see."

"Heaven is right here," I exclaimed. "Don't you see?"

I looked into their eyes, and for a moment I could swear that their veils had also dropped away. We shared a shiny heavenly vision and then a minute later I saw in their eyes a cloud of confusion, the veil returning. They thanked me and hurried outside.

I believe the power of my "seeing" opened their eyes, even if it was just for a moment. As each of us rises to the spiritual challenge of "seeing" clearly, the singular vision we are given can affect the mind-state and then the perception of others so that together we can acknowledge the fullness of the Reality that has been set before us.

Guidance for Practice

Pilgrimage

Portion Re'eh *ends with the commandment to make three pilgrimages a year, "to appear before God in the place that God chooses." Those three pilgrimage times are Passover,* Shavuot, *and* Sukkot. *We are commanded not to come empty-handed, but to bring an offering "according to the blessing you have been given."*

Our vision gets clouded by habit. We begin to see our lives as ordinary and mundane. Every so often a pilgrimage is necessary so that we can awaken to holiness and open our eyes to the extraordinary, and see that "Heaven is right here."

Richard Niebuhr says, "Pilgrims are persons in motion, passing through territories not their own, seeking something we might call completion, or perhaps the word clarity will do as well, a goal to which only the spirit's compass points the way."[4]

Every pilgrimage is a journey inward, even if we travel clear across the world. The particular festivals that the Torah commands us to mark with sacred journeys are both agricultural and historical festivals. With our journey to center, we integrate these two aspects of religious practice. With one foot I walk through the blessed cycle of plantings and harvests. With the other foot I journey with my ancestors, re-enacting the drama that moves us from slavery to freedom. The journey is both personal and collective. With one foot I walk my singular path towards clarity. I open my eyes wider with each step, awakening to my personal destiny. With the other foot I fall into step with my people, and with spiritual seekers everywhere. My journey becomes a celebration of shared blessing.

Our practice for this week of *Re'eh* is to let "spirit's compass point the way," and begin to open to the call of pilgrimage. We can practice the meaning of pilgrimage by making a small journey to a sacred site near home. It could be a shrine or a waterfall or a grave, a monument or a quiet park, a place significant for its History or Nature.

Begin the journey consciously by becoming aware of your deepest longing, setting an intention for the journey, surrendering your expectations, and asking an elder for a blessing. Let every step of the journey be a spiritual practice, remembering that every pilgrimage is a journey inward. And you never know exactly what you will find.

With each step your eyes and heart must open a bit wider to receive the unexpected.

Don't forget to bring an offering with you, "according to the blessing you have been given."

The Sufi poet and mystic, Rumi says,
"As you start on the Way, the Way appears."

---

[4] Quoted in *The Art Of Pilgrimage*, Cousineau, Phil, p.14

Shoftim
(Judges)

DEUTERONOMY 16:18 - 21:9

Shoftim *defines the status and function of Judges, the King, the Priests, and the Prophet in Israelite society. The people are commanded to set up Cities of Refuge where someone who has killed accidentally can find sanctuary.*

THE BLESSING

THE PORTION *SHOFTIM* TAKES US ON A JOURNEY through the inner landscape – giving us a vision of four aspects of Self that must be discovered, cultivated and refined. To receive the blessings of *Shoftim*, we must look within and do an accounting of these aspects of Self. As these aspects are acknowledge and honored, we are blessed with a life of consciously growing ourselves in Holiness and Wholeness.

THE FIRST ASPECT comes to us in the symbol of JUDGE, the Administrator of Justice. It represents the Power of Discernment. As we step onto the spiritual path, we learn that a basic and essential component of consciousness is the ability to discern. There are so many voices within that vie for our attention, all of them claiming to be the TRUTH. Our perceptions of Reality are colored by our conditioning, passing moods, hormonal changes, habits... and by the prejudices of the cultures that have shaped us.

In the pursuit of Justice, our Judge-within takes into account all the pushes and pulls of these forces of bribery. In the pursuit of Justice, she balances the powers of Love, Generosity, and Expansiveness, with the power's of Rigor, Limits, and Boundaries, while keeping the eyes of the heart wide open.

We rely on the Judge-within to discern and make audible the subtle voices of wisdom that might otherwise be drowned out by the din of fear, jealousy or habitual patterns of thought. He points us towards those subtle perceptions so that we can make room for their wisdom to be manifested in our lives. In the panoply of inner conversation, the Judge learns to be suspicious of certain voices, and to give absolute trust to others. A keen discernment of the forces of the inner landscape allows us to see the outside world with a new clarity. When our prejudices have been unmasked and our reactivity tempered by understanding, then we can pursue Justice wholeheartedly. Our hearts can remain open even in the face of difficult choices.

The Torah portion *Shoftim* tells us, "Justice (within, and), Justice (without) you must pursue," and then you will receive the blessing of Life and "inherit the Land (the opportunities of incarnation) that God is giving to you."[1]

THE SECOND ASPECT comes to us as KING, representing Mastery and our identification with the God-spark. When the aspect of Judge is refined enough to discern the inner voice of mastery (that part of us which is fully identified with the expanse of Soul), then the Judge, using utter discernment, raises up a King. The King rules by merit of his connection and identification with the Source of Wisdom and Compassion. The aspect of Self that is King speaks from that Source-point and can from there, access the widest possible perspective. *Shoftim* cautions us that the ever-present danger to this aspect of Self is inflation.

The blessing of the King connects us intimately with the Source of all wisdom, power and riches. Yet there is a danger in accumulating those gifts as if they, rather than God, were the goal of our quest. Jeremiah articulates this danger well when he says, "Let not the wise one glory in his wisdom, and let not the powerful one glory in his power. Let not the rich one glory in his riches. But let one that glories, glory in this: That he understands and knows Me."[2]

The aspect of Self that is called King is the part that consciously "knows" God. It is the part of us that is intimate with the Mystery behind Creation. Through that intimacy the King dons the robes of mastery and the crown of sovereignty. In knowing God and in recognizing ourselves as a spark of the Divine, we learn to exult in the majesty of the cosmos and bask in the radiance and nobility that is our inheritance. This aspect of King allows us to embody spiritual authority when necessary.

THE THIRD ASPECT of Self that we are called upon to discover, cultivate, and refine is symbolized by the PRIESTS and LEVITES. This aspect represents our commitment to Spiritual Practice, Ritual, and Artistry. Just as the Judge-within discerns the true and faithful King that shines through us, that King shows us a vision of the Unity and Integrity of all-that-we-perceive. The vision flashes and fades and is given to us in bright glimpses that inspire and encourage the holiness that we are. How do we sustain that flashing vision? How do we unfold the implications of that awesome glimpse of the Unity of All?

---

[1] Deuteronomy 16:20

[2] Jeremiah 9:22-23

The Priests and the Levites within us rise to this challenge and bless us with practices, rituals, and forms that are meant to imprint that vision onto the fabric of our lives. The Priest stands between Life and Death and shows us the Pathways of Holiness and Balance. She is the healer who sends us to face our own disease. The Levites give us the song that will lift our hearts into generosity and give us the courage to see the Truth and act righteously. They show us the dance that will sanctify each step on our journey. The Priests and Levites minister the forms of our religious life. They teach us how to celebrate and how to mourn; how to return when we have fallen away from ourselves.

Yet even these beautiful forms inspired by revelation and majesty can become rigid and confining. Pulled into the details of ritual and form, we can sometimes lose track of the "big picture;" and the intention that created the ritual in the first place can get lost in the particulars of practice. We may also find ourselves seduced by the beauty of the song or the cleverness of the text.

Then God raises up, from deep within us, the fourth and last aspect of Self, which is called prophet. The essential quality of the Prophet is that she is whole-hearted before God. The true Prophet has not been corrupted by ambition, has not become lost in the forms or influenced by the passing fashions of the age. The Prophet's mission is to be a clear channel for the Divine flow and to identify the ways in which that Divine flow is being obstructed. He cuts through self-deception and shatters the defenses so carefully constructed by the personality. The Prophet cares nothing for nostalgia, sentimental attachment, reputation, appearances, or the norms of society. He shakes things up when we get too comfortably complacent. He calls us back to our true essence when we have wandered too far. The Prophet calls us back to our depths when we become infatuated with those "other" gods of the surface world.

The Spiritual Challenge

After blessing us with the fullness and richness of our inner aspects of Judge, King, Priest and Prophet, *Shoftim* sets forth a challenge. Each of these aspects emerges consciously as we step forth to deal deliberately with the situations that life presents. But it is the nature of Mind to babble on in a reactive chain of association, habit and contention. The mind has a comment or argument about everything. One thought compels the next and we are caught in an endless cycle. What do we do with the reckless power of our unconscious? How do we break free from the tyranny of Mind?

In order for the voices of wisdom to emerge we must interrupt that cycle and enter a place of refuge from the cacophony. From that place of spacious refuge a new voice can emerge, a new course can be set, a new song can be heard.

To describe this unconscious thought that captures our awareness and leads to a reactive and compulsive chain of babble, we use the language of Torah, and name it a "murderer," because its chokehold on the mind kills all possibility for true wisdom to emerge. This murderer is one who kills accidentally, without evil intention. Thus we designate the random thoughts that flit through the untrained mind without clear or deliberate focus. One thought compels the next, just as the avenger of the one murdered is forced to set in motion a cycle of violence that is endless.

The only hope we have for interrupting this cycle and giving our Mind the spaciousness that is required for wisdom to emerge, is in our establishing places of refuge within us.

We are commanded to set aside Cities of Refuge so that there may be an escape from the tyranny of the Mind. So important are the Cities of Refuge to the inner landscape that the Torah repeats this commandment three times. The establishment of these Cities of Refuge, in each corner of the inner landscape, ensures that wherever the mind wanders, and however far the sense of being lost in the labyrinth of Mind, we can find a way back to Center.

Guidance for Practice

There are two practices for this week of Shoftim.

Building a Fire-Tower in the Forest of the Mind

The first practice for this week of *Shoftim* is to notice carefully the workings of the Mind. Set a timer and spend five minutes each day just watching thoughts. Notice how one thought connects to and compels the next.

Learning to notice the processes of the Mind is like building a fire-tower in the forest. The process of thinking is like wandering through that thick forest, where your only view is of the trees immediately before you. When you build the tower, it is possible to gain a clear view of the whole forest, with all its interesting trees and animals and pathways. You may still be thinking yourself through the wooded landscape, but part of your attention watches from the tower.

THE NEXT STEP after noticing the machinations and patterns of your thoughts is to practice interrupting those patterns. When, during meditation, I notice that I have been captured by a rogue pattern of thought, or by a tape-loop that is compulsively repeating the same thoughts, the watcher-in-me knows that it is time to revisit the City of Refuge.

I GENTLY AND SILENTLY SAY THE WORD "*ATAH*," which means "You." I have programmed this word to release me from the content of Mind and send me to the City of Refuge where I can rest in pure Being.

CHOOSE A SACRED WORD that can be used as a reminder to let go of the content of thought. The more you use this word the more powerful it becomes in the process of un-sticking you from the stickiness of thought. At some point you won't even have to say the word to yourself. The awakening of the watcher and the mere impulse to say the word will effectively release you from the thought and send you to the place of Refuge, the place of simply Being. This practice will build upon itself in time. As you better know the workings of your own mind, your periods of being lost in thought get shorter; you catch yourself sooner and returning to the place of Refuge inside becomes a compelling and nurturing experience.

GIVING VOICE TO THE FOUR ASPECTS OF SELF

ANOTHER PRACTICE FOR THIS WEEK OF *SHOFTIM* is to identify and give voice to the aspects of Self that the text describes: Judge, King, Priest, and Prophet.

WHICH OF THESE ASPECTS OF SELF IS ASKING FOR YOUR HONOR and attention? When an aspect of Self is not fully honored by simply being acknowledged and given its rightful place in your awareness... its shadow may emerge. The Judge may become over-critical; the King may become inflated; the Priest may become rigid and overly attached to the forms; and the Prophet's righteousness may become "self-righteous."

WHICH OF THESE SHADOWS have you observed in your own personality?

WRITE ABOUT THESE ASPECTS OF SELF in your journal or share about them with a spirit-buddy.

Ki Tetze

(When You'll Go Out)

DEUTERONOMY 21:10 - 25:19

Ki Tetze *consists of a series of laws concerning family relations, acts of kindness and propriety, equity, and moral behavior.*

THE BLESSING

ACCORDING TO MOSES MAIMONIDES, there are 72 *mitzvot* in this portion. A *mitzvah* is literally a "commandment" from God, but it can also be understood as an opportunity for "connection," an opening to holiness. (The Aramaic form of this root means "to connect.")

When we receive a *mitzvah* as a pathway to holiness, and then step onto that path, we have the opportunity of bringing blessing into the world through our actions. When we perform these actions with heightened awareness and clear intention, simple acts of everyday living can have a transformative impact on both inner character and outer universe.

When we dedicate the energy of living to the wholeness and holiness of Creation, our lives become a source of blessing.

KI TETZE IS A DIVERSE COLLECTION of social, ethical, legal, and ritual laws. Through these *mitzvot* it is possible to cultivate the qualities of clarity, stability, wholeness, kindness, compassion, generosity, honesty, and justice. The blessing comes through us when we integrate those qualities and begin expressing them through our every word, thought and interaction. But first we must receive the deeper meaning and power of a *mitzvah*, take it personally and learn to apply its principles to our real, everyday lives.

With these words, "When you go out to battle against your enemies," *Ki Tetze* begins by acknowledging the struggle. It's much easier to be a decent human being when you are at peace... but there is a battle to be waged and that battle will try our decency, challenge our integrity and put every good intention to the test.

THE SPIRITUAL CHALLENGE

THE FIRST TEST of *Ki Tetze* comes not from losing the battle, but from winning it. The very first commandment of *Ki Tetze* warns us that when we win that battle and bring away the spoils of war, we will try to acquire the beautiful woman who has become our captive. We will want to own her. And when the lust and delight for new acquisition has waned we may be tempted to sell her.

The commandment of *Ki Tetze* replaces the subjugation and acquisition of the captive woman with the requirement to establish a binding relationship with her, to know her as "Thou" rather than use her as "It."

To know our captive "Thou," we are commanded to take her into our home, and let her be stripped of all the outer trappings of seduction. Her hair and nails are cut, the clothes of captivity are put aside, and she must be given a month to set her own heart in order.

Only after witnessing the simplified essence and subjective reality of our captive bride may we "come in to her," and live in sanctified relationship.

As I TAKE THIS COMMANDMENT UPON MYSELF, I ask, "What is the victory that leaves me vulnerable to the forces of my own lust and greed?" As I take this commandment upon myself, I ask, "Where is the pathway to holiness?"

I GREW UP in a land of shopping malls surrounded by advertisements, inundated by commercials. No matter how we hide from the mainstream culture or create alternatives to the norms, consumerism is the *de facto* religion of the land. Though it may seem that this religion might open us to the beauty, peace, and satisfaction of acquiring and owning material wealth, in actuality consumerism sets us at war with the material world. Because of our addictions and insatiable desires for "MORE," we are in almost constant battle with ourselves over how much is enough. This battle affects our relationship to beauty, wealth and the Earth itself. Consumerism degrades our relationship to all we see or touch in the world, because it teaches us that rather than just enjoy this beauty, we must try to acquire, own, and subjugate everything for our own use. We are conditioned to reach for the next thing, rather than taking the time to appreciate, honor, and celebrate what is already in our hands.

My world becomes a "captive bride" whose seduction lies in the fact that I have battled to own her; she is mine, to use, keep or sell. When my world is a "captive bride," then the Earth and all her riches become commodities. That which is beyond price becomes nearly invisible. When everything in our lives becomes a thing that is to be grasped or appropriated for our own use and pleasure… then the ungraspable, unnameable, indefinable (in other words – God) ceases to exist for us. When my world is a "captive bride" I stop noticing the "spaces" between things where the mysterious force of relationship exerts its power, forming the connective web of Life. When my world is a "captive bride" then I am a slave to desires and aversions but true Love eludes me. *Ki Tetze* challenges us to acknowledge the destructive nature of this relationship and to transform it into one of loving mutuality. This is the pathway to holiness.

When I look at my own relationship to the "things" that I accumulate, I am reminded that the Hebrew name for Deuteronomy, *D'varim*, also means "things." Though I take exquisite delight in the things of my life, I also feel that I am in an almost constant battle with clutter. If I don't stay vigilant, it feels as if I will be buried in piles of paper or get lost in the things that I cannot manage to put in their proper place. One voice inside keeps saying that if only I would be more organized then the battle with clutter could be won. Another voice whispers that perhaps the problem is deeper and the solution more radical.

Ki Tetze challenges us to re-examine the very foundation of our relationship to the world. It says that as we transform our perception of the world-as-"Captive-Bride" to the World-as-Beloved-Manifestation-of-God, the path to holiness opens up before us.

"The Promised Land is a state of mind," says a favorite reggae song.[1] The commandments of Deuteronomy are preparing us to enter that state of mind where milk and honey flow from the nurturing, simple and sweet relationship that we establish with all of Life.

Guidance for Practice

How is that nurturing relationship with the world established?

Only after witnessing the simplified essence and subjective reality of our captive bride may we "come in to her," and live in sanctified relationship. This witnessing is accomplished through a period of stepping back from the entanglement of compelling desire.

I will suggest three practices from our inheritance that help us to step back from our habits and complicated attachments in order to establish and renew our relationship to material existence.

Passover Practice

The Festival of *Pesach*, Passover, is our first practice. Passover commemorates our journey from Slavery to Freedom.

[1] "Promised Land" by Majek Fashek, on his 1997 *Rainmaker* album.

To celebrate, we are commanded to simplify our diets, eliminating all leaven. We return to the most basic food of *Matzah*, remembering that our freedom depends on our willingness to leave the securities of enslavement and venture into the wilderness where our faith can be renewed.

Instead of buying all those complicated Kosher-for-Passover highly processed foods, I make it a practice to spend that week (after the seder) eating simply. I eat mostly fruits and vegetables and do a kind of internal "spring cleaning." Simplifying my diet and going back to the basics helps me to become conscious of the land's rebirth and of my relationship with the earth. The change in diet breaks the patterns of habitual eating. I remember both my Freedom and my interdependence.

During this one week, I re-sensitize my palate and become more conscious of how and what I consume. This practice, of returning to the basics, can influence my awareness as I continue through the rest of the year.

Sukkot Practice

The second practice is the celebration of Sukkot.

We are commanded to build a simple hut – just three walls and a flimsy roof, and live there for the week of the holiday. We remember our journey through the wilderness and the nomadic ways of our ancestors.

The practice of Sukkot is a practice of remembering that we actually don't need so much. Our return to the basic pleasures of celebrating the harvest and basking in the moonlight as it shines through our roof, reminds us that all of our elaborate appliances and furnishings are extra. It is a time of interrupting our patterns of addiction to technology; it is a time of stripping away the artifice of civilization. On Sukkot we renew our relationship with simplicity. We sanctify our relationship with the sheltering wings of Shekhina, the Divine Presence.

When we return to our sturdy houses, we bring with us the knowledge of our fragility, the realization of just how temporary our possessions are, and the remembrance of our True Refuge in God's Hand. We transform the "captive bride" of our possessions into a holy, simple, and grateful relationship with Home.

Shabbat Practice

The third practice that I will suggest in order to rise to the challenge and receive the blessing of *Ki Tetze*, is the celebration of Shabbat.

Every week we have the opportunity to simplify our lives and remember what is essential.

On Shabbat we take a break from being a consumer and allow ourselves to simply delight in the gift that is right before us. We put down the struggle, relax our desperate grip on the external world and just let it be. My friend Rabbi Arthur Waskow, who works so passionately for social justice throughout the rest of his week, turns off his computer before Shabbat and says, "The world will just have to save itself for the next 25 hours!" In that gesture of trust and surrender, the world as "captive bride," is given her freedom. In freedom, her inner beauty shines out to awaken our unconditional love.

Our practice for this week of *Ki Tetze* is to relax our manipulations and release the "World-as-Captive-Bride" to her subjective experience and simple essence. Then we just may fall in love with each other and let that love inspire how we live.

Spend one day this week fasting from media and consumerism. Do not watch TV, read the newspaper or listen to radio, etc. Do not buy anything. For one day honor and celebrate the simple pleasures of the world before you.

Ki Tavo

(When You Enter)

DEUTERONOMY 26:1 - 29:8

This portion describes two rituals that the Israelites are commanded to perform when they enter the Land: the ritual of the first fruits, and the ritual of ratification of the Covenant.

THE BLESSING

THERE IS A TIMELESS MOMENT called "Enlightenment," that we experience as a beacon shining forth and piercing right through our constructed reality, calling us to awaken, inspiring us to expand beyond imposed boundaries of identity. That timeless moment is our inheritance. It is the Promised Land flowing with milk and honey.

Ki Tavo means "when you enter." It describes two amazing rituals enacted in that timeless moment of enlightenment. These sacred ceremonies are performed in "ritual space," which is a kind of dream-time, so that their power and blessing can enter our ordinary waking consciousness. When God-the-Beloved says to us in the Song of Songs, "Honey and milk are under your tongue,"[1] he is reminding us that the Promised Land is so very close. It is there for the tasting whenever we are willing to "enter in" and be intimate with Life. The power of that intimacy is shown to us through an act of ritual. The blessing of ritual-work is that it underlines and thus activates what we already know to be true. It reminds us of that truth we have forgotten amid the clutter, distraction and busyness of our lives.

THE FIRST OF THESE RITUALS holds such a clear imprint of the Freedom of enlightened consciousness that it is recited as part of the *Haggadah* each year at the Passover Seder – our celebration of Freedom.

We are instructed to do this ritual "when we enter the Land," when we experience that state of enlightened expansion of consciousness. We gather up the first fruits – the deliciousness and nurturance, even the terror of those experiences – and bring them before God. On our spiritual journey we move through many states of consciousness. Experiences come and go. It is only when we bring awareness to those states (laying their fruit before God) that we can fully receive their blessing and benefit. It is not enough to enter the land. We must bear witness to the miracle of the

[1] Song of Songs 4:11

journey and acknowledge the One who brings us out of slavery, guides us through the wilderness and opens the way to expanded awareness. When the flow from God opens up for us, we are instructed to bring an offering, to return that gift to its source. The flow then becomes circular and we are blessed, purified and made transparent by it.

When engaged in ecstatic practice, the Divine flow opens up and spills into and through us. This moment of blessing is also a danger if we ignore the instruction of *Ki Tavo.* When the gifts of ecstasy are merely consumed, without giving anything in return, the false-self (or surface identity) is fortified and every experience of spiritual "high" decorates and glorifies that fortification. To prevent this, we are taught that the moment of receiving must be transformed into a moment of offering. Our ritual of offering is a way of acknowledging a truth that can sometimes be obscured. The truth is that our bounty comes from God, and we can connect ourselves to the Source as we receive Her gifts. That connection is even more precious than the gift itself.

The blessing of *Ki Tavo* is the connection that happens when we offer up the "first fruits" – those flashes of joy or insight that come to us in practice.

The second ritual that is commanded describes a magnificent landscape – a valley surrounded by two great mountains. Six tribes are positioned on one mountain and six on the other. The Levites, arranged around the ark in the center of the valley, alternately call out blessings and curses to the people on opposing mountains who respond with a rousing, "Amen!"[2]

That awesome scene described in *Ki Tavo* is a rare view into the inner landscape of enlightened consciousness. When we stand as Levites in the valley of enlightenment, it becomes so clear and obvious what it is that blesses our existence, and connects us with our Divine inheritance, and what it is that curses us, thus separating us from that inheritance. Our normal state of consciousness in contrast, feels like stumbling through the fog, our inner landscape shrouded in bewilderment. As the mists of confusion clear, the blessing and the curse of our lives rise up like mountains, and in the valley between we sing, "Amen."

In *Midrash Raba*, Rabbi Judah son of Sima said, "Amen contains three kinds of solemn declaration: oath, consent, and confirmation."[3] The blessing of *Ki Tavo* enters us when we say, "Amen!" to that moment of enlightenment, that taste of milk and honey. With the saying of "Amen,"

[2] Deuteronomy 27:11-26

[3] *Midrash Raba*, Deuteronomy, 7:1

we make an oath to be moved by the force of that moment; we consent to its power and confirm its reality.

The Spiritual Challenge

The timeless moment of enlightenment, of entering through the doorway to the Promised Land, is shown to us through Ritual and through the *Shaarei Tzedek*, the "Gates of Justice."

The first spiritual challenge of *Ki Tavo* is learning how to enter "ritual space," how to step outside of Time and access the "Eternal Now" of mythic truth that includes, and yet transcends, our ordinary daily rhythms. The obstacles at the doorway to "ritual space" are cynicism, self-consciousness and the drab, solemn decorum that has so often masqueraded as ritual.

True ritual is serious work, yet cannot be accomplished without a twinkle in the eye. It is holy play, solemn joy. True ritual can be powerful enough to change our perception of Reality, put us face to face with Death… and yet there is a certain unmistakable lightness in it that keeps us just at the edge of laughter.

Ritual requires both inner and outer preparation. The inner preparation allows us to set aside the narrow version of "self," and step into the persona of High Priest or Levitical singer. The outer preparation for ritual involves a complete dedication of the physical realm to the fulfillment of a spiritual purpose. All of the elements – Earth, Water, Fire and Air, (and the aspects of Life they represent) – become our allies. Using our imagination and aesthetic sensibilities concerning color, fragrance, music, and drama, we engage the senses in service to the purpose of a particular ritual.

After all the preparation is completed, the spiritual challenge of ritual is to remain open to the unexpected, the unplanned, and to receive the soul's wisdom. That wisdom and inspiration can then be embodied and integrated onto our everyday lives.

Often when we study Torah, we separate the writings about ritual from the parts that legislate justice… but in the text they are interwoven. No distinction is made between the commandment to enact ritual and the decree for Justice. Between the two great rituals of *Ki Tavo*, we are given another doorway to the Promised Land. It is the doorway of Justice.

"Pitchu-li
Sha'arei Tzedek
Avovam OdehYah" [4]

Open for me
the gates of Justice
I will enter them and thank God.

After the ritual offering of the First Fruits, we are commanded to give a special tithe to benefit the Levite, the refugee, the widow, and the orphan. Elsewhere in Torah when we have given tithes, it has always been in lieu of taxes or gifts for the maintenance of the Sanctuary and its Priests. This tithe is different. It is given purely in the name of Justice, to benefit those who have been disconnected from the wealth of the land.

To receive the milk and honey of the Promised Land, to enter into its mystery, we must share the wealth with those who have none.

The spiritual challenge of *Ki Tavo* is to enter through the gates of Justice by opening our eyes and hearts to the disenfranchised and sharing with them generously the riches we have been given.

Guidance for Practice

A Ritual for Entering the Land

Preparation: Gather together a small group (or even just one spirit-buddy to act as your priest or priestess). Build an altar at the center of your Holy Space and decorate the space with fruit, flowers and a special box for *Tzedakah*. Each person prepares a basket and fills it with symbols of their prosperity. (Examples: a dollar to represent material wealth, a book to symbolize knowledge, pictures of family and friends to remember the treasure of our relationships, etc.) Also decide on a charity that benefits some disenfranchised population – refugees, the homeless, hungry etc. and set aside some money as *Tzedakah*.[5] Prepare a meal that includes milk and honey to share afterwards.

Begin by chanting together:

"P'tach libi
Open my heart!"

[4] Psalm 118:19

[5] *Tzedakah:* literally, "Righteousness," but colloquially - as here - Charity

Everyone: "Open our hearts that we may enter the Promised Land, flowing with milk and honey!"

Priest/Priestess: "And it shall be, when you come in to the Land that *YudHeyVavHey*, Your God, is giving to you as an inheritance, that you shall gather the first fruits, set them in a basket and bring them to this chosen place."

Each pilgrim steps up to altar and says: "I declare today to *YudHeyVavHey* my God, in the presence of these witnesses and the witness of Heaven and Earth, I have come into the Land of Promise. These are the fruits of my Life."[6] (Show and explain what is in your basket.)

The Priest/Priestess takes the basket and places it before the altar.

After each offering everyone chants:

For in joy will you go out,
In peace be led across the Land,
Mountains and hills will burst into song,
And the trees of the field will clap their hands.
Ki v-simcha tate-tzay-oo,
Oo-v-shalom toovaloon.[7]

When everyone has given their offering, the Priest holds up the *Tzedakah* box and says: "When you have collected the tithe, you shall give it to the Levite, to the refugee, to the orphan, and to the widow. All who are hungry will eat and be satisfied within your gates."

The box is passed around and everyone puts in their tithe.

Priest/Priestess: "We ask for Your blessing as You gaze upon us from above, from the heights of the Heavens and support us from below, from the depths of this Holy Earth. Bless us as we enter the Land of our lives, the Land You have given us, a Land flowing with milk and honey."

The ritual concludes with a sacred meal. Include foods that contain milk and honey.

---

6 Based on the verse Deuteronomy 26:10

7 Isaiah 55:12

Nitzavim
(Standing)

DEUTERONOMY 29:9 - 30:20

The Israelites stand before God and receive the covenant. They are encouraged to step up to the blessings and challenges of Torah.

THE BLESSING

NITZAVIM TELLS US that we stand before God in our wholeness. This completeness infuses us with the fullness of vitality, presence and beauty that is necessary in order to receive and give the blessings of covenantal love.

THE PROPHET EZEKIEL gives us a glimpse of the passionate partnership suggested in the meaning of covenant. We stand before God in our most fragile and raw vulnerability. From there we are lifted up into sovereignty:

> **"I let you grow like the plants of the field; and you continued to grow up until you attained to womanhood, until your breasts became firm and your hair sprouted. You were still naked and bare when I passed by you and saw that your time for love had arrived. So I spread My robe over you and covered your nakedness, and I entered into a covenant with you by oath – declares the Lord God; thus you became Mine. I bathed you in water, and washed the blood off you, and anointed you with oil. I clothed you with embroidered garments… dressed you in silks. I decked you out in finery… I put a ring in your nose and earrings in your ears, and a splendid crown on your head. Your food was choice flour, honey and oil. You grew more and more beautiful, and became fit for royalty."**[1]

When we stand in our wholeness (including all our disparate parts – from the elder and honored aspect of self, to the most lowly woodcutter/water-carrier aspect[2]) we are privileged to pass into a covenant with God. To stand and receive this honor is to be given a splendid crown, be

[1] Ezekiel 16:8-13

[2] Deuteronomy 29:9-10

robed in finest silk, enjoy a royal repast and grow into our beauty. Covenantal love washes us clean and anoints us with the oil of our sovereignty. The path of covenantal love requires the maturing of our humanity as we become "fit for royalty," as we grow into our essential Divinity. Through covenantal love we are lifted up, ennobled.

The prophet Hosea describes that day of covenant, the day when we stand before God in our wholeness. The covenant that we establish with God blesses the whole world, opens our hearts to all creatures, and ends violence.

> **"In that day, I will make a covenant for them with the beasts of the field, the birds of the air, and the creeping things of the ground; I will also banish bow, sword, and war from the land. Thus I will let them lie down in safety."[3]**

This "safety" that Hosea describes comes in remembering that we are intimately related to all beings. We are part of them and they are part of us. We can lay down our weapons, put away our armor and clothe ourselves in the silks and embroidered garments of covenantal love.

The Spiritual Challenge

As we stand before God we are challenged to reclaim all the shards of self that have been broken off in trauma, all the lost pieces of self that we project on the "other," all the parts of self that lie hidden behind walls of shame or pride. As we stand up in our integrity, the blessings of covenantal love begin to shine through our lives.

These blessings of covenantal love come as we stand before God and rise to the challenge that has been put before us. We grow into spiritual adults by standing up to face this challenge and not shying away from it. "I've put Life and Death in front of you, Blessing and Curse."[4] The challenge that God gives us is to choose Life and Blessing, to turn away from Death (the force of destruction) and Curse (the negativity that limits us). Yet what sounds so very simple becomes so very confusing in the moment-to-moment choices that we face. The Mind becomes an expert in rationalizing whatever choice might bolster the ego's ambitions

[3] Hosea 2:2

[4] Deuteronomy 30:19

or defenses. What looks like a blessing in one moment may turn out to be a curse in the next. What seems like a choice for Life entangles us in the forces of Death. The simple challenge of "choosing Life" becomes infinitely more subtle.

This spiritual challenge of *Nitzavim* can only be taken up when we learn how to "stand before God." In standing fully before God, we can finally embrace our whole selves completely. We can take responsibility for our choices. In standing before God we become true partners in the work of Creation.

I WAS ONCE ASKED to lead High Holy Day services at a large Mindfulness retreat that was to be taught by Thich Nhat Hanh, a Vietnamese Buddhist teacher whose reputation for gentleness and wisdom drew hundreds of followers. The retreat was scheduled during the Jewish Holidays, and the organizers thought there might be some Jews at the retreat who would benefit from the presence of a rabbi. In preparing for the retreat, I wrote to Thich Nhat Hanh to explain what we'd be doing at his gathering and I sent him a few books about Judaism so that he'd have a better understanding of the importance that these days held for his Jewish students.

At the opening session, he welcomed the Jews who would be celebrating their holy days at the retreat. In a tone that was both incisive and tender he said, "It is my understanding that the purpose of all Jewish practice is to live every moment in the awareness of God's Presence... and that is Mindfulness."

He understood that to stand in God's presence means to stand outside the whirlwinds of change, anchored in the stillness of center, shining out the fullness of our own presence, attentive to the truth of this moment. From that still center, from that open-hearted awareness, the choice between Life and Death, Blessing and Curse at last becomes clear. Until we can stand before God in a state of calm, alert clarity, all the layers of distraction, turbulence and conditioning will rob from us the freedom of choice. And so as we rise to the challenge of choosing Life, we must learn to stand before God, or as Thich Nhat Hanh explained, "to live every moment in the awareness of God's Presence."

I LIKE TO IMAGINE that Thich Nhat Hanh's exposure to Jewish teaching deepened his understanding of the core practice of Mindfulness meditation, just as my own experience with Buddhist meditation has given me insights into how I might "live every moment in the awareness of God's Presence." One way that I might live up to this ideal is to bless the Source of every gift I receive – each awakening, each meal, each opportunity for celebrating this unique moment as a culmination of my life's journey. (The Tradition advises us to say 100 blessings a day in order to affirm our awareness of the Divine Presence, in an attempt to remain conscious amid the constant stream of distractions and acknowledge the unseen miracles that are the foundation of existence.)

The challenge of *Nitzavim* goes a step further. The continual awareness of God's Presence, which we affirm through the act of blessing, leads us to truly stand before God and pass into a covenantal love affair. Covenantal love requires that we stand up, accept our soul's mission and take action to manifest our purpose and calling. *Nitzavim* reminds us that we reject that mission at our peril, and not only at our own peril. Nitzavim tells us that when we "walk in the stubbornness of our heart, (that is, resist our true destiny and work) the wet will be swept away with the dry."[5] (The innocent will suffer because of our negligence.) *Nitzavim* raises the stakes. Covenantal love calls forth the wisest and best from us and then warns us that there are consequences when we ignore that call.

Guidance for Practice

There are three signs of the covenant that serve as reminders of our obligations and tools for awareness as we enter into partnership with God.

The first sign of the covenant is the rainbow, which God establishes as a remembrance of the love and commitment between the Source – and all of Life, forever. The Rainbow is a reminder that renewal follows devastation; and that beauty is born from opposites (sun and rain) converging in paradox. We are reminded by the Rainbow that our covenant with God is large enough to include all the colors or aspects of faith, even the ones that seem to contradict each other.

The second sign of the covenant is *Shabbat*. We are given this sacred time of renewal each week so that we might rest and enjoy the fruits of Creation. We are bathed and anointed, dressed in silks, decked out in finery. The splendid crown of Shabbat is placed upon our heads. We become fit for royalty. On Shabbat we are led to the place where covenantal love may be consummated.

The third sign of the covenant is circumcision. Most literally, circumcision is the ritual cutting away of the foreskin which covers the glans of the penis. It is a ritual that dates back to prehistoric times and till this

[5] Deuteronomy 29:18

day is practiced by many peoples. For Jews it became not only a religious practice but a national one, representing a sign of tribal inclusion.

At a time in our history when women are standing up to claim their rightful and honored place in the tribe, how is it possible to put forth a sign of inclusion that is by definition, exclusively male?

Fortunately, there is another kind of circumcision described in Leviticus, Deuteronomy, and in the writings of the prophets which is called the "circumcision of the heart." Earlier in Deuteronomy, we are commanded to circumcise our hearts,[1] and here in Nitzavim we are told that God "...will circumcise your heart and your descendants' hearts so you can love God with all your heart and with all your soul, so that you will live."[2]

Here it sounds as if it is God performing the circumcision. How do we reconcile this apparent contradiction? Who is to perform this most important ritual for which our lives and love depend, God or us?

Because circumcision is the sign or reminder of covenantal love, which denotes mutuality, I believe it requires a sacred partnership in order to accomplish it. We must lay our hearts bare, become aware of just when and why our heart closes, confess to our own hard-heartedness, and offer up our stubborn heart to the Power-that-transforms.

Circumcision of the Heart

The practice for this week of *Nitzavim* is to take special care to notice when your heart closes. Really notice. Does your heart close when you feel judged? When you are in the presence of suffering? When you are stuck in traffic? When you disagree? When you get too busy? When you're in pain? When you read the newspaper?

In the moment when you notice that your heart is closing, take a slow gentle breath into the heart and ask God for help.

[1] Deuteronomy 10:16

[2] Deuteronomy 30:6

Vayelekh
(And He Went)

Deuteronomy 31:1 - 31:30

Moses begins to prepare for his death by empowering Joshua as his successor and establishing regular readings of the Torah. He again warns the people about the perils of forgetting God once they enter the Land and instructs them in methods of remembrance.

The Blessing

Our holy text begins with the words, "And Moses went...."[3] Where did he go? Instead of gathering the people to him, Moses goes out to them. His message is too important, his mission most vital; he dare not risk missing his mark.

Remember that Moses is the part of us that is awake, that is connected to the power of prophesy, that is linked inextricably to its Divine source. "I was asleep but my heart stayed awake,"[4] cries the Song of Songs. Moses is that awakened heart that beats at the center, but whose song is usually well-muffled by layers and layers of Self.

Moses goes out on a mission of empowerment. He travels to the edges of our awareness in order to awaken our potential – to call us into our power. The Talmud describes this aspect of the inner landscape by saying, "The face of Moses was as the face of the sun; the face of Joshua as the face of the moon."[5] Even through the dark night we can receive and reflect some measure of wisdom, joy and true grace. In the presence of all the people (every facet of awareness), Moses empowers Joshua to activate his full strength and courage on behalf of the whole. And though the light of the moon may wane, it will wax again bright and round. Even though we will forget the essential truth of our Oneness and Glory, we will remember again, just as surely as the moon's light forever returns... returning us to our fullness, to our remembrance.

The blessing of *Vayelekh* is the pathway of *Teshuvah*, the ever-present possibility of "return," no matter how far we've strayed, no matter how extreme our forgetfulness. And the blessing of *Vayelekh* is that we, like Joshua, have been empowered to boldly reflect the Divine light, to step

[3] Deuteronomy31:1
[4] Song of Songs 5:2
[5] *Bava Batra* 75a

into leadership, to open ourselves wide to receive our inheritance – in spite of our inconsistencies, volatilities, uncertainties, and tendencies towards absentmindedness.

Vayelekh commands us to set up regular, public readings of the Torah, so that everyone can hear, learn, and come into a state of awe before the Great Mystery.[6] We are each invited to stand at the foot of Mount Sinai and receive the blessing of Revelation. When we encounter Torah at regular intervals, we are turning our moon-faces towards the light to receive and reflect and remember our inheritance. It is said that for Joshua the sun stood still.[7] We, like Joshua, are blessed with that timeless moment of Revelation as we stand before the sacred text and receive its light.

The Spiritual Challenge

Vayelekh describes, in vivid detail, the perils of forgetfulness. In our forgetfulness, we will feel abandoned; God's face will be hidden from us and in our confusion we will turn to "other gods," thus breaking the connection with Source and cutting off the flow of covenantal love. *Vayelekh* warns us that when we enter the Land flowing with milk and honey and have eaten our fill, we will "get fat,"[8] which means we will become complacent and inevitably forget the miracle before us. We will be devoured by the Land that we had set out to conquer.

God instructs Moses to compose a song, and teach it to us, to "put it in our mouths."[9] The Song is planted within us as a witness, an antidote to our inevitable forgetfulness. For even when we forget everything else, we will remember the Song.

The advertising industry understands this maneuver so very well. We are easily manipulated by the power of Song. A clever rhyme married to a catchy tune can be planted through repetition in the soil of our vulnerable minds to grow a sudden and inexplicable thirst for a certain soft drink or a craving for fast food.

The spiritual challenge of *Vayelekh* is to consciously use the power of Song, to deliberately plant the remembrance that will become vitally important when the forces of forgetfulness pull you into that familiar labyrinth of complacency, distraction, self-righteousness or confusion.

---

6 Deuteronomy 31:9-11

7 Talmud *Ta'anit* 20a

8 Deuteronomy 31:20

9 Deuteronomy 31:19

You must first fully acknowledge the nature of forgetfulness – its power to seduce you, its familiar deceptions, and its insidious influence that can send you to addictive behavior or unconscious destructive reactivity time and time again. Only when you have understood the poison, can you begin to know and apply the antidote.

Guidance for Practice

In a Jewish court of law, witnesses are called to reflect the scope of Reality and discern the path of Justice and Love. Here, on the banks of the Jordan, as we harvest the wisdom of our Torah Journey from the narrowness of slavery to the freedom of the Promised Land, we call three witnesses who can safeguard the Truth in all its enormity and subtlety. We trust them as sworn witnesses to then give that Truth back to us when we have the presence of heart, mind and soul to call upon them. The three witnesses that *Vayelekh* calls are the Song, Heaven, and Earth.[10]

Appointing the Song as witness means that in the moment that we come into remembrance of God's Presence, we ask for the words, rhythm, melody, tone, and cadence that can celebrate that moment of knowing. The words may be a phrase from liturgy or scripture that suddenly makes perfect sense in the light of this holy moment. The melody can be quite simple. The rhythm is linked to your own heart-beat, the ebb and flow of Life pulsing through you. To establish the Song as witness, you must anchor your heart in the experience of intimacy with God and then open your mouth, trusting that the song that emerges carries the feeling-tone and memory of a precious truth.

Establishing Witnesses

The practice for this week of Vayelekh *is to establish the Song as witness against our forgetfulness. Through persistent and artful repetition of a sacred and delicate truth, we plant the seed of remembrance so that on the day of our forgetfulness, it will be there to call us back.*

In a moment of calm, ask yourself the question, "What is it that I know so clearly in my moment of wisdom, yet seem to lose sight of again and again in times of forgetfulness? What is the Song that embodies and expresses that truth?" Sing that song again and again till the song begins to sing itself inside you. Record it or teach it to a friend.

---

[10] Deuteronomy 31:21,28

The difficult conundrum of spiritual practice is that exactly when we need it the most, we are least likely to do it. When I feel restless, angry, worried, too busy, depressed or anxious, I'm likely to forget all about my spiritual practice… even though it is precisely the antidote to the poison at hand. That is why it is so important to establish a routine, a set time and place each day for practice. That is why it is so important to surround yourself with beautiful reminders – *mezuzot* at the gates of awareness. That is why it is so important to establish Spirit-Buddies – friends who can perceive, magnify and reflect back to you your deepest intention, hidden beauty and buried essence.

Once we have appointed the Song as witness – empowering that song to be a loyal servant of remembrance – we must call two more witnesses to preside over the proceedings of our inner life.

Heaven and Earth represent the two great forces that form the fabric of existence. By calling Heaven and Earth as witnesses we are opening ourselves to the vast intelligence of Creation, to the consciousness that is alive in our world. How do we actually do this as a practice? How do we establish Heaven and Earth as our witnesses?

Each morning whenever I can, I watch the sunrise. My attention is drawn to the horizon, where Heaven and Earth meet. When I can become still enough, when I can suspend the chattering flow and commentary of mind-wanderings, I begin to sense an immense, benevolent and articulate presence – Creation bearing witness to its Creator. The Book of Proverbs, *Mishlei*, personifies and gives voice to that presence and calls her, Wisdom. "My fruit is better than gold," she says, "better than fine gold, and my produce is better than fine silver. I walk on the way of righteousness, on the paths of justice. I bequeath those who love me existence itself! I will fill them with treasures."[11]

When Heaven and Earth are called as witnesses, they show me how to receive existence itself as the most precious of treasures. The key to attaining those treasures lies in cultivating an inner stillness.

During this week of *Vayelekh*, set aside some time to be in a place that is spacious, beautiful and relatively quiet.

---

[11] Proverbs 8:19-21

Even if there are sounds, listen in to the silence. Be attentive to the spaces between the sounds. Instead of focusing in on particular objects, expand your gaze to encompass the widest scene possible.

Bring your full power, receptive presence and alert awareness as you open to the forces of Heaven and Earth, who stand before you as witnesses, at your service.

Ha'azinu
(Listen)

DEUTERONOMY 32:1 - 32:52

This portion consists of the final farewell song of Moses.

THE BLESSING

HA'AZINU BEGINS with Moses addressing Heaven and Earth, exclaiming the nature of Torah and the character of Divine blessing as it manifests in our world. It is like the rain that falls, giving Life to the Land. It is like the dew that moistens Reality itself, making it supple, fragrant, alive and fluid. After blessing us with these succulent and watery images of Divine generosity, *Ha'azinu* returns us to the Ground of Being, to the solidity on which we stand. Seven times in this poem, God is called "*Tzur*," The Rock.

Through the wilderness of our lives we are called to return again and again to the Presence of God who supports us, who is the ground beneath our feet. Because of the solidity of this Rock, we can stand upright. Each time we stumble, each time we fall into distraction, forgetfulness, confusion or complacency, we can again find our bearings and push against the Rock of God beneath us in order to stand upright. In fact, in *Ha'azinu*, "Upright," Jeshurun[1] becomes our name.

And so *Ha'azinu* blesses us with these images or ways to understand and receive God's Presence. God is like the rain and dew, giving Life to all. God is like the Rock on which everything rests, allowing us to stand upright and find our footing as we traverse this wilderness. Rain and dew are Heavenly images, while Rock is the essence of Earth. Heaven and Earth are the aspects within us that are called upon to hear this final sublime message. Heaven and Earth receive the blessing of *Ha'azinu* through their attentive witness.

AND WE ARE GIVEN YET ANOTHER METAPHOR that includes and transcends both Heaven and Earth:

---

[1] Jeshurun is a poetic name for Israel/Jacob that appears just 4 times in the Bible: Deut: 32:15, 33:5, 26, Isaiah 44:2. While the name Jacob hints at deceitfulness, Jeshurun contradicts that tendency. It is probably derived from the root Y-Sh-R (*yashar*) which means "direct/straight/upright," or "righteous." Perhaps we become Israel when our inner drama leads deceitful Jacob to become fully integrated with righteous Jeshurun.

Back in the Book of Exodus, God was a mother eagle who carried us on her wings to our Freedom. And now that same Mother Eagle God has returned to stir the nest – that tangle of branches where we doubt, procrastinate and hesitate. She urges us to Flight, exhorting us to receive the legacy of our Freedom. The Mother Eagle God reminds us, her fledglings, that we are not limited to either Heaven or to Earth. We are blessed with both the fluid and the firm. And we are blessed with the ability to soar between them.

As we return again and again to the Rock on which we stand – feeling God beneath our feet supporting us on this journey – we might be deceived into thinking that this Rock is unresponsive, without love or tenderness. We might even be tempted to strike the Rock in frustration or anger. Laboring under this misapprehension, we would be missing the sweetest mystery… for, when we come to the highest places, the places of remembrance and true presence, the delicious bounty of Life will be ours. We will then suckle and be nourished by honey from that very Rock, and we will be anointed with the choicest oil from what had once seemed the hardest crevice.

Ha'azinu BLESSES US with this remembrance: The hardest and most difficult places on our journey may ultimately become the greatest sources of our Redemption and Nourishment. Only when we rise to the spiritual challenges before us, do we receive Life's bounty. Our awareness can transform those difficult places on our journey into fountains of blessing.

The Spiritual Challenge

Ha'azinu DESCRIBES those difficult places. These are the spiritual challenges we are given – times of great suffering – which are the result of our forgetfulness.

We forget to turn back to our Source, the only true font of sustenance. We forget to trust the Rock beneath us… and instead search for God somewhere faraway and remote. We grasp after something external and remain unsatisfied.

Ha'azinu describes this state of alienation from our Source in vividly stark and cruel language:

**"Outside: A sword will bereave,
and Inside: Terror"**[2]

[2] Deuteronomy 32:25

We have somehow become drunk on the wrong wine – a poisonous brew made from the grapes of Sodom and Gomorrah (a place famous for its hatred and meanness.) Wisdom means understanding the future that you are creating for yourself with your present actions … and this wine, which is called serpent's venom … dissolves that understanding.

"Outside: A sword will bereave." Every time we close our hearts and lift our hand against another, we ourselves will be bereaved. We will lose access to the power of goodness at our core. Every time we raise our voice in blame or hatred, we wound ourselves with our own sword.

"… and Inside: Terror." Every act or word of violence or cruelty conceals the growing terror within.

It's easy for me to acknowledge this state of alienation in the world, where my country wages war after war, concealing its terror of "the stranger," and where genocide and the brutal domination and destruction of cultures and of the earth itself are the norm. I can see that war against the "other" as an easy option, serves to conceal the terror that hides within our own borders, within our own hearts.

It is easy for me to acknowledge our culture's addiction to violence and the meanness of politics that feeds our own cynicism. At times like this, God's face is hidden behind the mask of a cruel warrior… which is merely the reflection of our own hidden terror. It's easy for me to become comfortably self-righteous and join with like-minded rebels to build up our case against the powers-that-be.

What is harder for me (and here lies the true spiritual challenge of *Ha'azinu*) is acknowledging my own complicity. At times, I also drink from the poison wine. I wield the sword which is the cause of my own bereavement. I hide a terror within. I am a microcosm of the world that I so adeptly criticize.

Ha'azinu challenges us by warning, "It is not a worthless thing… it is your life." It is not possible to avoid the pain of life… but when we react to the inevitable pains and difficulties of life by becoming bitter, negative and judgmental or by blaming others… then we turn our pain into suffering. Suffering is the magnification and reification of pain. When we become that pain and spiral down into an identification with negativity… then our lives become a "worthless thing." We lose sight of the cosmos of which we are a part. We lose touch with our own power and essential goodness. *Ha'azinu* lifts up each moment and says, "It is your life! What will you do with it just now?"

Guidance for Practice

Ha'azinu instructs, "Remember the days of old." I have planted this memory of innocence in you. It may be a memory of childhood or of the childhood of humanity. Remember a time when My teachings could be received in the nurturing rain, when My Torah was simply understood in the morning dew. Remember when I led you through the wilderness and showed you the secret high places. And there you ate directly from the soft and nurturing breast of the field. There you suckled honey from the rock. The wine you drank was pure and its intoxication opened your eyes wider to My Presence everywhere.

And then something changed. Somehow you were corrupted and began to take the Rock for granted, ignoring the very foundation of existence.

Whenever some aspect of our being is forgotten or ignored or denied, its Shadow inevitably emerges. In *Ha'azinu*, the Shadow-God is a bloodthirsty warrior intent on vengeance. "I'll make my arrows drunk with blood and my sword will eat flesh!" The God that you have denied will destroy you.

The spiritual practice of *Ha'azinu* is to "Remember the days of old," to journey back to the innocence that is buried in our personal and collective memory. We must take this journey without sentimentality or nostalgia… for now we return to the wisdom of childhood as fully conscious and responsible adults.

The morning liturgy says:

"Elohai neshama shenatata bi, tehorah hi."
My God, the soul/breath that
You place in me is completely pure.

Remembrance Meditation

Our practice for Ha'azinu is to take this journey to our essential purity so that we can re-member the Rock beneath our feet and re-connect with the Source of sweet honey that flows from that Rock. These words from the liturgy can help us to take that journey.

I ALWAYS BEGIN THIS PRAYER WITH A FEW MINUTES OF CONCENTRATION ON MY BREATH, following the in-breath all the way to the place deep inside the Heart/Temple that is called "The Holy of Holies." Whatever corruption or confusion or cynicism that has entered my life has not penetrated to the Holy of Holies, that place of essential purity.

I BREATHE IN – to the Holy of Holies within me – and breathe out from those depths. With each breath I am remembering that in spite of the ways I have been corrupted, there is a core goodness waiting to be acknowledged and re-birthed.

WHEN I SING THE WORD "*ELOHAI*," I am calling on my God, not necessarily the God of my ancestors, or the God that I learn about from others. When I sing to "my God," I open to the Force that embraces, supports and sends me just now.

WHEN I SING THE WORD, "NESHAMA," ("SOUL") I remember that there is an opportunity given to me with each and every breath[1] to come into greater awareness and compassion.

WHEN I SING THE WORDS, "SHE'NATATA BI," ("THAT YOU HAVE PLACED IN ME") I remember to open myself in gratitude for this gift of my life.

AND WHEN I SING THE WORDS, "TEHORAH HI," ("SHE IS PURE"), I remember the truth of who I am at my core. I visualize myself as a newborn baby, completely innocent and pure and connected to the Source… and I know that this newborn still lives inside me as a teacher, as a savior. She is teaching me to be reborn, to be fully alive and open to God in this moment. She is saving me from my own corruption, showing me the Rock of God beneath my feet.

---

[1] The Hebrew word *neshimah* means breath and is from the same root as *neshamah*-soul.

Vezot HaBrakha

(And this is the Blessing)

DEUTERONOMY 33:1 - 34:12

Moses blesses each of the tribes and then gives his blessing to the people as a whole. He goes up the mountain, gazes upon the Land and dies.

THE BLESSING

THE FIRST WORD of this final portion of the Torah, the first step on this last leg of the journey, is "*Zot*," which is the feminine form of the word, "This." In mystical language *zot* refers to The *Shekhina*, the immanent, sparkling Divine Presence that is hidden and waiting at the center of all manifest being. She is waiting to be discovered, embraced, honored, and redeemed, longing for us as we long for her.

Throughout our lives we receive the light, the blessing of *Shekhina* in flashes of terror or beauty. The light of the Infinite shines through this finite world. A veil is lifted. Our physical existence is unwrapped to reveal a splendor and brilliance that is the soul, the "innerness" of all things. These flashes awaken in us a yearning for Truth, an aching desire that tears our hearts open in surrender to the Beloved.

But then the veil drops, the light fades, and we are surrounded once more with seemingly dead and dense matter. We return to the task of manipulating the material realm even as the details slip beyond our control, and everything that we try to grasp passes away or changes.

MOSES CLIMBS THE FINAL MOUNTAIN of his life and blesses us "*lifnei moto*,"[2] as he faces his Death. Sogyal Rinpoche, in his book, *The Tibetan Book of Living and Dying*, says that Death is "… a mirror in which the entire meaning of life is reflected." Moses looks into that mirror and opens to blessing. "For Love is as strong as Death."[3] In the presence of Death, those veils of the superficial and trivial drop away and the power of Love is revealed.

Each of us must climb that same mountain. And if we are to unlock the blessing, the transforming love that is in us, we must stand without flinching,in the presence of Death. "If a man tried to buy love with all the wealth of his house, he would be despised."[4] In the presence of Death

[2] Deuteronomy 33:1

[3] *Shir HaShirim* 8:6

[4] *Shir HaShirim* 8:7

all bets are off. When faced with Death we stop trying to buy love or prove ourselves. When reputation, wealth, success, and worldly power are stripped away by the reality of Death, the blessing that we give and receive is of the purest essence.

In facing Death we are given a key to the locked garden, the garden of our innocence. There, we address *Shekhina* directly. We call to the ultimate Reality that until this moment has been disguised beneath the layered garment of our lives, "Oh woman in the garden, all our friends listen for your voice. Let me hear it now!"[5] Facing Death, we receive Life in its fullness. The blessing of *Vezot HaBrakha* comes as we open to the Divine Presence in "This!": this life, this step, this breath, this moment. "Let me hear it now!" In facing Death, I open to receive the abundant Now. As I lay down my fear of Death, my arms are free to embrace and treasure each day.

Psalm 90, which is attributed to Moses says, "Teach us to treasure each day that we may acquire a Heart of Wisdom...." When we treasure each day and acknowledge how precious Life is, the Heart of Wisdom opens and expands, receiving into it the blessing that is our inheritance.

The Spiritual Challenge

The Death of Moses represents the ultimate and most profound spiritual challenge that God gives to each of us. The vast body of literature, poetry, and midrash that describe the death-scene and burial of Moses stand in contrast to the actuality of the stark and spare text in Deuteronomy that says he died (by the mouth of God) was buried, and that no one knows where his grave is.[6]

The fact that Moses' gravesite is unknown, poses a major challenge in the development of Judaism. Religions tend to develop as the glorification of some great man. "He was so great and we are nothing. Let us worship him, or pray at his grave, or receive the merit of his goodness."

But here the message becomes, "Don't look to Moses… it is not really about him… The Torah is about you."

Once during a meditative journey I asked, "Show me where Moses is buried". I was told, "It's not out there. Moses is buried within you." Upon hearing this, I sat very still, took a long slow breath and turned even deeper within. The moment I found stillness, a flower opened up inside my heart. The flower grew to fill me with its essence. Then *Ruach*

---

[5] *Shir HaShirim* 8:13

[6] Deuteronomy 34:5-6

HaKodesh, the "Holy Spirit" blew upon me, scattering seeds and fragrance into the world.

THE CHALLENGE FOR EACH ONE OF US is to plant and tend the seeds of prophesy. Each of us must stand up to Pharaoh, take our shoes off at the burning bush, receive the Divine Name, sweeten our bitter waters, and journey courageously through the wilderness. Each one of us must come to Sinai and receive Torah for ourselves.

And each one of us must face Death. Through that initiatory encounter we receive the fullness of Life and are able to finally give ourselves wholly to God. That complete giving of Self and receiving of Life is expressed in the image of the Divine Kiss. Moses dies "by the mouth of God."[7]

In that kiss we give our lives away. Everything that we have been clinging to and grasping is finally released in that kiss. All the fearful power that has been devoted to pushing away pain and death is finally released. In that kiss we can finally love God "with all our heart, with all our soul and with all our might." In that kiss, giving and receiving become One.

THE KISS OF DEATH is not something that is passively received. The challenge of *Vezot HaBrakha* is to surrender our lives in loving generosity. This means working wholeheartedly for justice while letting go of attachment to the outcome of our efforts. It means loving with abandon even when there is no guarantee that the love will be received. It means writing books whether or not others will read or appreciate them, singing songs that perhaps no one will hear. It means dying to your ambitions, dying to your personality and preferences.

Dying again and again.

For me the dream of love had to die before I could open my eyes and embrace true love. My fantasies, expectations, ideas and beliefs about romance, and past disappointments, all obscured the view.

THE VERY FIRST LINE of the *Song of Songs* says, "He kisses me with the kisses of his mouth." Each kiss is another death (and another re-birth.) Each kiss is practice in letting go. And yes, each kiss is an initiation into more abundant Life.

Yet the ego-self is such an expert at holding on. She is the consummate survivor and preserver of the status quo which is in her eyes the only "sure thing." The great spiritual challenge that *Vezot HaBrakha* gives us is to risk the known in order to step into the unknown. Moses is commanded to "Die," even though "his eye was not dim nor his natural force abated."

---

[7] Deuteronomy 34:5

In the stories about his death, Moses turns away every messenger that is sent to claim his soul. Only the Divine kiss can claim him.

Only the consummation of our soul's desire can allow us to surrender the fortress we have built and defended for a lifetime.

"Only when you drink from the river of silence shall you indeed sing. And when you have reached the mountain top, then you shall begin to climb. And when the earth shall claim your limbs, then shall you truly dance."[8]

Guidance for Practice:

There are two practices for the week of Vezot HaBrakha.

Rabbi Eliezer, one of our great sages, taught his disciples, "Turn (repent) one day prior to your death." And his students said to him, "Master, how can anyone know what day is one day prior to their death?" His response to them was, "Therefore, turn today, because tomorrow you may die." [9]

All of the small spiritual deaths we suffer, all of our griefs and losses point to the fact of our physical death, which will ultimately and definitely happen to all of us. Instead of walking through our lives in denial, we can use the power of the Reality of Death to turn – turn towards God, turn towards the deliciousness of Life's precious gifts, turn towards each other in compassion and friendship.

Right now, imagine that you are lying on your death-bed, surrounded by everyone you have ever known. Your heart is filled with memories of the life you have led. What do you regret? What are you proud of? What seeds have you planted? What are your priorities "one day prior to your death?" Now, turn towards the faces that witness you – family, friends, bosses, employees, co-workers, enemies, neighbors, strangers. Perhaps the meaning and fullness of your life can only be expressed through the blessing that you impart to them.

The practice of conferring blessing requires you to open your eyes and heart to the one who stands before you, to acknowledge and honor the unique gift that they carry.

---

[8] Khalil Gibran, *The Prophet* (1923)

[9] Talmud Bavli, *Shabbat* 153a

When I turned 50, I gathered with my family to celebrate. They are wonderful people, yet are uncomfortable with religious language. I wanted to bless them and receive their blessings. I asked everyone to share 3 things: one fond memory of being with me during the last 50 years, one wish for the future, and a poem or a song. As each person shared a memory, I gave each one a blessing by reflecting back to them how uniquely precious they have been to my life.

To my older brother I said, "I remember how you were there for me when I needed you, how you lent me money when I was broke, how you drove me places when I needed a ride. You are such a solid presence. You are someone I know I can always count on."

To my sister I said, "Remember how when your dog died, your heart was broken open and you turned to me for support? Even though I shared your sadness I was also so grateful that we could begin talking about what mattered most. It means so much to me that the conversation continues. I am inspired by your passion and humor and generosity."

To my younger brother I said, "Remember how we used to play in the gully behind our yard, exploring every secret place, sharing our love of the land? That love has stayed with me. When we watched the sunset together, you showed me how to speak to the clouds so that they would make a beautiful painting of the sky. You opened my eyes to color."

To my mother I said, "Remember when I picked flowers from the neighbors' yards and gave them to you as a gift, telling you that I had found them in the gully? You took me by the hand and patiently asked me to show you where. We walked and walked until I burst out crying and told you the truth. You weren't angry but you were resolute in teaching me the importance of telling the truth. That lesson has stayed with me and I am so grateful for all that you have taught me about honesty, integrity and the gift of direct teaching."

We all cried and ate birthday cake. It was such a simple thing. Yet most people wait until they are lying on their death-bed to tell the truth, to express their love and gratefulness, to forgive or to bless each other.

Conferring Blessing Practice

The practice given to us by *VeZot HaBrakha* is to first imagine the blessings you might give from your death-bed, and then begin communicating those blessings. "Therefore, turn today, because tomorrow you may die." Write a letter, make a phone call. Or perhaps the person you'd like to bless is sitting in the next room.

And now, we arrive at the last words of our journey – "Never again did there arise in Israel a prophet like Moses, whom YHVH singled out, face to face…" But wait! Don't you remember that this is not a story about someone else or some other time? It is a story about you right now. Never before and never again will there arise a prophet like YOU. God has seen your true face. God has sent you to confront Pharaoh. God has blessed you with great might and awesome power.

Receiving Blessing Practice

The final practice of Torah Journeys is for you to receive this blessing as God says to each of us, "You are My Beloved, unique and precious to Me. I will draw you from the waters of unconsciousness; I will lead you through the wilderness; I will mourn your passing and celebrate your incomparable life; I will lift you up on eagle's wings and welcome you home."

Appendices

Chant as a Core Spiritual Practice

Chanting is the melodic and rhythmic repetition of a Hebrew phrase drawn from our sacred text. It is a practice that allows for the exploration of the deeper levels of meaning and experience that lie beneath the surface of our religious lives. For many, chanting has become an important method of opening the heart, connecting with the community, quieting the mind and viscerally embodying our liturgy and scripture.

Why We Value this Practice as a Core of Contemporary Jewish Spirituality

It is important to bring our sustained and loving attention into building and refining our inner lives. Chant is a practice that connects the outer dimensions of sound and group dynamics with inner dimensions of awareness. As we grow and nurture our inner lives, it is important to have ways to express and share with our community the gifts we have received in the solitude of our personal practice.

Chant is the bridge between the inner life and the outer expression; between the solitary practice and the shared beauty of fellowship. When we chant, we use the whole body as the instrument with which to feel the meaning of the sacred phrase. We study the meaning of the words and the context from which they are drawn. We explore the range of our feelings so that they can be dedicated to the purpose of the chant. And we use the power of the practice to enter into the silence and stillness at our core. Thus the practice of Chant integrates our spiritual, intellectual, emotional and physical energies.

The Relation between Chanting and Other Spiritual Practices

Mindfulness Meditation

For many, the practice of silence can be daunting. Our minds are so filled with clutter and our thoughts tend to move in habitual circles. By focusing our intention and gathering up our attention into a form that is both compelling and beautiful, the practice of Chant can provide an entranceway to the silence. In the silence after a chant, many people experience an inner spaciousness for the first time. Because the chant is often energizing, they are able to sustain that spacious silence for much longer than ever before. The silence after the chant invites them then to rest and be renewed in the sanctuary that the chant has built.

Prayer

The practice of Chant takes the words of prayer and uses them as doorways into deeper meanings and into the spaces of our own hearts. It does this through the clarifying and refining of our intention. Sometimes the sheer volume of prayers, collected over the centuries, itself becomes an obstacle to delving more deeply into their meaning or using their power for transformation. The practice of Chant allows us the luxury of exploring one phrase at a time, igniting the fire of our enthusiasm and pouring our passion into those particular words. Our prayer-life will start to reflect the personal and passionate experience we have had with those words. Chanting wakes up our liturgy and brings it to life within us.

Text Study

The practice of Chant allows us to begin to approach the text from an expanded understanding – from our hearts, bodies, and experience, as well as from what we know intellectually. In addition to preparing us for text study by expanding our perception of the words in front of us, chant may also be used as a tool for comprehension. We take a phrase from the text that holds some power or mystery for us, and experience it with melody and rhythm and repetition until it unlocks its secrets for us.

Spiritual Direction

Often during the ongoing practice of Chant, the complexities of our inner life are brought to the surface. For this reason, it is recommended that one who engages in Chant also seek access to a Spiritual Director who can acknowledge the mysteries and challenges that are called up by the chant and help us to appreciate the complexities of the inner life as they are revealed by the practice. Both Spiritual Direction and Chant deepen our capacity to listen and in turn encourage us to express the truth of our inner knowing.

Yoga

Like Yoga, Chanting is an embodied practice. As chanters, we are encouraged to feel the sounds we produce resonating in every part of the body and to use that sound to work on places of tension or resistance.

Chanting supports the practice of Yoga by energizing the body, opening the heart, and clearing the mind. Chanting has often been used in conjunction with Yoga to put our efforts into the context of a Devotional Practice.

Midot (Character Traits)

We are dedicated to supporting the work of cultivating *midot* (qualities) such as: the conscious awareness of God's presence, compassion, wisdom, love, open-heartedness, justice, spiritual community and humility. Chanting can be an effective and powerful tool in this work. In the practice of Chant, we choose a phrase that expresses or embodies a quality that we wish to cultivate. As we chant, we can step inside that quality, feel its beauty and also explore the obstacles that arise in response to its presence. For instance, in exploring the *midah* of patience, we might chant from the psalms, "*Dom l'Yah v'hitchollelo.*"[1] (Be still and wait for God.) As we repeat and embody that phrase, we experience both the feeling of patient waiting AND our rising impatience. In the practice of Chant, we can strengthen and appreciate the stillness of waiting as well as explore the roots of our impatience. This exploration can be done with compassion and understanding as we direct the beauty of the chant to soften hard places in the heart and melt our defenses.

Spiritual Community

When we chant together with a community we create something so much more beautiful than any one of us could accomplish alone. We begin to appreciate the shared project of a chant and see that it is a microcosm of our lives. We can shape our differences to create fascinating harmonies. We can time our varying rhythms to create counterpoint. Each of us learns to bring the fullness of our presence to the group in ways that will enhance the overall feeling and tone of the chant. Even people who feel that they cannot sing can learn to chant and contribute their unique tone and feeling to the whole of the shared creation. As we enter the silence after the chant, each of us lays down our differences and experiences a collective silence that is framed by the highest intentions of everyone in the group.

[1] Psalm 37:7

Where to find these chants

Rabbi Shefa Gold has composed melodies for some of the chants in this book. Several are available on her CDs:

The chant from ***Bereshit***, *"Hineni Osa et Atzmi Merkava le-shekhina,"* is called "Hineni" and is recorded on ***Chants Encounter.***

The chant from ***Chayei Sarah***, *"V'ikvotecha Lo Noda-u,"* is called "Echad" and is recorded on ***Chants Encounter.***

The blessing and challenge from ***Vayetze*** refers to "How Awesome," which is recorded on ***Hymnanence.***

The chant from ***Vayechi***, *"Mah Tovu,"* is recorded on ***Enchant-meant.***

The chant from ***Vayikra*** and ***Massei***, *"Kosi R'vaya,"* is recorded on ***Chanscendence.***

The chant from ***Vayikra***, *"Hashiveynu,"* is called "Let Us Return" and is recorded on ***Chanscendence.***

More chants are available at http:/www.RabbiShefaGold.com (look under "Specific Practices").

Spirit Buddies: Theory and Practice

The Kabbalists of S'fat began their prayer with the following intention, which formed the foundation and measure for all practices:

> **"For the sake of the union of The Blessed Holy One with the *Shekhina*, I stand here, ready to take upon myself the *mitzva*, 'You shall love your fellow human being as yourself,' and by this merit may I open my mouth."**

Our practice of Spirit Buddies is the concrete embodiment of this abstract intention. The daily practice of kindness, compassion, and service to each other helps to keep us from the dangers of inflation, isolation, delusion, and greediness. We check in with our own souls in the presence of a discerning friend. We can also dedicate the energy that we receive from our practice to our partners. This gesture of dedicating energy in service has the effect of opening our channels further for more and finer energy to flow.

Working with Spirit Buddies requires us to practice "presence." This requires letting go of judgment, letting go of the need to "fix" our partner or to offer solutions. We search beneath the layers of personality and invite the pure soul/essence of our partner to be revealed. Together, we create the safe and sacred space in which healing, self-realization and transformation can occur. It means "trusting the process."

Spirit Buddies

... become anchors and grounding for one another
... create the container for practice for each other
... pray for each other
... serve as windows for each other into the infinite divine expanse

Through our Spirit Buddies we are loved unconditionally by the "Great Love."

Our Spirit Buddies listen with warm delighted attention, witness our dreams and commitments, take us seriously, and hold us accountable for our promises. In this relationship we experience "safe space" which makes possible the leap into the unknown. We see the strength, essence and potential of our Spirit Buddies and share our vision with them; sending them with confidence and joy to the work before them.

May this *mitzvah* of love be fulfilled for the sake of the unification within ourselves, between us and through all the worlds.

Spirit Buddy Guidelines

Sacred Space = Safe Space

Create sacred space between you with a chant, meditation, blessing, or rhythm that moves you from mind-space to heart-space.

Listen to your Spirit Buddy with respect and openness, delighting in his uniqueness.

Encourage your Buddy to say what is in her heart.

Honor confidentiality.

Remember that you cannot judge and serve at the same time. Since we are here to serve one another, continue to let go of all judgment.

Don't interrupt or give advice or try to fix things. Don't say, "That reminds me of…," and then tell your own story.

Allow for silence to deepen between you.

Tune in to the breath of your spirit buddy.

Make sure each of you gets equal time for expression.

Before you go to sleep each night, pray for your Spirit Buddies. Your prayer can be as simple as visualizing them shining with their particular and beautiful light, or calling on God, the Great Mystery to let the very best unfold for them for the period of time you are together.

Before the end of your time together, express your intention for deepening or expanding your spiritual practice, (prayer, meditation, *tikkun olam* work, study, etc.) inspired by what you've been doing.

Witness each other's commitments.

Calendar of Torah Portions

		2006-7	2007-8	2008-9	2009-10	2010-11
Bereshit	Gen. 1:1-6:8	Oct 21, '06	Oct 6, '07	Oct 25, '06	Oct 17, '06	Oct 2, '10
Noah	Gen. 6:9-11:32	Oct 28, '06	Oct 13, '07	Nov 1, '08	Oct 24, '09	Oct 9, '10
Lekh Lekha	Gen. 12:1-17:27	Nov 4, '06	Oct 20, '07	Nov 8, '08	Oct 31, '09	Oct 16, '10
Vayera	Gen. 18:1-22:24	Nov 11, '06	Oct 27, '07	Nov 15, 08	Nov 7, 09	Oct 23, '10
Chayei Sarah	Gen. 23:1-25:18	Nov 18, '06	Nov 3, '07	Nov 22, '08	Nov 14, '09	Oct 30, '10
Toldot	Gen. 25:19-28:9	Nov 25, '06	Nov 10, '07	Nov 29, '08	Nov 21, '09	Nov 6, '10
Vayetze	Gen. 28:10-32:3	Dec 2, '06	Nov 17, '07	Dec 6, '08	Nov 28, '09	Nov 13, '10
Vayishlach	Gen. 32:4-36:43	Dec 9, '06	Nov 24, '07	Dec 13, '08	Dec 5, '09	Nov 20, '10
Vayeshev	Gen. 37:1-40:23	Dec 16, '06	Dec 1, '07	Dec 20, '08	Dec 12, '09	Nov 27, '10
Miketz	Gen. 41:1-44:17	Dec 23, '06	Dec 8, '07	Dec 27, '08	Dec 19, '09	Dec 4, '10
Vayigash	Gen. 44:18- 47:27	Dec 30, '06	Dec 15, '07	Jan 3, '09	Dec 26, '09	Dec 11, '10
Vayechi	Gen. 47:28-50:26	Jan 6, '07	Dec 22, '07	Jan 10, '09	Jan 2, '10	Dec 18, '10
Shemot	Ex. 1:1-6:1	Jan 13, '07	Dec 29, '07	Jan 17, '09	Jan 9, '10	Dec 25, '10
Va-eyra	Ex. 6:2 - 9:35	Jan 20, '07	Jan 5, '08	Jan 24, '09	Jan 16, '10	Jan 1, '11
Bo	Ex. 10:1-13:16	Jan 27, '07	Jan 12, '08	Jan 31, '09	Jan 23, '10	Jan 8, '11
Beshallach	Ex.13:17-17:16	Feb 3, '07	Jan 19, '08	Feb 7, '09	Jan 30, '10	Jan 15, '11
Yitro	Ex. 18:1-20:23	Feb 10, '07	Jan 26, '08	Feb 14, '09	Feb 6, '10	Jan 22, '11
Mishpatim	Ex. 21:1-24:18	Feb 17, '07	Feb 2, '08	Feb 21, '09	Feb 13, '10	Jan 29, '11
Terumah	Ex. 25:1- 27:19	Feb 24, '07	Feb 9, '08	Feb 28, '09	Feb 20, '10	Feb 5, '11
Tetzaveh	Ex. 27:20-30:10	Mar 3, '07	Feb 16, '08	Mar 7, '09	Feb 27, '10	Feb 12, '11
Ki Tisa	Ex. 30:11-34:35	Mar 10, '07	Feb 23, '08	Mar 14, '09	Mar 6, '10	Feb 19, '11
Vayakhel	Ex. 35:1-38:20	Mar 17, '07	Mar 1, '08	Mar 21, '09	Mar 13, '10	Feb 26, '11
Pekuday	Ex. 38:21-40:38	"	Mar 8, '08	"	"	Mar 5, '11
Vayikra	Lev. 1:1-5:26	Mar 24, '07	Mar 15, '08	Mar 28, '09	Mar 20, '10	Mar 12, '11
Tzav	Lev. 6:1-8:36	Mar 31, '07	Mar 22, '08	Apr 4, '09	Mar 27, '10	Mar 19, '11
Shemini	Lev. 9:1-11:47	Apr 14, '07	Mar 29, '08	Apr 18, '09	Apr 10, '10	Mar 26, '11
Tazria	Lev. 12:1-13:59	Apr 21, '07	Apr 5, '08	Apr 25, '09	Apr 17, '10	Apr 2, '11
Metzora	Lev. 14:1-15:33	"	Apr 12, '08	"	"	Apr 9, '11
Acharey Mot	Lev. 16:1 - 18:30	Apr 28, '07	Apr 19, '08	May 2, '09	Apr 24, '10	Apr 16, '11
Kedoshim	Lev. 19:1-20:27	"	May 3, '08	"	"	Apr 30, '11

Emor	Lev. 21:1-24:23	May 5, '07	May 10, '08	May 9, '09	May 1, '10	May 7, '11
Behar	Levi 25:1-26:2	May 12, '07	May 17, '08	May 16, '09	May 8, '10	May 14, '11
Bechukotai	Lev 26:3-27:34	"	May 24, '08	"	"	May 21, '11
Bamidbar	Num 1:1-4:20	May 19, '07	May 31, '08	May 23, '09	May 15, '10	May 28, '11
Naso	Num. 4:21-7:89	May 26, '07	Jun 7, '08	Jun 6, '09	May 22, '10	Jun 4, '11
Beha`alotcha	Num 8:1-12:16	Jun 2, '07	Jun 14, '08	Jun 13, '09	May 29, '10	Jun 11, '11
Shelach	Num. 13:1-15:41	Jun 9, '07	Jun 21, '08	Jun 20, '09	Jun 5, '10	Jun 18, '11
Korach	Num. 16:1-18:32	Jun 16, '07	Jun 28, '08	Jun 27, '09	Jun 12, '10	Jun 25, '11
Chukat	Num. 19:1-22:1	Jun 23, '07	Jul 5, '08	Jul 4, '09	Jun 19, '10	Jul 2, '11
Balak	Num. 22:2-25:9	Jun 30, '07	Jul 12, '08	"	Jun 26, '10	Jul 9, '11
Pinchas	Num. 25:10-30:1	Jul 7, '07	Jul 19, '08	Jul 11, '09	Jul 3, '10	Jul 16, '11
Mattot	Num. 30:2-32:42	Jul 14, '07	Jul 26, '08	Jul 18, '09	Jul 10, '10	Jul 23, '11
Massei	Num. 33:1-36:13	"	Aug 2, '08	"	"	Jul 30, '11
D'varim	Deut. 1:1-3:22	Jul 21, '07	Aug 9, '08	Jul 25, '09	Jul 17, '10	Aug 6, '11
V'Etchanan	Deut. 3:23-7:11	Jul 28, '07	Aug 16, '08	Aug 1, '09	Jul 24, '10	Aug 13, '11
Ekev	Deut. 7:12-11:25	Aug 4, '07	Aug 23, '08	Aug 8, '09	Jul 31, '10	Aug 20, '11
Re'eh	Deut. 11:26-16:17	Aug 11, '07	Aug 30, '08	Aug 15, '09	Aug 7, '10	Aug 27, '11
Shoftim	Deut. 16:18-21:9	Aug 18, '07	Sep 6, '08	Aug 22, '09	Aug 14, '10	Sep 3, '11
Ki Teitze	Deut. 21:10-25:19	Aug 25, '07	Sep 13, '08	Aug 29, '09	Aug 21, '10	Sep 10, '11
Ki Tavo	Deut. 26:1-29:8	Sep 1, '07	Sep 20, '08	Sep 5, '09	Aug 28, '10	Sep 17, '11
Nitzavim	Deut. 29:9-30:20	Sep 8, '07	Sep 27, '08	Sep 12, '09	Sep 4, '10	Sep 24, '11
Vayelekh	Deut. 31:1-31:30	"	Oct 4, '08	"	"	"
Ha'azinu	Deut. 32:1-32:52	Sep 15, '07	Oct 11, '08	Sep 26, '06	Sep 11, '10	Oct 1, '11
V'zot Habrakha	Deut. 33:1-34:12	Oct 5, '07	Oct 22, '08	Oct 11, '09	Oct 1, '10	Oct 21, '11

V'zot Habrakha is read at the end of Sukkot, on the holiday of Simchat Torah (which takes place on the 8th day of Sukkot in Israel and in the Reform tradition, and on the 9th day elsewhere). We have indicated the traditional Diaspora date.

On holidays, the cycle is interrupted in favor of a special reading appropriate to the day.

Because of the hybrid nature of the Hebrew lunar-solar calendar, in which years can range from 355-384 days, there are some portions that "double up" during the shorter years to fit all the readings into the calendar. Those portions are indicated with a ditto mark.

Hebcal.com provides dates of Torah readings and holidays, as well as candle lighting times.

Glossary

Adam kadmon (Ah-**dahm** cod-**mone**): the primordial "first man," a mythic figure in Jewish mystical literature.
aliyah (ah-lee-yah): to "go up," designating the act of being called up to bless the reading of a section of the weekly Torah.
covenant: God's binding agreement with humanity.
emunah (eh-moo-nah): faith.
ephod (eh-fode): part of the vestments of the High Priest, as described in Leviticus. Its exact appearance and nature is unknown.
Jewish Renewal: An innovative movement within contemporary Judaism that seeks to reinvigorate Jewish practice and spirituality.
Kabbala: Jewish mystical tradition.
kavanah: Intention.
Kohen: Descendant of the first Biblical priest, Aaron.
korban (pl. ***korbanot***) (core-bon): Sacrificial offerings
manna: The miraculous food sent by God to feed the Jews in the desert.
midrash: Expounding of scripture through legends, tales, and literature.
minyan: Quorum of ten needed for public prayer and Torah readings.
Mishkan: The tent built by Moses at God's command to house the Indwelling Presence of God amidst the people in the desert; later replaced by the Temple in Jerusalem.
mitzvah: Literally, commandment; also connotes good deeds.
Ner Tamid (nayr ta-**meed**): Eternal flame, in the synagogue, modeled after the continuously-burning fire in the Mishkan.
niggun: A wordless tune, sung as ecstatic practice.
Rebbe (**reh**-bee): Rabbi, spiritual teacher.
Sefat Emet: Title of collection of lectures on the Torah by Polish Rabbi Yehuda Aryeh Leib Alter of Ger (1847-1905). Also used to refer Rabbi Yehuda himself.
s'firah (pl: s'firot) (sfee-rah / sfee-rote): One of ten aspects or emmanations of God, as delineated by the mystical teachers of the Kabbala
Shabbat (shah-bot): The Jewish Sabbath, which extends from sundown Friday until after dark on Saturday night.
Shekhina: The indwelling Presence of God.
shul (shool): Synagogue.
sparks: Refers to the mystical notion that all of Creation contains pieces of God, which can be "elevated" and returned to their Source.

tikkun olam (tee-kune o-lahm): the "mending of the world," combining mystic ideas of repairing the universe with the practice of acting to improve the world.
treif (trayf): Not kosher; unfit to be eaten according to Jewish tradition.
yeshiva: Jewish religious school.
Zohar: A mystical commentary on the Torah and the primary text of Kabbala.

Notes on Hebrew Pronounciation

ch, kh: a guttural, like the Scottish "loch" or German ...
a: as in father
e: as in bed

About the Author

Rabbi Shefa Gold is a leader in ALEPH: Alliance for Jewish Renewal and is the director of C-DEEP, the Center for Devotional, Energy and Ecstatic Practice in Jemez Springs, New Mexico.

Shefa received ordination both from the Reconstructionist Rabbinical College and from Rabbi Zalman Schachter-Shalomi.

Shefa composes and performs spiritual music, has produced ten albums, and her liturgies have been published in several new prayerbooks. She teaches workshops and retreats on the theory and art of Chanting, Devotional Healing, Spiritual Community building and Meditation.

Shefa combines her grounding in Judaism with a background in Buddhist, Christian, Islamic, and Native American spiritual traditions to make her uniquely qualified as a spiritual bridge celebrating the shared path of devotion.

More information, including her teaching schedule, can be found at http://www.RabbiShefaGold.com

CPSIA information can be obtained at www.ICGtesting.com
Printed in the USA
241306LV00001B/178/A

9 780976 986263